THE PROTOCOL EXPERIMENT

JAMES ZOLLERN

Self-published through:
Amazon
Barnes and Noble
IngramSpark
Lulu

TikTok: @zollernwolf | Instagram: @zollerwolf

ISBN 9798261772507
ISBN 9798260397701
ISBN 9798279109005
ISBN 9798234001146
ISBN 9798234046581

Subjects: Adult Science Fiction | Techno Thriller | Alien Invasion

https://www.theprotocolbookseries.com/

Cover art by: **Miblart Book Cover Design**

Two possibilities exist: either we are alone in the universe, or we are not. Both are equally terrifying. – Arthur C. Clarke

TWINKLE, TWINKLE, LITTLE STAR
HOW I WONDER WHAT YOU ARE

0. Prologue: Genesys

If we knew which paths to take on the road of life, and where each one would lead us, which would we choose? Some say if anything can go wrong, then it will. Others believe these circumstances are up to us, and that, despite widespread belief, there was truly no such thing as a coincidence. Someone from one part of the world may become important to someone else in another, and never even know it until destiny wove their lives together. From a higher vantage point, however, this becomes obvious. Humanity is flawed, but these flaws allow relationships to form. Without them, there would be no need for growth or development. It was all a grand experiment, so the question then becomes, who, or what, designed it?

There were those who saw no grand plan, no intelligent design, and no one behind the steering wheel of creation. They believed all was chance. It was one of the many paradoxes of the human experience. Everything needed a beginning and an end, and it was not possible to create something from nothing, but all of existence was once nothing. So, the provocative question then becomes, which came first? The nothing, or the something?

A star shone in the sparkling heavens, twinkling brightly, yet hidden by the light of day. It was beautiful and luminous, carrying a dark, sinister presence. Soon, more stars appeared, all of them twinkling and sparkling like diamonds. Humanity was unaware that these stars, however slowly, were coming closer.

On July 28, 2036, a worker at SETI received a unique signal from space, one that hadn't been detected in fifty-nine years. It lasted for seventy-two seconds before stopping abruptly.

William jolted awake in his chair as the signal came through. "Jeez, I do *not* get paid enough for this. Maybe this discovery will change that," he said breathlessly. One of the satellites went offline, and William remotely accessed its server to diagnose it. His computer behaved erratically, showing signs of a dangerous virus.

An NSA agent named Dale monitored William due to his criminal record. Since William's computer became infected, so did Dale's. Dale scrambled to contain the virus, and despite the struggle, he was successful.

The NSA decided to study the virus to determine how it reached the satellite and breached their systems, but it quickly adapted to their quarantines and firewalls. It escaped, infecting nearby NSA computers spying on people throughout the globe. The silent spread had begun. The weight of this infection would be felt across the Earth, which didn't stand still, but was ever so slightly slowed.

UP ABOVE IN SPACE SO HIGH
SHINING BRIGHTLY IN THE SKY

1. Murphy's Law

Hannah Morgan began her day like any other, with a smile and a thankful prayer, unaware of the coming events. It wasn't just her world that was about to change; it was everyone's. Hannah was raised by parents who regularly did drugs, so she didn't have the best upbringing. Still, she healed from her trauma and helped other people overcome their addictions. This was the final step of her healing. She suffered from health problems due to prenatal drug exposure, so she had regular doctor appointments.

A week prior, Hannah had suffered a heart attack, during which her life flashed before her eyes. This made her quickly realize fifty-five years wasn't enough time. Once her life was saved, she planned to use what time she had left to make a difference in the lives of others. She even handed her doctor a book she wrote about overcoming drugs, addiction, and the generational cycles they create. Unfortunately, something dark was coming, and it wasn't slowing down.

"Thank you, and have a wonderful day, Mrs. Morgan," the doctor said, dismissing Hannah with a smile. She walked out of the clinic and embraced the bright, glistening sun and the brand-new day. Hannah was a vibrant woman. Her long, curly blonde hair blew lightly in the wind, and her blue eyes reflected the sky. Her medication waited for her at the local pharmacy, and she decided to pick it up while she was out.

As she walked to her car, she noticed how beautiful the environment was around her: birds singing as they chased each other in the sky, the sun gleaming down on the sidewalk, and the alluring aroma of fresh coffee in her car's cupholder.

The clouds in the sky were sparse, and the radio played an upbeat, peppy song, accentuating the beauty of the day. Hannah couldn't resist a smile as she sang along and drove to the store, silently thanking God for such a blessed day.

After a quick drive, she walked into the pharmacy at 12:01 p.m. and greeted the pharmacist with a pearly smile, clearly still left over from her natural, euphoric high of the morning. "That's quite the smile you have there, ma'am," said Ron, a hint of flirtation in his voice.

"It's the little things," Hannah replied with joy.

An error occurred on Ron's coworker Ricky's PC, his irritation peaking. "Ahh, shh—" he started, slowly stopping himself, but he already realized it was too late for Ron not to say something.

"Ricky, what did I tell you about watching your language?" Ron asked, smiling.

Ricky sat up. "Sorry," he said. "I can't figure out how to resolve this error. It keeps screwing up. It's saying something about an intrusion, but when I run the scans, I don't get any results. My stupid computer isn't working, and I can't figure out what's wrong. Can I just use yours?"

Ron pulled Hannah's information up on his computer by running a quick query. "Here, see the green button at the bottom?" asked Ron, pointing at the screen. "That's how you save.

Click it and wait a couple minutes. It can take a while sometimes," said Ron, his tone deep with mockery, making Ricky roll his eyes.

"So," Hannah began, "is my medication ready? It's supposed to help lower my cholesterol. I know I look too young, but I had a heart attack about a week ago. Guess I pushed myself too hard," she said with a nervous laugh. "My name is Hannah Morgan."

"Yes, ma'am. I have it right here. One moment, please." Ron clicked a button on the screen, and the computer generated the medication, synthesizing the prescription into pill form. He bagged Hannah's Crestor and handed it to her. "See, Ricky? You just don't have the touch that I do. This PC is working fine." Ron tapped the computer tower twice on Ricky's desk, while Ricky rolled his eyes again and shook his head. "Alright, Mrs. Morgan, here you are. Have an enjoyable day."

"Thank you!" Hannah joyfully walked to her car, with her medication and a light snack in tow, then took the first pill from the container when she climbed in. Her car's radio roared back to life, and she sang along with it again.

The instructions on the bottle of capsules stated not to take them while driving, but her house was around the corner, a ten-minute drive, at most. Hannah surmised she would have time before the medication kicked in. She had no way of knowing what an unwise decision she had made.

✧

"Hey, Ron. I finally got the error to go away. Look," Ricky called to Ron at the pharmacy, smiling wide with his chest puffed out.

"Yeah, you did. Nice, man. See? Just gotta have patience, brother… and, you know, a manly touch never hurts," teased Ron.

"You sound like my wi—" started Ricky, but he looked back at the computer screen and noticed an issue. His brows furrowed, and he observed the computer closely to help him focus.

Ron noticed the same problem on his own PC. "Wait, I think we gave Hannah the wrong medication. Damn it," he scoffed.

Ricky raised his index finger with a smirk on his face, but didn't turn around. "Language!"

"Ricky, this is not the time for your smart-aleck shenanigans," Ron barked. "I could've sworn we gave her Crestor. My computer even showed the name when it generated the pills."

"Wait, so, what did we give her instead? How do you know it's not Crestor? Why did the computer generate it, then?" asked Ricky.

"Too many questions, Ricky. Ohh, wait." Ron noticed the error and pointed at a chart on the computer screen. "Look, see this here? It's the chemical compounds button. When you click on that, it shows you what the medication consists of for security's sake. It won't tell you specifically what's in it, but it gives you colors based off what's inside it. See this yellow line here? That's the stuff to reduce cholesterol. Now look at the red line there, see that? Those are inhibitors. I'm not sure what kind, but mixing any inhibitor with Crestor is potentially lethal. It could increase the chance of a heart attack. It is Crestor. I was wrong about that, but its composition is all wrong. It's like the computer generated it incorrectly, but how?"

"Oh, God. Did we just kill this woman?" Sweat poured down Ricky's cheeks, and his hands trembled as he felt his blood turn cold in his veins.

"Not if I can help it." Ron grabbed his phone while his heart rate increased and his stomach churned. "Come on, come on. Pick up," he yelled, his fear mounting. He frantically tried calling Hannah, but her phone was in the backseat in her purse on vibrate, and she couldn't hear her buzzing phone over the music.

Hannah sang her heart out to a song in her car as the sky rapidly turned gray, and rain fell. She rolled up her window so the rain wouldn't get in her car, because even though she loved the rain, her philosophy was that it didn't belong inside.

After about five minutes, she felt nauseated and weak. Hannah pulled the car over and stopped, getting out briefly to feel the fresh air and rain on her face. It brought sensation and cleanliness back to her senses, and so she climbed back into the car after a few minutes. When she reached back for her purse and checked her phone, it flickered and died. "Oh, great," she whispered to herself, "and here I was thinking today was going to be a *good* day."

Hannah was glad no one could see her in those moments of self-doubt. Everyone saw her as a peppy, upbeat woman, and she wanted it to stay that way. People were happier with the mask of happiness, or at least that's what she told herself. Knowing her house was only a little further up the road, she continued.

Unbeknownst to Hannah, her phone flickered back on, at which point she was already half asleep at the wheel. Her car swerved, and it only took her a couple minutes to pass out. There was a wreck in the middle of the road up ahead, in which one car had T-boned another.

Hannah, still passed out with her foot on the pedal, traveled over eighty-five miles per hour. With nothing to stop her, she crashed into the wrecked car. Her airbag didn't deploy, and her head slammed into the steering wheel at full speed. The sky billowed with smoke and flames as loud sirens from emergency vehicles approached the scene in response to the former wreck. A star shined in the sky briefly, then stopped.

Ron turned on the television when he got home, after finally giving up on reaching Hannah. He had left her two voicemails, in which he begged her not to take the pills until they could conduct further study, and had tried calling back another five times throughout the day without success. As he sat down to watch the news, there was a story about Hannah's wreck.

"Police have identified one of the deceased as Hannah Morgan, an astronomer from Babylon, New York. Upon inspection of the accident, it appears her airbag failed to deploy after she crashed at full speed into a wrecked car on Deer Park Avenue, wherein that driver also had a wreck in a similar fashion.

"The Centers for Disease Control has launched an investigation to discover why Hannah was asleep at the wheel, as the driver of the earlier wreck was asleep as well, though no links between the two people have been definitively confirmed.

"The CDC is investigating the possibility of an airborne chemical agent at this point in the road, and an autopsy of Mrs. Morgan's body is scheduled for some time next week. Until this situation is resolved, officials have warned residents to stay away from this road, and it will remain blocked until further notice. In other news, a local bunny has learned how to use a toaster. More on that story when we return."

Ron shut off the television and panicked, fearing incarceration, but he knew what he had to do. The morality of the situation is what truly haunted him, as he felt responsible for the loss of the woman's life. Ron's trepidation built slowly, growing rapidly with each passing second and increasing his anxiety. His palms sweated, and his whole body shivered nervously, feeling a sensation of hot and cold simultaneously. Ron eventually found the courage to do the right thing, and nervously dialed the Suffolk County police department, despite something in his gut telling him not to.

The phone rang one time before someone picked up. "This is Officer Dooley."

"Officer Dooley, this is Ron Lupin. I'm calling about Mrs. Hannah Morgan. Her body was found today in a wreck on Deer Park Avenue earlier this evening," Ron said, rushing the words out before his brain had time to stop him.

"What can you tell me about her? Do you know something?" the officer asked.

"Yes, sir," said Ron, his hesitation festering. "It's my fault, at least indirectly. I gave her volatile medication by mistake due to a computer glitch. I believe it may have affected her judgment or vision, which, uh…" he started, struggling to find the words, "led to her death. It's also highly possible that, due to the erroneous chemical compounds of the medication, she suffered a heart attack while driving. I am terribly sorry, sir. I truly meant no harm. So, I'm turning myself in now." Ron continued sweating and shaking, which was obvious from the way he was breathing into the phone.

The officer was briefly silent. "Sir, please hold," the officer said, while he thought about what the pharmacist told him. Officer Dooley could tell Ron's breathing was uneasy. He knew it wasn't Ron's fault, but he also knew he had to at least bring him in for questioning. "Alright, sir. We have a unit dispatched to your location. Please remain calm and do *not* leave the premises. We just want to ask you some questions," the officer explained as he ended the call.

A car arrived after about fifteen minutes, and a deputy stepped out, pointing a flashlight at Ron. "Good evening. Could you please step over here, sir?" the deputy asked of him. "I'm sorry to ask this of you, but I need you to put your hands behind your back and your cheek up against the car." The deputy sighed in disgust, and Ron silently did as he was told.

"You have the right to remain silent," the deputy said unenthusiastically. His monotonous, emotionless words would have been amusing to Ron, had he not been in a situation so dire. "Anything you say can and will be used against you in a court of law.

You have the right to have an attorney. If you should refuse to hire an attorney, one will be appointed for you by the court. Do you understand these rights as I have read them to you?"

"Yes, sir," Ron answered.

"With these rights in mind, do you wish to speak with me?" the deputy asked.

"No, sir. I'm willing to comply."

"Good. Now, please get in the back of the car, sir," the deputy commanded. "You've got a long night ahead of you, I'm afraid. I know this wasn't your fault. This is just standard procedure, at least in our neck of the woods," the deputy said, shaking his head in contempt. "Once we're at the station, you can tell your story to the chief, and we'll contact the necessary parties to inform them of your story. We're gonna try to keep this under wraps for now, so hopefully the media doesn't hear about any of this. In other words, keep your mouth shut, and *remain silent*, understood?" the deputy asked firmly.

Ron began to vocalize his assent, but decided against it.

"Good man," the deputy praised, growing increasingly remorseful during the drive. The whole situation tore at his morals. He knew Ron didn't intentionally kill Hannah. It wasn't his fault that something went wrong with the medication. How could he have known? "Look, friend, sorry about all this. They told me to just do my job, not to ask questions, and to continue with my duties and service. But this doesn't feel like serving, at least not in the interest of those we serve. My job is important, but so is my moral high ground."

Ron stayed silent for a substantial length of time, considering the officer's words carefully. Although he wanted to take the olive branch, it had happened more than once that this turned out to be a trick. People would frequently offer him a beautiful rug, roll it out, and ask him to step on it, only to pull it from under his feet. It took him two years to become friends with Ricky.

Though the car ride was silent, the deputy noticed a change in Ron's demeanor. Ron seemed to relax more, looking out the windows instead of down toward the floor. "My name is Jim, by the way. Jim Dalton. Listen, I get why you're not saying anything, and honestly, you're making the right choice. I can't say I'd be as smart if this situation was reversed. If you don't say anything, then I don't know anything. Plausible deniability, you know?

"I don't even know why I'm rambling. This just feels… wrong. It's not what I signed up for. I signed up to help people, to fight the battles for them when they can't, and to serve them when they need the kind of help I can give, the kind any police officer should be able to give. Arresting you just seems like saving face."

Ron met his eyes in the rearview mirror. Was this it? Was his life over? Never finding the love of his dreams, starting a family, or finding a job he didn't despise working daily? He had once desired a life of fulfillment, but all he found himself hoping for then was freedom. "Thank you," he said quietly.

"You're welcome," replied Jim. "Don't worry, they're not gonna keep you. This is all for appearances, I promise you. I doubt it even goes on your record. Bright side of it is you get to tell folks you did time in the slammer. Might be of benefit to you eventually," replied Jim, laughing.

Though he tried to keep his composure, Ron couldn't help but smile.

TWINKLE, TWINKLE, BLINKING STAR
WILL YOU TELL US WHO YOU ARE?

2. The Foster Principle

PROFESSOR HOWARD FOSTER GAVE A LECTURE IN his cybersecurity class at Hybrid-Tech University in Applewood, Tennessee. "Think of how much faith we put into technology. Almost everything has an internet connection now. Most of our electronics depend on the internet. Even some of our refrigerators depend on it.

"Imagine, if you will," he continued, gesturing toward a slideshow he had prepared, "a computer virus strong enough to not only infect one device, but to also spread to others. If you had to live without technology, even just for a day, or if you really want to get scared, a *week*," he jested with an exaggerated look of mocking torture, met with quiet but cheerful laughter from the class, "we would be helpless. We wouldn't know the news or weather, so you'd have to do something as difficult as going *outside*," he mocked with an ersatz shiver. "Most of us would be out of touch with our friends and most of our family.

"There would be no way to look up your favorite recipes, perform your daily work, or find out what Star Wars character you are. I'm assuming everyone here is above eleven years old, so remember in 2025, when a famous cloud service went down? Half the internet was crippled for the day. Most services, and even some people, couldn't function. Then, a short time later, a separate one went down and caused the same issue! Most of the internet is dependent on external services to stay up consistently, and while this is convenient, it's also dangerous.

"For some of you, this wouldn't be such a terrible thing to happen again. I know what a lot of you use the internet *for*," he said with a smirk. The class erupted in laughter, and when they quieted down, Professor Foster raised his index finger. "Cats! You use it to look at cats."

One student raised his hand with a wide-eyed grin on his face.

"Not *that* kind of cat, Thompson," said Professor Foster, making the class laugh again. "Technology is a wonderful and powerful force, folks. I'm not saying it isn't, but these are the reasons why it's so daunting. Most, if not all, of your personal data is stored on a cloud network. Ideally, you wouldn't have personal information in the cloud, but practice rarely conforms to theory.

"Remember, the cloud is basically a personal, online hard drive, stored on remote servers. You can store and retrieve data using an account you've created. However, if someone were to somehow figure out your login information, or gain access through other means, you can imagine what would happen.

"Identity theft is only the beginning. Therefore, a strong password is always, always recommended. Furthermore, and I cannot stress this enough, there is no such thing as a computer that cannot be hacked or infected," the professor declared, gently hitting his desk with every word to emphasize his point. "Regardless of its security, a computer is still a computer. That means whatever software it has is compiled upon an algorithm, which can be analyzed and unraveled, much like the mystifying human brain itself. If it is computerized, it can be hacked, and if it can be hacked, then it will be. I call that the Foster Principle.

"We're going to talk about something a bit dubious now, but stay with me. What do you think would happen if there was a virus so formidable that it altered our daily lives, down to the things we put into our bodies? If—"

Professor Foster was interrupted by the school bell before he could finish his discussion with the class. "Alright, everyone. I'll see you all next week. Remember, study for the exam, because I will *not* go easy on you. Now, before you leave, remind me again what James R. Schlesinger said. 'We only have two modes'"

"'Complacency and panic,'" roared the class.

"Dismissed." Professor Foster waved his students off with a smile and a sparkle in his eyes.

As everyone else left the classroom, an older student named Sean Caldwell approached the professor. Sean was skinny with little muscle, about five feet ten inches tall, and his skin was filled with color. Normally, he had trouble keeping his hazel eyes fully open, but the lecture riveted him.

"Your lecture really made me think," he said to the professor. "I've always felt that we're too reliant on technology, and it does scare me to think of what might happen someday. Do you think such a powerful virus is possible?"

"Oh, without a doubt. I don't know if it's within our current computing capability, but never get too complacent." Professor Foster winked at Sean. "Remember, back in 2014, we had that Chameleon virus. The darn thing spread through Wi-Fi signals.

"Anti-virus software is, sadly, not as powerful as most viruses these days. New ones are popping up so fast that we barely have time to react. What saddens me, though, is someone willing to corrupt or steal information to boost their ego. That's the real calamity. An inferiority complex can make people do absurd things."

Sean smiled. "Yes, sir, so I hear. Alright, see you later," he said, walking out of the classroom with a wave. As he made his way down the hall, he noticed a woman crying after being handed a broken cellphone by the school staff. It was clear the woman struggled to keep a level head.

The woman appeared to be about Sean's age, in her early thirties, which wasn't common in most colleges in his area. She stood out with her long, wavy black hair, falling to her middle back. Sean noticed she wore a pink beret on her head and lavender shirt, which didn't go all the way down to her tight blue jeans, leaving her midriff exposed. Her skin seemed to sparkle and radiate elegance, despite her sadness, and her eyes mesmerized Sean. They might as well have been galaxies to him, each of them exploding into massive supernovas before collapsing again to form a bright, iridescent green.

Sean approached her as the staff member walked away, and she looked at him briefly, her eyes begging the question, "Why would this happen?" They locked eyes for a moment, then the woman darted out of the hallway past Sean, nearly knocking him over. "Excuse me," she said as she continued walking, her voice shaking. Hearing someone so broken threatened to rip his soul in two, especially someone he found so beautiful.

Sean's friend Dustin noticed the encounter, looking at him as he sighed a breath of sympathy. "Man, poor girl. Losing family is tough. It ain't easy to go through. I hope she's got somebody to help her cope."

"What do you mean? What happened to her?" Sean asked. He began to wonder why he felt so compelled to help her—besides the obvious. It was in his nature, he guessed. Sean could never stand to see someone suffering, mostly because he suffered often himself. His teenage years were difficult for him, but he turned those years around to make him stronger, and that led to him wanting to help others.

"Well, story is, her mom died in a car wreck about a week ago, but seems there's more to it. Rumors are floating around, saying results came up showing she'd been doing drugs. Pill popping and all, man. Hard stuff. They supposedly found medication in her system that she ain't have any need for. Word around the school is, there was a man dealing under the table. Intentionally gave her the wrong prescription. Now, here's where it gets interesting—"

"It was already interesting, Dustin," Sean said with a half-smile.

"Man, shut up and let me tell this. Okay, so, Rebecca, her daughter who you just met, says her mom wasn't that kind of person at all. She was even an activist fighting *against* drugs, trying to fight the good fight, man. Rebecca thinks something's up. I'm not sure who to believe anymore, but something does smell funny there.

"Anyway, they gave Rebecca her mother's phone. Took 'em a few days, but she convinced her father to send it down to her from New York. Forensics said they went through it, but didn't find a single call, text message, voicemail, nothing. Seems a bit peculiar to me. It's like someone wiped it clean." Dustin noticed Sean staring at him. "Why are you looking at me like that?"

"How could you possibly know all this?" Sean asked.

Dustin was always one for gossip, and he picked up an abundance everywhere. No one suspected him since he was always so quiet, staying back in the unseen areas, observing life as if through a microscope. "Got my ways, man. I told you, just because I don't say nothing, don't mean I don't know nothing." Dustin smiled and nodded his head. He was the muscle, and no one dared to question him. Some people were intimidated by his size alone, but unfortunately, what most people saw was his dark skin. It broke his heart how judgmental bias was still alive, and he did his best to soldier through it. Still, he shouldn't have had to, and Sean knew that. It made for a strong bond in their friendship.

Dustin thought about how earlier in the week, a bright-skinned woman in an elevator pulled her child to the other side of her and clutched her purse as Dustin walked in. Fortunately, Sean was there when Dustin got out, giving him a big hug, confusing the woman. Sean had looked at the woman and told her how much Dustin loved hugs and people, which seemed to soothe her.

An idea formed in Sean's brain while Dustin reminisced. "Cellphones keep a local history of all data going in and out, right?"

"Yeah, I mean, I guess so, but of what relevance is that to this?" Dustin looked around the room, then back at Sean in confusion, which occurred often between the two. Dustin studied sociology, so technology wasn't his specialty.

"Okay, stay with me here. There are digital signatures for every action performed on a mobile device. We could use those to check for data erasure. My cybersecurity professor gave us an assignment last week that could help. Its goal was to create a program to read through a device's data and find evidence of tampering. I'm gonna try talking to her. Here, hold this." Sean gave Dustin his backpack.

After Sean left, Dustin sighed. Searching through the backpack, he found a donut. "A'ight, Sean. This right here is gonna be my payment," he said with a wide grin.

Sean bolted past his friend and caught Rebecca weeping beside her car. His heart broke as he watched her clutching her tear-soaked beret in her hands. "Hey! Rebecca, right? My name is Sean. I know we're strangers, but I think I can help you. I think I might be able to tell if the data on your mom's phone was tampered with. I mean, if you're willing to give it a shot. Maybe it's nothing, but I've heard what they're saying, so I want to help. I'm sorry to just throw this on you, but I thought—"

Rebecca grabbed Sean by the collar of his shirt, sending a shockwave of sensation through his body. "Do it! Please, please help me," she begged, knowing there was no way her mom was doing drugs. It simply wasn't who she was. It appalled her how no one believed her, because these were once good people who knew her mother and talked to her daily. All it took was a little gossip for that to mean nothing.

Sean and Rebecca walked past Dustin munching on what was once Sean's donut, which Sean pretended not to notice. Dustin followed them into a computer lab, browsing through Sean's backpack as he walked. Sean hooked Rebecca's phone up to a random PC's USB-G five-point-two port on campus and installed the driver software. Sean plugged in a flash drive with the sniffer program, which ran and finished instantly, confusing Sean.

"That's weird," Sean said. "It's supposed to go through a six-step process. It just skipped four steps." Sean ran the program again, and it executed correctly, creating a new text file on the desktop.

The file confirmed there were seven missed calls and two voicemails. Since the data was erased, Sean was only able to recover an exceedingly minor part of the second message by using the phone's speech-to-text feature. Sean hoped to find more, but the rest of the files were corrupted.

"Thank you, Sean, so much. This gets me enough information to prove everyone wrong. I can't begin to tell you how much I owe you. Thank you so much." Rebecca quickly kissed Sean on the cheek.

Sean blushed, cleared his throat, and quickly composed himself, doing his best to ignore his physical reactions. "No problem, but you might want to go to the police with this and keep quiet to anyone else." He wasn't about to mention how Rebecca made his heart skip a beat. The pain he had been feeling was, for a moment, silent.

Rebecca nodded as she wiped her eyes with her sleeve and pushed back her hair. "I will. My dad's a sheriff back home. God, he must be going through so much. I'm gonna start packing tonight and find a way up there tomorrow. School is just gonna have to wait." She started to leave, but stopped, turned around, and walked back toward Sean. "Hey, Sean. Um, could I have your number, please? Just to keep you updated, like if I find out anything, or need some tech help or… something?" she asked as she looked down and twirled her hair, moving her body from side to side.

Sean found the way Rebecca moved irresistible. "Y-you want my number?" he asked, his voice rising several octaves, then making it sound deeper. "I mean, yeah, sure." They quickly exchanged numbers, though Sean had to retype hers a couple of times because of his shaking fingers. Dustin raised an eyebrow as he quietly observed.

"Okay, thank you again. I'll keep you updated," said Rebecca. She thought Sean was quite cute and sweet, but knew there were more important things to manage. One of the most magnificent women Sean had seen in a while smiled at him, walked to her car, and drove off. *Maybe next time,* she thought.

Once Rebecca was gone, Dustin smiled and nodded. "Yeah, Sean."

"Knock it off," Sean complained in embarrassment. "I did it because it was the right thing to do," he lied. "Wipe that grin away. You look high with all that donut powder on your face."

Dustin lightly punched Sean on the shoulder. "You're alright, you know that?" he said as they walked off.

Sean laughed and playfully hit his friend back. “Shut up, dude,” he replied with a smile. “You owe me a donut.”

WE SEE YOU SHINING IN THE NIGHT
BRINGING TO US ENDLESS FRIGHT

✧

3. Ghosts in the Machine

Ron woke up in a holding cell at the police station where he had spent the past week. Like every morning, he was given prison food for breakfast, and he devoured it like a ravenous animal. It wasn't like this at first—he was terrified and disgusted by the food, refusing to eat. The longer he stayed there, the more determined and desperate he became. After all, the police couldn't legally keep him indefinitely. He had rights, which he planned to exercise once he was free by suing the police department. Ron wore the same clothes for a week, had no privacy, and was treated worse than a chained-up dog. His claustrophobia ate him alive, and he rapidly became more willing to be a true criminal the longer he was kept locked up.

This day was different, though. Jim came by and unlocked the cell, gesturing for Ron to come out. As Ron hesitantly walked out, he gave Jim a nasty glare, silently daring him to make a single sudden movement. Despite Ron's frailty, he would use every bit of strength he had. After all, Jim was the officer who arrested him, and assured him he wouldn't be kept there. Ron was disgusted by liars because he was always honest, and he always admitted to everything he did wrong. As he turned to look at Jim, he reflected on whether his honesty was a mistake.

Jim sighed. "Hey, I know you're pissed, and you're right to be. I'm sorry. I wasn't trying to lie to you. I honestly didn't think they'd keep you here this long. Ron, it's disgusting here. I hate this job and what they've done to you. Humanity has so many problems. I don't understand how we've survived this long. You didn't deserve this, and I know that doesn't make it any better, but hang in there.

"Trust me, better days are coming. One way or another, things are going to change. They have to." Jim shook his head and looked down at the floor, then back up at Ron. "Someone, somewhere, is gonna make this better. Okay? I'm gonna fight for you, and I'll support you if you wanna fight this place. But for now, come with me."

Ron hesitated, but Jim's words partially calmed him. Desperate for freedom, he nodded and followed Jim into the sheriff's office, stopping to read the nameplate before he went in. It read, "Sheriff Darren Morgan." Ron swallowed the lump in his throat when he saw the last name.

The chief had stepped out for a while, and Darren was the only other officer there who was willing to listen besides Jim, who took off Ron's handcuffs. Ron's shaking hands then broke free. Jim looked at his fellow officers with repulsion and walked away. "I'm done for the night. Maybe I'll be in for my next shift," Jim bemoaned as he started to leave, but he stopped and turned around. "Shame on you all for keeping this man here. I know we're backed up and short-staffed, but it's no excuse for withholding the freedoms of an innocent man," Jim shouted before swiftly walking away, sick to his stomach and even feeling culpable, despite only following orders.

Ron was terrified, barely able to speak at first, but he was ready for any form of freedom. It took all the strength he had in him to speak. "Sir, my name is Ron, and I am so, so sorry for what happened. I had no way of knowing. Keeping me in that cell was wrong," he said, raising his voice. "I have rights, and believe me, I plan on using them, so you better—"

Darren raised his hand to signal Ron that he had heard enough. "What happened to my wife? I wanna know everything. Don't sugar-coat it. You will tell me every detail. If I should find out that you withheld *any* information from me, or if you lie to me, whether it's to cover your own ass or otherwise, I *will* lock you up for the rest of your life. Especially if you keep up your attitude. All I'm askin' for in return for your freedom is for you to inform me of absolutely everythin' you know, and then you're a free man." Darren was dressed in a black, highly decorated sheriff uniform. His black hair was slicked back, and his face was filled with wrinkles. He appeared to be in amazing physical shape and was much bigger than Ron.

Terrified but grateful, Ron sat down to explain. "Hannah—I mean, Mrs. Morgan, came to our pharmacy last week to pick up Crestor. Our computers experienced a glitch, some sort of system error. I thought it was limited to my coworker Ricky's computer, so we used mine instead, and everything seemed to work fine.

"It wasn't until she had already left and been gone for a good six to eight minutes that the computer showed signs of infection. It was as if this virus was trying to conceal itself. I shouldn't have given her the medication, sir, but again, I had no control over the situation. I'm not even sure how or why this happened." Ron sighed, deciding to give empathy a shot. "I am so, so sorry. I know you're hurting, but if I could just—"

"That's enough," Darren shouted. The sheriff composed himself shortly thereafter and continued his interrogation. "Did you try callin' her and lettin' her know?"

Ron perked up, hope budding in his chest. "Yes, sir. Seven times. I even left two voicemails."

Darren's blood boiled, and he glared harshly at Ron as though he was young, vulnerable prey, and Darren was the predator on the prowl. "I told you that if you lied to me, I would ruin your life. That is exactly what I intend to do." Darren stood and knocked on his desk twice. "Take him back and book him for good this time," he called to the surrounding officers, who yanked Ron from the chair.

"What?" Ron shouted. "Wait, I don't understand. I told you everything! What do you think I left out? Something's not right here. I swear I've told you everything and it's all true! Please, you must believe me," he begged loudly. "I have rights!"

Darren stormed toward Ron until their faces were inches apart. "You said you called her and left voicemails?" he asked, his anger festering.

"Yes, I did! I swear to you," Ron assured, trying to sound as genuine as he could, but he was too confused and upset to think straight.

"Well, that's interestin', because accordin' to forensics, her phone had no missed calls, no voicemails, and no text messages. You are a filthy, sickening liar. I warned you, and now you get to pay the price," yelled Darren.

"You can't do this to me. I-I-I'm supposed to have a trial," shouted Ron.

"You will, but not for a long time," responded Darren. "You killed my wife." Darren nodded at the officers as they grabbed Ron and began dragging him to a permanent cell.

Ron was shocked into silence. He knew he had called Hannah and left the messages, so why weren't they there? Was there something wrong with the phone? Was the police station corrupt? Ron found himself thinking of all the possibilities, no longer capable of speech.

Darren walked alongside his fellow officers until his phone rang. "Darn it, stop right here for a moment, guys. I'm gonna answer this call from my daughter," he said, answering the phone. "Hey, sweetie. I know you're upset, but I'm busy right now. I need you to—"

"No, listen to me! I met this guy, and he found hidden files on Mom's phone. The data was erased somehow, but the pharmacist did try calling her to let her know," Rebecca rushed out. "Those forensic reports were false!"

"You're kiddin'. This guy found all that out for you? How could they just disappear?" Darren stared at Ron as the painful rage briefly drained from his face, replaced by growing doubt.

"I don't know. He found it with some script thingy," Rebecca replied.

"Well, I've got the guy who prescribed the medication right here. I'm gettin' ready to lock him up cause I thought he was lyin' to me. Do you know anythin' else?" Darren asked.

"No, but don't you dare lock him up, Daddy. Shame on you! He's an innocent man. I don't know what happened, but it's no excuse to treat him that way. Mom would be so livid with you." Rebecca sniffled as she fought the urge to cry.

Darren winced from Rebecca's loud voice, her words echoing through his soul. "Okay, I understand. Becca, you just saved this man's freedom. Be careful, and I'll see you soon."

"Oh, that reminds me. I'm heading up there first thing tomorrow morning," Rebecca sputtered.

Darren was terrified of Rebecca driving so far by herself, or worse—by plane. "What? No, you stay there. I'll come to you, and this guy is comin' with me."

"Okay, Daddy. Bye, I love you," Rebecca bubbled, waiting for her father to end the call.

"I love you too. Bye." Darren ended the call and looked back at Ron again. "Let him go," he shouted. "This man is tellin' the truth." The officers released Ron and walked back to their desks.

After Ron was freed, he looked at Darren, confused. "I have no idea what just happened, so will you please fill me in?" he asked, rubbing his wrists.

"I don't know yet, but we're gonna find out. Come on, let's go for a ride." Darren walked toward the exit, and Ron started to follow him, but Darren stopped and turned around, Jim's words repeating in his mind. "Tell you what, we'll go by your place first, so you can get a shower and clean clothes. It's the least I can do. You don't have to come with me if you don't want to."

Ron was silent the entire drive, and they arrived at his house about fifteen minutes later. Once there, Ron hurriedly got out and ran inside, then closed and locked the door. When he was done with his shower, he thought about staying inside. After all, he had no reason to accompany the sheriff. He was off the hook, and it wasn't his responsibility anymore. Still, he had a strong moral compass, and it wouldn't let him leave this unsolved, especially with Jim's comment about his moral high ground. He was too curious, unable to turn away a good mystery. Despite wanting to stay put, he considered the situation and decided to ride with Darren. They nodded at each other and drove off.

Ron stayed quiet for most of the ride, occasionally glancing over at Darren. His eyes were baggy, and Ron noticed the wrinkles on the sheriff's face. An old scar struck through his right eye, and worried wrinkles displayed prominently on his face. A bead of sweat rolled down the back of Darren's neck, and Ron thought he saw a tear roll down his cheek. Ron wanted to say something to comfort Darren, to ease his emotions, but he was afraid it would only worsen things. His emotions were tumultuous, and he wasn't managing them well.

Ron pulled out his cellphone and loaded a news app. The headlines were as deceptive as always: "Local pharmacist drugs astronomer"; "Woman overdoses, toxicology reports indicate substance abuse." This confused him, as Jim mentioned he didn't want the media to learn of the incident, but all it took was a suggestion from someone, and the rest was history. Ron wondered if the information was leaked somehow, and didn't put anything past the cops after what he went through.

Normally, Ron wasn't one to read the vile comment sections. People were unusually cruel and obnoxious. Ron thought it was a breeding ground for negativity; a place to avoid at all costs, even for the happy posts, because inevitably, there was always at least one person who had something malicious to say. This time was different, though. This time, he was curious, and he knew Hannah didn't have a drug problem, based on her medical profile alone. Ron scrolled through the comments, reading testimonies from people who knew her, telling of how she actively tried to turn people away from drugs. Many of them shared how great of a person she was. Of course, these were also the same people blaming the good pharmacist. They talked about how he ended her life, about how he took a magnificent soul from the world. Ron felt his stomach drop in anguish, realizing how the world was coming to view him.

Darren slammed on the brakes to avoid hitting a deer in the road, while Ron absentmindedly scrolled through his phone, ironically something he often chided his relatives for doing. As he looked up to see what happened, his phone briefly flickered to a black screen before returning to normal. Ron breathed a deep, shaky sigh of relief, then relaxed back in his seat, unaware his phone had malfunctioned.

"Sorry 'bout that," said Darren. "Damn thing jumped right out in front of me. Fearless little buggers, ain't they?" he said, forcing a laugh. Ron stayed quiet and Darren sighed. "Look, Ron, I'm sorry. Things have been rough for Hannah and me, but they were just startin' to get better, and now…" he trailed off, a tear betraying him as it ran down his face. "You know, she had this quirk where she would just…" Darren gritted his teeth and forced out a smile. "She loved people, no matter what they said or did to her, and she would always go out of her way to make somebody smile. She could see a murderer feeling down about himself, and she'd still try to lift him up. That's who Hannah was. God, I miss her so much." Darren composed himself and spoke in a more professional tone. "Doesn't excuse what we did to you, though. I guess I needed someone to blame and punish, so I wasn't thinking rationally.

"My point is I came down way too hard on you, and I jumped to conclusions. I mean, the evidence was there, but I should've known better than treating you the way I did, so I apologize. You deserve better, and I don't want you to be afraid of me. I'm not a bad guy. Maybe not a great guy either, but not a bad one," he said as he pulled up to a stoplight, looking over at Ron. "If the public can't trust those sworn to defend them, then those who do wrong will only become worse."

"Thank you," Ron replied, but he had already decided to stay quiet. Ron was a timid man, and once confronted, especially by someone in a position of authority, it took him a while to recover. It was a result of his many years of being bullied.

Twenty more minutes passed before Darren grew uncomfortable with the silence. "Hey, if you want, you can turn on the radio," he said. "This quiet is killin' me. Might even help us find somethin' to talk about," he suggested.

Ron turned the radio on, changing it to a rock station, and they sang along with it for a couple of hours. As the sun rose, the radio turned off, and the rest of the car gradually shut down as it lulled itself to a stop.

"What's this about now?" asked Darren. Ron noticed the complete absence of traffic, and realized there had been maybe two cars passing them in the opposite lane for the entirety of the trip so far.

Both men exited the car and Darren checked under the hood, while Ron absentmindedly checked the tires, pretending he knew what to do. He shook his head as he started checking other parts. *I should have been a mechanic*, Ron thought. A sparkle in the sky grabbed his attention, but he thought nothing of it.

"Alright, think my car just needs a jump. She's a little over a decade old, and I'm too darn stubborn to get rid of her, so she's tryin' to die on me. There's gotta be somebody around here willin' to help us out. Stay here, and I'll be back." Darren grabbed his phone from the car's console, and prepared to walk up to the Burger King nearby, about a mile up the road.

Ron looked a little further the other direction and noticed a man near a Cox cable truck, working on an internet line. "Hey, Darren, over here. Look," shouted Ron, pointing to the man by the truck.

Darren ran back over. "Excuse me, sir? Sir? My patrol car died on us, and we think she just needs a jump. Do you think you could—" Darren was cut off as the police car's lights and siren suddenly activated on their own. "Never mind, what the hell?"

Darren and Ron darted back to the car, and once they both climbed inside, everything returned to normal. Before they could think about the situation, the Cox employee's van took off on its own and crashed into a nearby Waffle House, bringing most of it down, causing nearby people and cars to scatter in response.

UP ABOVE THE WORLD SO HIGH
YOU'RE A MENACE IN THE SKY

✧

4. THE CURVE

ABIGAIL FOCUSED AS SHE PERFORMED ANOTHER autopsy, her third for the day. "This is Medical Examiner Abigail Warren. Subject is, or was, Hannah Morgan, a fifty-five-year-old, female astronomer from our town of Babylon, New York. I am beginning the autopsy now."

She performed the autopsy carefully, steadying her hand and observing her findings with meticulous precision. Abigail knew the job wasn't for most people, and her mother made sure to show her disapproval, but Abigail loved what she did because she could help people. She could prove that a death wasn't a suicide, that they were murdered instead. It was always about the trivial things: diligence and details most people would have missed. Abigail was outstanding in her field, extraordinary even, with a stomach of steel and an empathetic heart for the work that most people lacked.

As she prepared to make a note, she took a deep breath and brushed back her long, flowing red hair, her green eyes focusing on every detail of the cadaver in front of her. "Internal organs show stress levels consistent with standard cardiac arrest. I believe she died before the crash. An added note to mention here is that I personally witnessed the crash from the side of the road while on my daily walk. It occurred at approximately 2:15 p.m. on Monday, July 28, 2036, and Mrs. Morgan's death seems to have occurred about two minutes prior.

"I also feel it is worth mentioning that the deceased driver of the other vehicle was also asleep. However, his drowsiness appeared to have been caused by sleep deprivation. Rumors have swirled online regarding fake reports before I've performed this autopsy. I would like to set the record straight. These rumors are false and undignified."

What Abigail didn't mention in her recording, though, was that as she checked her phone right before the wreck occurred, it went dark for a moment and flickered back on in a couple of seconds. She brushed it off as a technical glitch and approached the crash site to ensure everyone was safe.

"Toxicology screening shows evidence of medication ingested shortly before the use of her motor vehicle, which I believe to be Crestor. It's a medication normally administered for lowering cholesterol, usually to reduce risk of cardiac arrest. Chemical analysis shows matching compound structure.

"Oddly enough, this medication may have *triggered* her heart attack. Analysis of the medication shows signs of tampering, indicated by the inclusion of bundled inhibitors, specifically CYP3A4. The peculiarity about this discovery is how they seem intelligently laced with erythromycin. There are patterns about this peculiarity that could not have been accidental, as the methodology is too precise. This eliminates any correlation to the other victim."

Abigail stared off into the middle distance, remembering a lecture at a conference she had attended a few months back. "It's the erythromycin. When erythromycin becomes compounded with CYP3A4 inhibitors, it produces potentially lethal effects, quintupling the chance for cardiac arrest. Mrs. Morgan appears to have been supplied with a modified version of this medication, which appears to have been erroneously manufactured. I will send this to the CDC and report my official statement to management tomorrow morning. End of case file."

Six hours had passed since the autopsy. Abigail listened to herself on the tape repeatedly, proud of herself for a case being solved so quickly, though she did wonder if it was too quickly, considering it took them a week to get approval for it. It tore at her, though. She wondered how the medication could be so severely altered, and how the pharmacy had no idea. *Something better left to the authorities*, she thought. Abigail didn't want to become involved in matters that didn't concern her.

It was in her nature to help and to perform her duties, but she rarely left home. For all her talk to her younger colleagues about reaching out and embracing life, she was certainly the antonym of what she preached, and the world was all the worse for it.

She sipped her wine as she sat at her piano and played a melodic tune to soothe her worries and stresses away. Abigail never took lessons; she naturally knew how to play. Some people could play by ear, and it's what everyone assumed she did, but she didn't.

Her fingers simply knew where to go. They somehow knew what keys sounded harmonious together, which notes produced a beautiful, echoing hum, and how to blend them together into something resembling harmonic perfection. She never understood why, but it was as though she had taken lessons before;

lessons her soul knew and passed on to her body in her youth. Many people told her she should pursue a career in music, but she told them it wouldn't really help anyone, at least not in the way she wanted to. Abigail felt she had influence, that she saved lives by helping to understand how other people lost theirs. She made a living from death. Sure, it was morbid, but it was as though she could touch a withered flower, and from it, produce a garden. Sometimes, though, she wished she could prevent people from getting that far and save them before anything awful happened.

Abigail loved her time off, but it always left her so bored. There was nothing to do, no one to talk to, and nowhere to go. She typically stayed in the three-story home she inherited from her father, only going out for work, food, and the occasional date night, which was rare.

As the clock ticked from 11:59 p.m. to 12:00 a.m., she walked up to her bedroom to prepare for bed. She was a woman of habit, after all. Once she slipped off her nightgown, she climbed into her bed and drifted off to sleep, her bare feet and chest against the sheets soothing her skin, lulling her to rest. Her phone lay beside her, connected by a USB-G cable to a wall charger plugged into a wireless surge protector.

All was well for a few hours, until every electrical appliance inside her house activated at once. The lights flickered rapidly, the television turned itself on and off and changed channels and volume, radio stations came on and blasted nothing but static and white noise, blenders and coffee makers activated, her alarm blared loudly, and too many other things for her to keep up with all at once, overwhelming her senses.

She slipped back into her nightgown and proceeded to walk around the house in awe at everything she experienced, unsure of what to do. As she came across her laptop still sitting active on the coffee table, she noticed the nightly virus scan had quarantined something. As she went to inspect it, the computer shut itself off, and all activity in the house ceased. It was as though the culprit for the activity had felt itself caught.

Abigail wasn't really one to believe in the paranormal, but in this instance, she felt she didn't have much of another choice. "Hello?" she called out. *Get it together, Abby,* she thought. *This isn't ghosts. It's some weird problem with the electrical wiring, like a short, or maybe radio interference.* She grabbed her cellphone after retreating to her bedroom and dialed her brother. The phone rang six times before he answered. "Jake? Hello?" she said shakily.

"Abby? Why?" Jake squinted at the clock. "Jeez, Abby, it's four o'clock in the fricking morning. What's the matter? Who died? Because if someone didn't," he warned, yawning pugnaciously, "someone's gonna."

Abigail ignored Jake's faux threats and focused on the problem. "Look, be mad at me all you want, but something weird is going on over here at my place. Lights are flickering and devices are turning on and off. It's like Poltergeist here! I didn't know who else to call."

Jake smiled. "Have you tried the Ghostbusters?"

"Hilarious," Abigail replied, annoyed. "I think it's stopped, but I don't know how long. I'm… I'm really creeped out."

Jake laughed. "Okay, now I know you're screwing with me. My sister who does autopsies on human corpses is creeped out. Sure. We'll go with that."

"Darn it, Jake. I'm being serious. Can you come over? Please? You know I wouldn't call if it wasn't important." Abigail tried to instill fear in her words, but all she could manage was frustration. *Leave it to my brother to not care about anyone but himself*, she thought.

"Yeah, I can come over… in about six hours. Night-night." Jake ended the call and turned over on his bed.

Prick. Abigail eventually fell back asleep, and when she awoke the next morning at 11:37 a.m., she jumped as she realized someone stood beside her bed, facing the window.

Abigail screamed, making the man swiftly turn around. "Jeez, Abby. Scared me half to death," Jake said breathlessly. His tall and muscular build made him appear threatening from behind. His brown eyes widened when Abigail screamed, and the first thing he did was grab his head, messing up his dark brown hair.

"Me? Jake, you're standing in my *bedroom*. How did you even get in here?" Abigail pulled the covers up to conceal her chest.

Jake twirled a key in his hands and clumsily dropped it. "Oh, heck. Sorry," he said, holding his head low. "So what happened, anyway?" he asked as he bent down to pick the key up. "I mean, I got here by like six o'clock or so, and everything was fine. No poltergeists, ghosts, or whatever else. Honestly? I'm disappointed."

Abigail's skin crawled as she felt her body temperature drop. "You've been in my house for over *five hours*? How long have you been in my *bedroom*?"

"Only for a couple of minutes, and yes, I left earlier than I said I would. Once you woke me up, I couldn't get back to sleep. Just tossed and turned for an hour. So, finally, I got up, did my stuff, and headed here. I kinda passed out on your couch when I got here, though. That thing is *nice*," Jake said, a wide smile on his face. "What *wasn't* fun was driving through this crazy thunderstorm."

"You know, if you hadn't shown up, I could've blown this whole thing off as a dream, but now you're here, corroborating." Abigail took a breath to calm herself. "I'm sorry I'm so cranky, okay? I didn't sleep well either. It was a freaky night. Thanks for coming."

"That's what brothers are for," he crooned, wrapping his arms around her neck in a hug. Abigail clutched the covers tightly. "Are you—"

"Can you step out of here for a minute so I can get dressed?"

"Uhh, yeah," Jake responded as he bolted out of the room.

✧

"Is anyone hurt?" Darren shouted into the Waffle House through the gaping hole in the side of it. No response. As Darren stepped inside, he discovered the restaurant seemed to be empty, filled with rubble. Another tragedy would have been too much for him to manage. Darren sighed and wiped his brow. "Thank God," he said with a sigh of relief.

A cop car activated its lights and made its way to the restaurant, and when it arrived, a pot-bellied sheriff stepped out of the car. It was as if someone pulled the sheriff from the song The Night the Lights Went Out in Georgia by Vicki Lawrence. Darren snickered to himself at the thought. "You boys a'ight?" asked the sheriff. "W'happened here?"

Darren pointed at the van in the middle of the restaurant. "Heck if I know, pal. Darn thing just turned on and drove itself. I've never seen anythin' like it," Darren gasped out with disbelief, rubbing the back of his head in confusion. "Look, you got this? My friend and I really need to get goin'."

"Oh, yeah, I got—" the sheriff answered as he hiccupped. "Whew, sorry. Yeah, I got it. Y'all just b'careful. I was gonna get smothered, covered and buttered, but I guess that ain't happenin' now."

Darren backed away from the man and bolted for his car, nearly running into a little girl. "Oh sh—I mean darn, I'm sorry, little lady. Are you okay?" he asked as a woman came running by. "Ma'am, I'm so sorry. I didn't see your daugh—"

"Monica," the woman yelled over Darren. "Don't run off on your aunt like that, baby." The woman picked up her niece and looked toward Darren. "No, it's okay, she's always running off. I swear, she's just like her father. Cute and innocent on the outside, but nosey and mischievous on the inside." Monica laughed as the woman booped her on the nose. "Thank you for your kindness.

We really must be going." The woman walked away. "You *know* better," he heard the woman scold Monica.

"It's not my fault you're slow, Aunt Mandy," Monica playfully said back.

Darren breathed a sigh of relief, then walked up to Ron and grabbed his shoulders, startling him and making him scream. "Whoa there. Sorry, but we gotta go, alright? This guy here says he's got this handled, and we really don't have time to deal with it anyway. So let's get goin'."

"Are you sure? Is the car even gonna work?" Ron inquired, confused and afraid.

"Somethin' tells me it never really stopped. There's somethin' funky going on here, Ron. You and I are gonna find out what that is." Ron nodded in accord, and they got inside the car, which started up without issue. The two men looked at each other in mutual confusion.

Hours passed, during which time Ron and Darren bonded through more music on the radio. Darren turned the volume down when a commercial came on. "You know, I used to be an alcoholic," he admitted. "Hannah was the one who got me out of the hole. I met her at an AA meeting she hosted and we just… connected. It was obvious to me from day one that she was one of a kind. When anyone else looked at her, they saw an ordinary woman, but I saw my future. You got anybody?" he asked, looking over at Ron while at a stoplight.

"Nah, I've never been any good at that stuff." Ron looked down as he fidgeted with his fingers in his lap. "The most I've done is gone skinny dipping for this girl as a teenager because I lost a dare. It was fun, and I enjoyed it, but it didn't lead anywhere. I figured if something's meant to happen for me, then it will, and if it doesn't, that's okay. There are just too many things wrong with me," Ron said despondently. He reflected on his few failed attempts, and he could feel his emotional boat taking on heavy water as it threatened to capsize and fall to the abyss.

"Oh, come on. Everyone's got someone. Just give it time and put yourself out there. Stop waitin' for it to come to you, because that almost never happens. You're gonna find someone, and she's gonna love you for who you are. Okay?" Darren patted Ron's shoulder, and Ron smiled. He felt hope for the first time in a while as he started trusting Darren.

It was just after three a.m. when the car abruptly acted haywire again, the same behavior as before. This time, though, they were in the middle of the woods on an old road, the kind you can hardly make out in the dead of the night, save for the glowing lines on the asphalt, mandated for the world to use in 2030. There were no jumper cables in the car, and even if there were, the men had nothing to jump it with.

Darren and Ron tried opening their doors, but the doors would re-lock themselves every time they tried. The radio would occasionally turn on and off, but only static came from it. There were red lights up ahead that Darren assumed were brake lights. The lights burned increasingly brighter until the whole night was a shade of crimson. They could do nothing as they watched and became entranced by the glowing lights.

Darren decided to place a call to the nearest dispatch, but before he could, he felt a violent force fly through the car, which felt like a strong wind, but electrical. Once he composed himself, he called.

It took about seven rings, but someone finally picked up. "Nine-one-one, what is your emergency?" asked the dispatcher.

"I'm not sure. I think somethin' just… I don't know what it was, but somethin' hit my car, or washed over it," Darren stammered.

"Are you alright? What is your condition?" the dispatcher asked.

"I don't know. Somethin' attacked the car. Somethin' I couldn't see. The glass acted like it was about to break, there's cracks in the windshield, and the locks… I can't get out. My whole car just locked up on me. Somethin's wrong. Feels like my eyes fell victim to an arc welder. Everythin's gone red, I—"

All activity ceased as the call disconnected. The lights retracted, leaving the night pitch black again. Darren looked over at Ron, who was still passed out in the passenger's seat. It was for the best, he figured. Ron was a timid man, and Darren didn't want to make things worse.

Darren yawned and glanced at the clock on the dash. He had to do a double take as he read the time. It was 5:45 a.m. What felt like mere minutes turned out to be nearly three hours. He figured he must have dozed off, though he did not remember doing so. *The hell is going on*? he thought as he wondered if he was dreaming.

Ron finally rose from his sleep. "Any idea how much longer the ride is gonna be? I don't mind catching up on the shuteye, and I'm grateful not to be behind bars, but I wouldn't say no to getting up and walking soon. So, how much longer do you think?" He stretched in his seat.

"I'm… not sure. Did you feel any of that?" Darren asked.

Ron deliberated for a moment. "I didn't feel anything, but I had a weird dream. It was of this masked doctor wearing these weird, diagonal goggles giving me a shot in my wrist. It felt like a memory, but the dream was scarier. I can't really explain it," Ron elaborated. "I also remember seeing this super bright light, and I know this sounds crazy, but I think the light was red." Ron smiled nervously. "Should we call Mulder and Scully?"

Darren felt every hair on his body stand up and nausea build in his stomach, despite Ron's joke. "You're ridiculous. Anyway, for now, let's just keep moving and put this behind us. I'd rather not deal with it, frankly," Darren quavered, and Ron nodded in assent.

The men decided to keep on their current path and not acknowledge what happened. They were determined to get to Rebecca, and nothing would stop them. They may have delayed, but they would not be stopped. Darren felt a strong itch on the back of his neck and scratched it, but thought nothing of it. He resumed driving, and Ron soon fell back asleep.

✧

It had been a couple days since Sean helped Rebecca discover those hidden files. He started to text her, but decided against it. *It's just too soon*, he thought. The despair had overtaken him again, eating him alive like flesh-eating bacteria consuming the raw flesh of emotion. He called his sister in the hopes she could cheer him up, but there was no answer after five rings, so he ended the call before it could reach voicemail. He would just try again later.

Sean loaded his laptop and scrolled through news headlines, most of them about local robberies and murders, but at the top was a story about how at least two hundred people had been injured or died from tech-related accidents in less than a month, the majority of which arose from the volatile alterations to mass-produced medications and seemingly random computer glitches.

Sean turned on the television, and almost every channel was broadcasting a news story describing similar issues: cars randomly going haywire and crashing, doctors accidentally prescribing volatile or incorrect medications due to misdiagnoses or medicine being tampered with, computer viruses stealing and doxxing private and classified information, devices locking up and getting infected, and other miscellaneous tech-related incidents. Whatever this was, it was spreading, and fast.

Something clicked in Sean's mind as he remembered how his sniffer program had run and finished instantly. This was the result of a computer virus, he realized. "I'm an *idiot*," he groaned aloud to no one. Sean loaded various news stories about the virus on his tablet, recording the dates of incidents and the ones reported on the news and their web sites, with ideas turning in his brain as he connected them. The virus had begun spreading to other forms of transportation.

The first publicized attack started in New York, with Hannah Morgan's phone, which her daughter received in Tennessee.

Since the phone was infected, it was possible it spread throughout its journey, with several smaller paths branching from those. People who traveled to other countries contributed to the spread without realizing it through no fault of their own.

As Sean put everything together, his PC's antivirus caught something and put it in quarantine. *Darn news sites. So many viruses,* he thought, but he wasn't sure if it was the killer virus. It was possible, he surmised, perhaps someone drove by with an infected car, but he also remembered how Rebecca's mother's phone was infected when he was nearby. Sean inspected the virus closely, and though he originally decided against it, he followed the path to its executable file. Against his better judgment, he placed it into a decompiling program he had written.

This program took the executable apart a piece at a time, until several lines of code combined with external libraries written by known black hats came into view. The code appeared to be designed to insert random logic into the native code of whatever it infected, and different technologies would yield vastly different results. The coding method seemed random, but the further Sean dug, the more intricate and precise the code seemed to be. He could only understand so much of it, due to it being so heavily obfuscated, so what he learned was minimal. Still, it was enough to understand this virus was of a hyper-intelligent design.

Sean scrolled down in the code until he found a string of hexadecimal characters shaped like human DNA. *What the hell?* He stared at it, flummoxed, while the hexadecimal characters, arranged in a double-helix formation, rapidly changed. Every character gradually turned into a question mark before disappearing.

Eventually, the whole program closed itself, and the virus was no longer in quarantine. His computer flickered for a moment, then returned a message stating no problems were found with the computer.

A pang of trepidation built in Sean's stomach as he realized this computer virus itself was, somehow, intelligent. It was a neural network, the likes of which most people had never seen. It wasn't just learning. It was adapting to its surroundings. Whoever programmed it knew what they were doing, and they didn't want to be found.

TWINKLE, TWINKLE, PULSING STAR
ARE WE SURE THAT'S WHAT YOU ARE?

5. SYMPTOMS

AMANDA WASN'T NORMALLY AN APPREHENSIVE woman. She was a pragmatic elementary school teacher who did things her own way. Still, she saw the news and the footage. Watching all those people become unwell and die made her heart sink.

She tried hard to stay away from the news, to block it out, but she found herself drawn to it. What better way to stay informed? Amanda had to be careful about who her habits rubbed off on. Monica was still a little thing at nine years old, going on ten, but even in her fleeting time, Monica made an impact on so many lives. Amanda saw it, and it perplexed her how Monica's father couldn't see it too.

As she walked into the children's hospital, she took a deep breath, brushing back her short blonde hair and briefly closing her brown eyes in hesitation. She could feel the death and the sadness lurking in there; a voracious predator waiting to strike at any given moment. Her eyes were glued to the floor, occasionally peeking around, looking for one specific little girl who loved superheroes and monster trucks so much that she could put any boy to shame with her knowledge of the subjects.

This little girl was a hero herself. Monica took care of everyone else around her in the hospital, doing her best to ignore the pangs and sorrow she felt herself. Cancer was a villain children should never have to face, but Monica had to. Even in the early stages, skin cancer was painful, especially for a child.

"Monica, honey, are you ready to come home with me for a couple days?" Amanda called into the room. Several little ones ran to Amanda, all shouting excitedly for her to take them home with her too, or in her place; it varied. As much as she would have loved to, she couldn't. For one thing, most of the kids already had parents, and she wasn't about to rip them away. The hospital barely tolerated her taking Monica home, and she was her niece. They had already gone out sightseeing five days earlier, so the staff were apprehensive about her going anywhere at all, let alone going home.

Amanda had been watching Monica for years because of an arrangement made with her brother. Although she loved caring for Monica, she knew this sweet little girl needed her father, since her mother was no longer around. The voices of the children were heartbreaking, and it tugged at her heartstrings every time.

"I'll be your son," one emaciated little boy said hopefully.

"You seem like you'd be a good mommy," said a six-year-old girl in a wheelchair, her voice barely audible.

Amanda had told the children many times she couldn't take them home, especially since some of them were so far along that even if she did take them home, they wouldn't last much longer. It wasn't her right to take any of their days from their parents.

As much as it killed her inside, she tried to ignore the children's cries, which was easier said than done. Her husband had divorced her after the third miscarriage, and she wanted nothing more than to be a mother. Caring for Monica helped fill that vast, empty hole, though she also longed for someone else to care for her.

Monica came running up to her aunt, a fresh coat of face paint on her bald head. "Aunt Mandy! Yay," Monica shouted. They walked outside, climbed into Amanda's SUV, and took off down the road.

"So, what's with the butterfly on your head?" Amanda asked, keeping her eyes on the road.

"I saw one outside. It landed on the window right next to me! It was so pretty, and I wanted to pet it, so I put it on my head," she tittered, making Amanda laugh with her. Monica put on the wig Amanda had bought for her about six months back, so no one would ask questions or approach them.

"How are you feeling, baby?" Amanda asked as they traveled down the road.

"I'm okay. I am hurting, though. Not as bad as yesterday. Does that mean I'm getting better?" she asked with a bright grin on her face.

Amanda composed herself as best she could and kept her eyes on the road. "Yes, sweetie, I think so. Where are you hurting today? Do you mind telling me?"

"I don't mind. I'm hurting on the inside today. In my heart."

"Hang on, sweetie." Amanda pulled the SUV over into a store's parking lot. Once she stopped the vehicle and placed it into park, she turned to Monica. "You wanna talk about it?"

Monica looked at Amanda, questions in her eyes. "I was playing with a boy yesterday named Josh. He was there yesterday, but he wasn't there today, and his mommy and daddy were crying.

I don't know where he went." Monica was quiet for a moment, and Amanda was on the verge of breaking down. "Is that gonna happen to me?" she asked. "Am I gonna disappear, too?"

Amanda's composure evaporated as she broke down. She unbuckled them both and pulled Monica to her in a tight hug. "Don't talk like that, sweetie. You are never going to disappear," she cried softly, kissing Monica all over her head. "I won't let anybody take you. Nothing is gonna take you from me. All right? Do you hear me? Nothing." She tried putting the SUV into drive, but it turned itself off. Not one to give up, she tried a few times to turn it back on, and it finally started. Amanda drove to her house, and she made a note to take her SUV to the dealership.

The two of them shared a night of fun together, both forgetting about Monica's ailments for a while. Later, Amanda tucked her in and read Monica her favorite bedtime story, Goodnight Moon, until she fell asleep. She watched Monica lie there like an angel, one she hoped she could keep.

Amanda pictured Monica growing up into a preteen, when she first really started liking boys. Then, into a teenager, when she started coming home late. Next, an adult in college. Then, finally, at work, married with a family of her own. Amanda was determined to give her such a life, even if only in stories and fairytales.

All was peaceful for most of the night, until around 2:36 a.m., when a bright light gleamed from outside Monica's window. Monica woke and walked to the window, singing her favorite nursery rhyme, Twinkle, Twinkle, Little Star. She sang for a minute or two, then returned to bed. As she drifted back toward sleep, the star grew closer and louder.

Monica grunted as the low humming roused her from her sleep once more. As she woke up again, the shadow of a being loomed over her, its face mere inches from hers. It had a bulbous head on a long, skinny neck, and long arms with elongated fingers. She couldn't make out any facial features since it was so dark.

Monica tried to scream, but discovered her mouth couldn't move. In fact, she couldn't move at all, except for her eyes. The entity unfolded its hand, and resting in its palm was a tiny metal insect. It flew off the creature's hand and into her ear, making Monica black out.

The next morning, all Monica remembered of the previous night was a bright light, a bug, and being unable to move. She dismissed it as a nightmare, but she couldn't shake the strange feeling she experienced.

Monica awoke with a splitting headache and nausea, groggily walking down the stairs to greet her aunt, who was on the phone with someone. She only heard parts of the conversation, and only her aunt's responses.

"So, what am I supposed to do then, huh? Your *daughter* needs you right now," Amanda scoffed. "Are you serious? Do you really want me to keep her at home?" Irritated, she held her phone to her ear in one hand and put her other hand on her hip. "You have no idea how hard this has been on me. They barely agreed to let me take her from the hospital! Oh, don't give me that. That's not what I meant, and you know it. I love having her around, but you *need* to be here," Amanda shouted, admonishing the person on the other end of the line.

Monica stumbled to the bathroom and vomited violently. *A side effect of the chemo,* she thought. She couldn't help but feel like something was missing. It was as though a part of her was either gone or changed. Since she was feeling so groggy, she tried something she wanted to get away with. "Mom?" she called for her aunt, who put up her finger and whispered into the phone.

Amanda closed her eyes and spoke quietly. "Do you hear that? That's your daughter. She's calling me Mom now. *Your* daughter is calling *me* Mom," Amanda chided. There was a short pause as she gave the person at the other end a chance to speak. "Yes, I remember Clarissa. I know how difficult that's been for you and Monica, but come on. Your daughter needs you.

"Look, you're my brother, and I love you. I just wish you could be in Monica's life more, I—" Amanda finally looked over at Monica and saw how sickly she was, beyond what had become her new normal. She hung up on her brother and ran to Monica. "My God, baby, what happened?"

"I don't know. I woke up and felt different," Monica sputtered. She was unsure of how else to explain it.

"Different how, sweetie? How do you feel different? Are you hurting? Where? Show me, it's okay." Amanda checked all over Monica's body, and noticed she had a fever, but otherwise looked okay beyond her usual afflictions.

"No, I'm not hurting. I just don't feel good," said Monica, accidentally raising her voice.

Amanda stepped back, shocked by Monica's unexpected rise in her voice. "Okay, okay, calm down. It's okay. No need to get upset. We don't raise our voices at each other. Let's just get you back to bed, alright?"

"No," Monica spat, her tiny body growing cold and making her feel twice her weight. "I don't wanna go back up there. It makes me feel wrong," she said, her body trembling in fear, though she wasn't sure why.

"Why does it make you feel wrong, honey? What do you mean?" Amanda asked.

"I don't know. I just feel like I shouldn't be up there. Like something bad will happen if I am," said Monica as she continued shivering violently.

"Oh. Um, okay, sweetie. Here, come lie down on the couch next to me, then, okay? We'll pop in a Disney movie. Is The Lion King okay? I know you love the classic oldies." Amanda decided to check on her niece's room later once she was more pacified. If someone had gotten into Monica's room, she was going to make them beg for their life.

Monica's face brightened with glee as some color briefly returned to her pallid face. As her excitement built, she clapped and jumped up and down, a wide smile on her face. "Circle of Life, Circle of Life," she chanted, feeling far lighter and warmer.

Amanda was confused by the situation, but she would do anything for Monica, and she didn't want to add to her niece's already-heightened stress levels. It was a shame her brother couldn't be there for his daughter, but like all things, she knew he believed he had good reason.

It didn't take long for Monica to doze off. The movie was barely halfway started when she fell asleep. Amanda stroked her niece's head, rubbing her thumb across her cheek to comfort her. She dozed off herself soon thereafter, the two of them wandering peacefully into the land of sleep while it stormed outside and Scar finished singing *Be Prepared* in the movie.

A SHINING STAR OF DOOM AND WOE
TO CHALLENGE WHAT WE THINK WE KNOW

6. Reality Check

Sean became so obsessed with the apparently sentient, adaptive computer virus that he had shut off all his surroundings. It made him jump when his phone rang again, set to the tune of Europe's The Final Countdown, his favorite song. "Hello?" he said into the phone before even answering it. Sean stifled a chuckle and answered it for real. "Hello?" he repeated, a little more cheerfully, trying not to laugh.

"Hello, Mr. Caldwell. This is Candice from Dr. Connors' office. I'm calling regarding your CAT scan and blood tests from a couple of weeks ago. There's been a major development, and we need you to come in immediately."

Sean didn't respond. He thought about all the people who were getting sick and dying after visiting their doctors, and debated whether he should go.

"Sir?" Candice implored. "If you'd like, given the current situation, we can give you the news over the phone, but it would be best for you to come in to hear this." There was a long pause. "Sir?"

"Just tell me," said Sean. "Please."

"Mr. Caldwell, I'm so sorry, but preliminary results show that you have a cyst right at the base of your brain. It appears to be growing based on our simulations, and we'd like to run a few more tests. When would be a suitable time to schedule—" Sean ended the call before Candice could finish, dread burning in his blood.

It's fake, he thought. *It's totally fake, just like the rest.* Even if it wasn't, it was still in the preliminary stages, so he had time. People were dying because of technological problems, something he had some ability at, so he had to at least try saving them. Sure, other people may have been more qualified, or had a better idea of what was going on, but Sean believed Rebecca was led to him for a reason. If everyone always thought someone else would do it, nobody ever would.

Sean turned on the television because he needed a distraction. There was another story about people dying because of medical mistreatment, and the reporter talked to a group of pharmacists and doctors that were called together from around the world. One of the reporters approached a younger male doctor and stuck a camera and microphone in his face as he spoke to someone.

"So, tell me, sir. How can this be happening to people on a global scale? What do you think is going on?" the reporter asked.

"Well, I don't know, honestly. The strange thing is that none of the illnesses are consistent with our models," the man replied.

"Can you elaborate?"

"I can try. Look, even with these volatile ingredients combined, the results shouldn't be this bad. It's simply not making sense. I think there's something else going on. There's almost no consistency in any of the strains. None of our simulations have been able to produce a match. It's entirely unfamiliar territory, and we're not even sure where or how to continue."

The reporter looked at the time and tried to hurry the interview along before she got in trouble. "Okay, well, we don't have a whole lot of time left, so can you tell us what this has been like for you personally? Do you think your career will survive?" the reporter read from the script. She realized how the script read after that, nausea burning in her stomach. It made her livid that the station sent her out there with such inconsiderate wording.

"That's a bit of an insensitive thing to ask someone right now, don't you think? We're all doing the best we can. Everyone is, not just us. I know people around the world think we're somehow complicit with all this, but we're not. We want answers as badly as you do, but that takes time.

"It doesn't help when the media is blatantly saying doctors and pharmacists are universally evil. We're not all conspiring to kill you, despite what the media wants you to think. Trust me, we want everyone to get better, and let's not forget that we're suffering too. I'm not worried about my career or even myself. I'm worried about those people out there who still need help. You know, the ones who are dying? I'm worried about them, because that's my job. To help people, not make them sicker. Right now, that's a bit backward for some reason. As soon as we hear something, we'll let everyone know. Hopefully, your career survives," the man scoffed as he turned and walked away.

The reporter forced a smile, and though she wasn't the one who wrote it, she did say it. Guilt assailed her mind and heart, but she let the comment pass. "Okay, thank you for your time. Brad, back to you," the reporter said icily.

Sean cut the television off. As he mulled about the situation, an idea formed. If he could get into the doctor's office with his sniffer and decompile programs on a flash drive, he could show the doctor what the code was doing. He believed he could catch it in the act of manipulating the computer. Sean called the doctor's office back, acting on his idea before it was too late.

"Hello, thank you for calling Navajo Health. This is Beverly speaking. How may I help you?" the receptionist asked cheerfully.

"Hey, this is Sean Caldwell. I received a call earlier from somebody named Candice asking me to come in for an appointment, but I kind of freaked out and hung up on her. So, I'm sorry, and I was wondering if there's a way I could still schedule an appointment?"

"Oh, that's alright, hon," said Beverly. "Candice went out to lunch, but I can look for you. Yes, sir, we have your file right here. One moment, please."

Beverly placed Sean on hold for what felt like hours, and the incessant elevator music played through the phone, mixed in with the occasional "Your call is important to us. Please stay on the line and a representative will be with you shortly."

Sean was almost asleep when a surly male voice came through the phone. "Hello? Sean, are you still there? Sean?"

Sean yawned. "Yeah, I'm still here. Sorry, I think I may have dozed off," he replied.

The doctor laughed heartily. "That's quite alright, I understand. I hear you're looking for an appointment, if you're sufficiently woken from your stupor?"

"Yes, sir, please. I need to find out what's going on. I was told I have a growing cyst on my brain. The weird thing is, I feel fine, and with all the medical issues going on in the world right now, I don't know if it's even safe to seek treatment. But I have a theory, and I'd like to see what our local medical community thinks."

Dr. Connors was silent for a moment, considering Sean's words. "Uh… alright. How's nine a.m. tomorrow? That work for you?"

"Yeah, that'll do it. See you then." Sean hung up the phone, going over everything he knew in his head.

First, there was the computer virus. It was somehow responsible for the outbreak. He knew that in his gut.

Second, the virus could adapt to its surroundings, including firewalls and antivirus programs. That claim was going to require a lot more convincing, because people wouldn't be comfortable believing a computer virus was somehow changing.

Whoever programmed the virus knew what they were doing by coding an adaptation matrix into an extraordinarily complex neural network. There were AIs, but none so powerful as this one. This was something else entirely. It wasn't just learning. It was *evolving*. It was the equivalent of the microbe evolving into the first land-dwelling creature, but not over thousands of years. This was overnight. No one had seen anything like it, not quite. At least, not that most people knew about.

Third, the virus's code seemed like a simple usage of hexadecimal notation, strangely shaped into a double helix, yet somehow, there seemed to be more complex algorithms underneath. Code learning from code and rewriting itself.

Finally, the virus could self-encrypt its contents to prevent its code from being analyzed and even change it at will. This was most assuredly a rogue AI, one with too much knowledge and power, but not unlike one Sean had heard of before.

Sean experienced trouble sleeping. He tossed and turned half the night, going over theories and paradigms in his head. None of them made sense with the virus's behavior. What little sleep he managed was filled with nightmares about the outbreak. All he could see was people's faces on the news, and all he could think of were the saddened families. Sean saw Rebecca's grief-stricken expression in his dreams and thought of the children who just visited the doctor for a routine checkup, then died varying days later.

He awoke around six-thirty a.m. the next morning in a cold sweat, unable to get back to sleep. *The outbreak*, he thought while he showered. That's what the news media decided to call it, which he found disgraceful.

Sean arrived at the doctor's office a bit earlier than his allotted time slot, and upon entering, he found the parking lot was completely empty. The offices opened at seven a.m., and it was eight thirty. Where could everybody be? Confused but not deterred, he walked inside. The building was empty too, save for one lady at the desk.

"Hey, I'm Sean Caldwell. I called yesterday and—"

"Mhmm." The lady waved her hand in the air, but remained fixated on her phone, occasionally brushing back her braided hair with her other hand.

"Ma'am, should I just go on back—"

"Boy, what's wrong with you? Just g'on back there. I ain't got time for this, can't you see I'm busy? Lord have mercy. Someone help this child."

Sean rolled his eyes and walked into the deserted offices, noticing the dimmed lights. Not one soul could be seen. He walked quietly throughout the building and silently jumped as he came across a mirror he bumped into.

"Excuse me," he said to it instinctively, not realizing what it was. He slapped his head with his hand and shook his head. *I'm losing it*, he thought. Sean pulled out his phone to scroll through social media as a distraction, needing to calm himself. It wasn't a healthy habit, but it worked, albeit temporarily.

Dr. Connors put his hand on Sean's shoulder, and Sean screamed, throwing his phone out of shock, to which the doctor laughed loudly. "Thanks for that. Been dead as a nail and as boring as tumbleweeds all morning. Needed the laugh. Now then, let's look, shall we?"

Sean nodded, grabbed his phone, and followed the doctor into a room. "So, what does a cyst mean, really? Is it a tumor or something different?" Sean asked.

Dr. Connors cleared his throat. "Well, most cysts are just little air pockets that form and are usually noncancerous, but given the current situation, we can't be too careful. It's also important to remember that most cancers do produce cysts. Some cysts are malignant, but others are benign, albeit annoying or messy.

"A tumor is an abnormal mass of tissue or some other form of swelling. It can, like a cyst, form in any part of the body. Most are cancerous, which is bad, obviously, but some of them are harmless. A lot of people don't know this. Most people, when they hear the word 'tumor,' automatically associate it with cancer. To be fair, they're usually right, but not always.

"I had a patient once who had a mass right on the base of his brain, same as you. We found it when he was five, and eventually discovered it was responsible for his tic disorder and other neurological problems. His family had it checked every five years until he turned fifteen, and it hadn't grown any. What we discovered was undeveloped fetal tissue, part of a twin who never matured. The mother had two miscarriages before him, you see.

"The kid was super claustrophobic, too. MRIs were how we watched it, and he insisted on sedation every time. The first time he went through it at five years old, he dreamed he was on a spaceship," the doctor said with a laugh. "Started making these beeping and rocket ship noises. Man, it was funny. We tried it with him awake once to save time, and that was a bad idea, let me tell you. Kid nearly destroyed the machine trying to get out. He didn't even remember much about it afterwards. The poor boy was traumatized so badly. Good kid, though. I hope he's doing well. That was over thirty years ago," the doctor finished.

Sean smiled and thought about how Dr. Connors reminded him of his grandfather, with how he used to get so wildly off topic and start rambling about stories to anyone who would listen.

"That's a remarkable story, Dr. Connors. Thanks for telling it, but back on topic, how bad do you think this is? Should we really trust these models, given the circumstances? What happens if it *is* real? Is there a chance, if it's real, it's nothing?"

"All of those are excellent questions, Sean. You're just as inquisitive as your father," said Dr. Connors.

Silence hung in the air. "You knew my father?"

"I know him still. He comes to visit me occasionally, and he's the one who asked me to look at you. That's how you got the call so fast. I know you won't believe this, but he does care about you." Dr. Connors already knew what kind of response he was about to get, but realized it too late.

Sean had heard that line too many times, and he always pushed it down, letting it run off his back, but not this time. This time, there were too many emotions, and the dam finally burst. All his bottled-up feelings and thoughts came bursting through the seams. Sean couldn't contain them any longer.

"Then where was he?" Sean shouted. "I needed a father. My mother could only do so much for me, and man, did she ever. I needed to talk to another guy sometimes, you know? Growing up without him was rough, especially as a teenager. I had questions, man. Every so often, I could get something out of him, which was rare, but even then, it was only when I saw him. That was even more sporadic. When he was in a good mood, he was a great dad, but often, he was just this distant, emotionless person who seemed not to care about anyone else, and half the time, he had anger issues. It's like he was two or three different people. He—"

Sean saw the doctor's concerned face and noticed he was offering him a box of tissues, discovering he was crying without realizing it. "I'm sorry," he muttered as he wiped his face. "It's a sensitive subject for me."

"You don't have to apologize to me, Sean. I've known your father since he was your age, you know. I'm sorry you've had to deal with this. Hopefully, your own next of kin has a better life. Don't follow in your father's footsteps, or in his father's. You have a chance here to break the cycle, so take it."

They were silent for a moment, soon erupting into cathartic laughter. "Thanks, Doc. I'll pay you extra for the talk if you want."

"Nah, it's all good. I don't want your money. My concern is you. I've known your family for a while now. When you've been around seventy-four years, you learn to appreciate moments like this. They're worth more to me than money. No, this visit is free of charge."

"Thank you," said Sean. "So, about those questions…"

"Ah, yes! So sorry, my boy, I completely forgot. Yes, there's a chance this is nothing. As you know, it's only a cyst at this point, assuming it's even real. Hard to tell right now, for sure. You should also be aware that if this does turn out to be a developing mass, it could be fatal. There's extraordinarily little we can do for it, even in 2036. We still haven't progressed since the Standstill of 2028.

"Since it's right at the base of your brain, it's inoperable without risking permanent brain damage or full-body paralysis. There are experimental procedures, but they're extremely dangerous, even under normal circumstances, so hopefully there's nothing to be worried about. I want you to know the dangers, at least."

Sean sulked, but nodded in agreement. "Yes, sir, I understand. Just scary, you know? Having all these ambitions, things I want to do with my life, but then I realize I may not ever get there. It's not just about losing my life. It's about never having the real chance to make my life worth losing."

Dr. Connors placed a hand on Sean's shoulder. "A life is *always* worth something. I must ask, though. If things do go south, are there any dependents we should be aware of? Also, you should know that if you ever have children, there's a chance they'll have cancer too. Maybe not the same kind, but the chance does increase."

Sean became despondent and sighed heavily. "Actually," he started, "there is someone. I… I um—"

"Save it," Dr. Connors soothed. "I can tell you're not comfortable telling me, and you don't have to. Anyway, I'll watch this and keep you updated as it develops. Now then, you said you had a theory?"

"Yes, sir, but it's a little crazy." Sean's blood ran warm, as he was unsure if what he was about to do was in his best interests, but he knew something had to be done.

"That's okay, so am I," Dr. Connors retorted with a chuckle. "What ya got?"

Sean cleared his throat. "Okay, so, I believe these deaths, misdiagnoses, and whatnot are because of a computer virus, one powerful enough to completely rewrite the software governing the factories where medicine gets manufactured and synthesized.

I think it's forcing the software to combine volatile ingredients on purpose, which otherwise seem normal on the surface."

Dr. Connors sat back and folded his arms. "That *is* a bold claim, Sean. Do you have any proof?"

"Sort of. I bet you put my information into that computer, right? Along with my medical history, my prognosis, and everything?"

Dr. Connors nodded. "Of course, it's just standard—"

"Policy, I know. I suspect that's the point. I'm willing to bet this virus is on your PC right now, waiting for you to send the data to an external location, at which point it will alter the data."

"Okay, so, what, I run a virus scan, and it just disappears?" asked Dr. Connors.

"I'm not so sure. See, the thing is, this computer virus is… changing." Sean articulated the words carefully, trying to ease into the bombshell.

"Changing how, Sean?" Sean could sense Dr. Connors' skepticism building. He didn't want to scare him away, or worse, make him think he was going crazy as a side effect of the potential mass.

"It's adapting. Rewriting itself. Think of it like a fast-tracked version of evolution. Through the years, species gain and lose traits they need and no longer need, respectively. This virus is doing the same thing, but rapidly. It's like it was programmed to evolve, kind of like John Conway's Game of Life. I think it's learning the firewalls and security systems, then rewriting its own code to prolong its lifespan and propagate."

Dr. Connors remembered something he had heard not so long ago. "You know, now that you mention it, I remember my grandson saying something about there being experimental code they were assessing in the tech community. Something about an AI, one capable of rewriting itself. It was about nine months ago, but they called it—"

"Protocol. Yeah, I remember. It was an ambitious experiment, and they named it that because the idea was to challenge the accepted protocols of technology. They eventually considered the program too dangerous, so they shut it down. Everyone believes the program was abandoned, but what if it wasn't? My cybersecurity professor went over something like this. I think whatever this is, it's somehow built on top of the Protocol AI. Maybe it reactivated on its own." Sean jumped up from his seat and pulled out his flash drive from his pocket. "May I?"

"I'm not supposed to let you do this, but go ahead," said Dr. Connors.

"Thanks." Sean plugged the drive in and ran his sniffer program, specifically modified to help it locate a single string from the decompiled virus's code. The sniffer found the code almost immediately. While Sean had it quarantined, he studied the information intently, trying to learn all he could. The virus adapted again five seconds later, escaping quarantine completely. The doctor glared at the screen with his mouth agape.

"That's what I thought. This virus is using our AIs to evolve. It's Protocol." Sean turned away from the computer to face Dr. Connors. "It's gotten loose."

The doors burst open as officers and special agents surrounded the room. "FBI," one of them shouted. A woman pointed a gun at Sean. "This is Special Agent Winona Reyes. I am actively detaining the designated person of interest. Surround the building and guard all exits. No one gets in or out," she said into her radio. "You," she said, pointing the gun at Sean. "On your knees, hands above your head. Step away from the doctor."

"What is this even about?" Sean shouted as he reluctantly complied. "What the hell? I haven't done anything wrong," he barked.

"That's classified. All you need to know is you're a person of interest to someone particularly important who wants to speak with you," said Winona.

"Yeah? Who the hell would that be?" Sean demanded.

Winona's face was stoic as she put her gun away. "The president." Sean was ushered out by the FBI agents. "Thank you for your cooperation, Dr. Connors," said Winona as she swiftly walked out.

Another man came in from a connecting room after waiting for a couple of minutes, and Dr. Connors sighed, holding his head low. "I'm sorry, John. I tried. He just doesn't seem ready."

"It's alright, Daniel. You did your best. Has he really figured that much out already?" John asked, impressed. He was bulky, with a blonde buzzcut and goatee. His tired green eyes analyzed everything in the room.

"Seems like it. John, listen. I don't know what you and your guys got going on, but Sean's not wrong. You could've been there more for him, and you still can. He needs you right now," Dr. Connors chided.

"I know." John sighed, pinching the bridge of his nose. "It's GAIA. They've got me watching this closely for some reason. I don't understand what this has to do with us. The only thing I can figure is that they want me to watch my son, but I have no idea why."

"I thought your agency only dealt with—" Dr. Connors started.

"Shh, keep your voice down. And yes, that's true. There's something they're not telling me, like always," John griped, shaking his head. "I'll talk to Sean when the time is right, but he's not the only one. His sister matters too.

"I know I've committed a lot of wrongs in my life, especially with my kids. I'm gonna make it right, but I was told to have no contact with Sean until they approve it, despite me supposedly being the one in charge. I've got a briefing tomorrow at noon, and I plan on asking questions." John unfolded his arms and sat down, holding his head in his hands.

"Didn't you tell me you left, though? How did you get involved with them again?"

"It's a long story," John replied wearily, shaking his head again. "We got reports to keep an eye out for a rise in activity about a month before all this started. They didn't give me a choice."

Dr. Connors placed a hand on John's back. "You need to get away from them, and you're probably gonna have a hard time explaining all this to Sean."

"You just gave me an idea. This whole thing falls under GAIA jurisdiction, so what's the best way to keep an eye on him and let him know what's going on?" John asked with a smile on his face.

"Beats me," the doctor yielded with a shrug.

"By bringing him in," said John. "I think he's ready, and this could work."

"Be careful, John. You're already trapped with them. Don't let him get trapped too."

"He won't. I'll make that crystal clear, but he has talents we can use, and he's smart. I'll make the call right now," said John, pulling out his phone. "Trust me, this is the right path, and he's going to *love* it."

So you glimmer without pause
Defying all of nature's laws

✧

7. Signs of Life

JAKE DECIDED TO STAY WITH ABIGAIL TO HELP HER feel safe. They spent a lot of time together, but luckily, Abigail's house was large enough for them both. It was stocked to the brim with groceries, so there was plenty of produce for them to cook with nightly. There were a few times when their electronics would malfunction again, but it never lasted long, and they weren't yet successful in pinpointing the cause.

"I wonder if what happened a few weeks ago had something to do with this computer virus thing," said Jake.

"What do you mean?" asked Abigail. "What computer virus?"

"Well, I was talking to a friend of mine this morning on Discord. Guy's a programmer at NASA. We catch up every weekend or so. Anyway, he was saying something about a deadly computer virus he heard of, supposedly a sentient one. Of course, I thought he was making stuff up, but now I'm thinking maybe he was on to something."

Abigail perked up as Jake piqued her curiosity. "You know, since you mention it, my phone flickered when I was near that wreck. That's how it got compromised! Don't you see? Hannah's phone must have been infected and passed it to mine. Then, it infected my computer when I got home. I still don't understand how it managed to manipulate all my other electronics, though. It doesn't make any sense. Then again, I'm not a techie of any sort. My experience is more with the biological system."

"Maybe it does make sense," said Jake. "What if it used your computer to send out some sort of signal? Maybe it sent out a pulse using special techy waves and it affected everything else, causing everything to surge."

Abigail was silent for a moment. "I don't know," she said as she pondered Jake's words, "but it was incredibly disconcerting."

Jake turned on the television and switched to the news, which played a report about a plane crash.

"...of a plane going down in Japan. There were one hundred and eight passengers on board, and authorities say there were no survivors. It's unclear what caused the crash. However, the NTSB has reported several electrical failures. Unfortunately, this is all we know about the incident currently. Disasters like this seem to be happening globally now. Tim, back to you."

The newscaster cleared his throat and composed himself the best he could. "This outbreak comes only weeks after the death of Hannah Morgan in Babylon, New York. It's undetermined currently what's causing these issues in the medical community, but we still advise you to see your doctor. Do *not* avoid medical treatment if you are ill or suspect that you may need medical assistance.

"Medication manufacturing facilities and automated pharmacy companies are still investigating their systems to determine what caused this outbreak. Sources are now saying that somehow, the chemical makeup of these medications has been severely altered. Workers are claiming they had no knowledge of this, and are working around the clock to discover the cause. No one has ever witnessed anything like this before. Even over-the-counter medications are affected. There's been a list of medications recalled, and we will have that list for you shortly.

"Now, we go live to the White House, where the president, accompanied by a few FBI agents, has recruited a professional software designer who may have some answers."

As soon as the newscaster finished speaking, the screen changed to static on every channel. It was clear this broadcast wasn't meant for public viewing. "Do you think this was a top-secret government project gone wrong? You know, a clandestine black op gone rogue?" Jake asked as he turned to Abigail.

Abigail rolled her eyes, but pondered the question.

✧

Sean was accompanied by a slew of FBI agents to the White House to sit down for a meeting. "Okay, what's going on, Mr. President? Why am I here?" Sean asked before anyone else could speak.

"I understand your confusion, Sean, but hear me out. We've been monitoring the infected systems, during which time we discovered someone managed to decompile the virus, and by someone, I mean you. Others have tried, but the virus adapted before they had a chance. We knew then that you understood something about this outbreak. Something essential to humanity's survival. So far, we've lost hundreds of thousands of lives in just a few weeks. I want you to explain to me everything you know. Start at the beginning, and leave nothing out."

Sean sweated as his mind pled with him to go home and forget about the situation. His nerves were shot, but of course, this was understandable, given the situation. Surely, someone else had managed to do what Sean did, effortless as it was. Then again, he did write the program he used to decompile the virus. Perhaps the virus wanted Sean to find it, and this was part of its plan. *Don't be silly*, he thought, but he still wondered.

"Take your time, Sean. You're not in any trouble," President Matthews assured, making certain Sean felt at ease.

It's now or never, he thought. Maybe he could get answers this way. "Well, the first incident I heard of was one of my classmates having her mom's phone tampered with. She told her father about what happened and cleared the pharmacist's name, since he was believed to have intentionally poisoned her. I have this program on my flash drive that I wrote. It searches any device for evidence of tampering. The program ran and failed when I first tried it, and I believe it's because the computer got infected. It executed flawlessly on the succeeding attempt, and showed results of data erasure.

"The next thing I know, after I get home, my computer catches this virus. It's likely because it infected my phone and even my flash drive. I followed its executable to its root path and put it into a program to deconstruct it into its native code, something I wrote as a personal project about a year ago.

"What I saw was remarkable. The program was made up of several complex strings of augmented matrices, each of which was in hexadecimal notation. They exhibited the shape of a double-helix formation in the terminal, like human DNA. It was obfuscated code hidden behind standard encryption.

"I was studying it when everything started turning into question marks, and then it was just gone. It's like it learned my security system and adapted. I think this virus is adapting to its environment. In a sense, I think it's evolving. It behaves as though it's alive. I know it sounds crazy, but that's been my observation."

"Alright, slow down, Sean. Let me get this straight. You think this thing is learning? That, somehow, it's *alive*?" asked President Matthews.

"Yes, sir. I know how it sounds, but I believe it to be possible. There was a dangerous project months ago that the tech community scrapped called Protocol. It was an experiment involving a series of programmable neural networks to create a singular master AI. They wanted it to teach itself how to adapt to its surroundings, and not only learn how to avoid dangers to itself, but also teach any other systems it touched the same thing.

"It was an open-source, community-funded project any programmer could submit to. Originally, it was meant to help bolster computer security and actively catch threats. Someone built this on top of the Protocol AI, but how they did it, the way they changed it, it's unlike anything I've ever seen. The thing is, Protocol was deemed too dangerous after it began building its own AIs and infecting major systems. I remember reading how it almost caused a nuclear war, but someone was able to prevent it just in time. Thankfully, it was easy to shut down. I thought it was abandoned, but what I'm afraid of is that it may have turned itself back on.

"The biggest thing I've noticed is how this new version spreads. We're all familiar with how you can transmit a bodily virus. This virus, AI, or whatever it is, is doing the same thing on a digital level. Even being near any other electronics has the potential for infection. It gets weirder, though. It's picking its targets. It cares about what it infects and when. It's not just infecting everything it touches, only the ones it wants to."

"Do you think you could trace its origin using our federal equipment?" asked the president, not skipping a beat.

Sean was taken aback by how quickly the president processed everything he explained. "Honestly, I'm not entirely sure that's possible, even this day and age. Twenty-five years ago, criminal forensics had basic software to somewhat trace where threats originated, but it was primitive, and it took an exceptionally long time. That's something we don't have a lot of right now. Since the Standstill, we haven't progressed."

The president leaned forward in his chair. "Well, that's not entirely accurate. There are new, top-secret technologies the public has no knowledge of. We can let you use it if you sign the paperwork first. Typical NDA. No one can know about this. No friends, no family, no one. Just sign these papers," the president commanded, handing a stack of documents to sign from under his desk.

Sean signed all the documents and silently handed them back. *What is happening?* he thought.

"Two years ago, several exceptionally talented programmers wrote software that took us giant leaps forward. One of these programs can be used to trace the origins of this Protocol virus.

So I'm told, anyway," said the president, shooting a glare at one of the people sitting at the table before looking back at Sean. "We knew most of the information you shared, but I needed to see what you knew about it. I'm happy to say that so far, I'm impressed."

Rendered speechless and confused, Sean simply nodded his head. President Matthews and his Secret Service took Sean to a black car. The trip lasted a little under an hour, and Sean was ushered out when they reached their destination. Once inside, Sean marveled at all the technological wonders. There were giant, glowing computers that made low, humming noises and were shaped like teardrops, an AI leading the center, and so many more indescribable, fascinating things. There were even what looked like intelligence and teamwork testing courses.

"Where do you keep the cake?" Sean joked.

"What cake?" replied one of the agents in confusion.

Sean grinned. "So it's a lie?"

"What are you talking about?" the agent asked, annoyed.

"Never mind," Sean said defeatedly, realizing the reference was lost on him.

"Plug your flash drive into that PC to your left, Sean. It'll automatically search the drive and scan the data you've collected," the president ordered.

"Alright." Sean's blood pressure spiked, his head spinning. He had never seen anything like what was in that room. It astounded him, and he wondered how they were capable of such advanced technology.

Sean plugged his flash drive into the main computer, and in an instant, the supercomputer displayed the paths of the virus. It was like looking at a star-map. Every device or car infected was listed on the screen. This kind of technology was believed to be impossible, but there it was in front of him. The question was, how?

After mere seconds, the computer located the origin of the virus, and one of the FBI agents pushed Sean out of the way. "Sir, we've found the origin of the virus. It came from somewhere within the NSA."

"Uh, ow." Sean's eyes widened. "How is that possible?"

"I'm not sure. Let's go find out," said the president. Sean was ushered along to another black sedan and placed in the back, where the president got in alongside him. "Head to the bunker, Jack. We're gonna pay someone a visit and see what in the blue blazes is going on."

The bunker, he thought. *Probably some other confidential place with ultramodern technology*. The car ride was quiet, and Sean passed out an hour later, drifting into the land of dreams. There was a dream that was also a memory. Someone his size led him out of the woods when he was lost as a child. As he turned to thank the person, they were gone. He was awoken by Winona a few hours later. "Let's go," she demanded as she forcefully removed Sean from the car.

"Easy," said Sean, rubbing his forearm. The agents led Sean and the president into a dome-shaped building, which opened with giant doors that silently slid upwards. They were taken to a black jet with a strange logo on the side of it. It was a giant V with two big dots in the middle, one on top of the other, and evenly spaced. Each part of it had an orange outline. *That's a strange logo*, Sean thought. They climbed inside the aircraft, and it immediately lit up.

"Please input your desired destination," an electronic voice commanded.

"NSA headquarters," commanded the president from a seat in front of Sean.

"Confirmed," the voice replied, and the ceiling of the building opened.

"Okay, how is all this possible? What secrets have you people been keeping?" Sean asked.

The president raised his hand and turned around, giving Sean a stern look. "Sorry, Sean. That's classified."

Sean shook his head. "Of course it is. Makes sense."

The jet was in the air within minutes, and it took off like a lightning bolt. Within minutes, the president stood. "We're here," he announced casually. Sean thought it better not to question the mechanics behind everything, and to simply let it be for the time being, but he would be asking questions later. First, he needed the words to use for them. He was also dizzy and nauseous from the quick trip. The agents stormed the NSA building, commanding everyone to step away from their computers. There was chaos all around as everyone scrambled to get away.

"Stand down," ordered the president as he entered the room. The agents lowered their weapons, but didn't let down their guard. "You there." President Matthews pointed at an NSA worker. "Dale Winston. Come over here, son." Dale moved slowly toward the president, his hands behind his head, sweating nervously.

"L-look, man, it was an accident. We couldn't anticipate what would happen, we—" Winona put a gun to Dale's back. "Uh, h-hey, is that necessary?"

"The virus. Why did you make it, and how was it built?" asked President Matthews.

"What? Sir, we didn't create the virus. It found us. Well, sort of. See, there's this guy, William, who has a criminal record. I was assigned to monitor him, and one day when I remoted in, something came out," Dale explained.

"Explain," the president commanded, folding his arms.

"Okay, the full story, sure. So, this William guy works for SETI. Don't ask me how they got someone there with a criminal history. I don't know how that stuff works, but his computer was the first to get infected. The first before ours, even. At first, we treated it like any other virus and did the usual stuff. You know, antivirus, malware cleanup, the usual. But it never detected anything, even though the program was there.

"Eventually, one of my coworkers helped me get it into quarantine using a custom script. We studied it for a while, trying to learn why this thing was so complex. Now here's where it gets freaky. This thing somehow learned how to escape quarantine on its own… while it was in there. We were studying it, trying to find out more about it, but somehow it escaped. I know it sounds crazy, but—"

"It doesn't sound crazy," said Sean. "I had the same experience in my investigation. As I studied it, it rewrote itself and somehow left my computer. This thing is evolving, adapting to its environment. Something I'm curious about though is that their tech said the virus originated here, not at SETI. How would it miss that?"

"Because by then, it had already changed its makeup to the point where it was a completely different virus. You could equate it to a person changing at a molecular level, like their fingerprints and blood type. There isn't just one virus at work here anymore, man. There are *millions*, all of which are quickly spreading. Each one of them is different in their digital footprint. If you want more answers, go to SETI. They're where it started. I didn't write this thing, man. None of us did. Our computers were infected like everybody else's."

"Of *course*. That makes perfect sense. From a strategic standpoint, it's genius. Infecting the NSA would be the start, and with how many computers they're tapped into… oh, wow," Sean said with a gasp, sitting down in a nearby chair with his hand over his mouth.

The president's brow furrowed as he grew enraged. "You were playing with something volatile, and it got away from you," he yelled.

"Sir, with all due respect, there's nothing we could've done. I'm telling you, we tried everything. Yes, we studied it and tried to dissect it. Maybe in doing so, it activated some dormant subroutine, I don't know, but it didn't come from here. This thing is alive. I don't know how, but this computer virus is a living thing." There were two loud knocks on the door. "What, your agents knock now?"

"I don't have any other agents in this area," replied the president.

Sean stood and looked over at the president, who nodded in approval as Sean opened the door. "Uh, hello?"

The man pushed Sean out of the way and swiftly walked into the center of the room. "My name is William Donovan. I'm here about the virus."

"I'm getting really tired of being pushed around," Sean muttered.

"That's him," shouted Dale, pointing to the man in the doorway. "He's the guy I got the virus from!"

"Sir, how did you even know where to find us?" asked the president. His Secret Service agents all pointed their guns at William, who begrudgingly raised his arms in surrender with a sigh of annoyance.

"I detected the NSA on my PC. It's not hard with the tech these days to know Big Brother is watching. A little script I wrote to text my smart watch whenever my PC gets accessed remotely. I was coming here anyway to ask why these people are still spying on me. I haven't done anything wrong in years. Imagine my surprise to find the president and FBI here when I arrive."

"Sir, we're under an investigation right now, and you have no authorization to be here, so I'm gonna have to ask you to leave, Mr. Donovan," the president demanded.

"Okay, but I really think you'll want to hear what I have to say," said William.

The president looked at his Secret Service and nodded, making them all lower their weapons.

William dropped his arms. "This virus didn't just come from nowhere, and Dale is right. It's a form of intelligent life." He paused to see everyone look at him in confusion. "What? Oh, I have a device that lets me listen to audio in any room. It's usually not so easy, so you might wanna consider beefing up your security. Anyway, we're not entirely certain where it came from, either, but there's something you should know. A week before all this started, SETI received a broadcast. It was an identical match to the Wow! signal from 1977."

"I'm sorry, hold on, the what?" barked Sean. All this information at once made his head feel tight.

William sat on top of a table. "Carl Sagan sent the Arecibo binary message into space in 1974, and three years later, they launched something called Voyager, which held information regarding our genetic makeup, music, and culture. On August 15, 1977, we received a signal from space. It came from somewhere in the Sagittarius constellation, which became famously known as the Wow! signal. Jerry Ehman analyzed the signal, then wrote and circled 'Wow!' on the results. It was picked up by a satellite named Big Ear, and lasted for exactly seventy-two seconds. The following month, Voyager was sent into space to further continue the search for intelligent life.

"One of our satellites went offline almost a month ago now, and then came back on, like someone rebooted it. I was the one to remote in and diagnose the problem, but as soon as I did, my computer started acting funky, showing all the signs of a ferocious computer virus," he began, looking at Dale, "which was *also* when I discovered my computer being remoted into. This virus came from the satellite. I hardly believe this myself. Still, I think we need to face the possibility that this isn't an ordinary computer virus. The possibility that it's not from… here."

"Wait, hang on a second," said Sean, shaking his head as dread set in. "Sorry, you're saying this computer virus came from *space?*"

"It's a strong possibility. All I'm saying is, this thing came from one of our satellites. Someone needed the clearance to do so. I've checked through every scenario, vetted every employee we have, and trust me, none of them did it. It's the only possible conclusion here. This thing came from space. It's no coincidence that we encountered this virus after receiving another Wow! signal," William explained.

"That signal was never proven to be alien in origin, though. You're assuming this is extraterrestrial based on backwater folklore and ufology," scoffed Dale.

"No, listen to me. The Wow! signal came through on a twenty-one-centimeter frequency no Earth satellites can use," said William.

"You clearly haven't read Jerry Ehman's official take on it then. Yes, initially, he thought it was alien, but after studying it more thoroughly, he changed his mind and concluded it was an earthly signal bounced off space debris," Dale carped as his frustration grew.

William laughed and shook his head. "Did you not hear what I just said? Earth satellites aren't permitted to use that frequency. Also, I have read Jerry's take on it, since he's the one who discovered it. He later revoked his skepticism due to it being unlikely to have come from us, given the requirements of a space-borne reflector being bound to certain, unrealistic requirements to sufficiently explain the signal. It was broadcast at 1,420 megahertz, which is problematic, because that is a *protected* spectrum. Meaning, it was using bandwidth reserved for astronomical signals, which terrestrial satellites are forbidden to transmit. Not to mention, it was *identical* to the hydrogen line, a mathematical constant throughout the universe."

"You can't prove any of that." Dale shook his head and threw his hands out in emphasis.

William laughed again. "I don't have to. We didn't have the power to produce such a powerful transmission then. That signal, coming from us, would've required a two-point-two-gigawatt transmitter, something vastly more powerful than we had. I don't really know if we could even do it now, but not in 1977. Besides, the frequency of the hydrogen line is 1,420.40575177 megahertz, the same frequency the Wow! signal came in as. That's awfully precise for a coincidence. Plus, it's the frequency an intelligent civilization would likely use to communicate. Granted, when we turned our radio telescopes back to the area after the signal, we didn't pick up anything again, but maybe they had moved or stopped broadcasting.

"There are too many signs here. It was alien in origin then, and it most certainly is now. The actual signal came in as 6EQUJ5. So did this one. The odds of it reflecting the same way twice are one in a trillion, maybe double that, but here we are. I'll also grant you that if it didn't come in the same way twice, there could have been a logical explanation for it we just haven't stumbled upon yet. As it stands, however…" William trailed off.

Sean felt his world flip upside-down. He tried to come to grips with the notion that not only was there now a heavy potential for intelligent life on other planets, but that such a civilization had attacked humanity, one much more powerful and advanced than we were. "So, you're saying *aliens* gave us a computer virus through one of our satellites, knowing we would investigate, and the virus would spread? My God."

Dale cleared his throat. "I get what you're saying, and maybe you're right. Heck, you're *probably* right, but couldn't this have just been a hacker screwing around? I imagine it wouldn't take much if they knew what they were doing, especially if they knew what to replicate. I mean, all this stuff has been public knowledge for decades."

"I doubt it," Sean muttered. "A prank to kill the entire world? I guess it's possible, but why has no one claimed responsibility? Usually, with casualties this high, someone wants to take credit." Sean hyperventilated and sweated, his vision spinning, so he sat down in a nearby chair to calm himself.

The president turned to Sean, unease dripping through his bones. "Sean, listen. I know this is a lot to process, but remember the NDA. Our goals haven't changed. We just need to stop this. We can worry about the cause of it later."

"Later? With all due respect, Mr. President, if we don't stop this thing now, there's not going to *be* a later," Sean yelled. "This isn't the time for political, bureaucratic nonsense. It's the time for action."

"Everyone, just, hold on a second, let's think this through," said Dale as he tried to rationalize the situation. "Why would an advanced alien race need our computers for such an advanced virus? Why not just use their own?"

Sean worked theories in his brain, which had become ingrained into him from years of software development. "I think it's a hyper-advanced neural network," he suggested. "An evolved AI, but one far more powerful than the Protocol experiment ever was. I mean, think about it. When we first invented neural nets, we had to send them through various iterations and feed them all kinds of data matrices for them to learn the difference between a cat and a dog, or a hello and a goodbye.

"Now we have AIs teaching AIs, even building their own. Our advantage is that we control it, at least when Protocol is deactivated. It's possible that this virus has been incubating and learning, and the more it learns, the more it's capable of. It's also possible that for us to fully believe it, it had to be born here. The best way to learn about your enemy is from within," Sean explained. "That makes the NSA the perfect target. A tactical breeding ground. It would explain how it escaped to the public. This is one of the consequences for violating individual privacy."

The president's gut sank. He wanted to dismiss the issue as a hoax, but alas, there was too much evidence. People were losing their lives, and the public was already in a panic, so lying would only cause more harm.

"Pardon me, uh, my name is Steve. I've got some questions of my own," another NSA worker interjected. "For starters, why would such an advanced alien race even want anything to do with us? We're probably like monkeys to them."

"Not necessarily," another NSA worker countered as he stood. "Hi, I'm Ryan. They'd see us more like ants. It's simply fun to crush us. If this really is a match to the Wow! signal from the seventies, then we shouldn't discount what we did in 2012. Everyone thought the world was gonna end, so we sent up a message from Earth. It was a greeting formed of posts and comments from social media outlets like X and Facebook. Back before Google bought them, I mean. The net has always been a hostile place, and we all know how people treat something they don't understand."

Ufology was not something Sean ever took seriously, even though he loved space. He couldn't wrap his head around the concept, slowly losing grip on reality. "So, you're saying aliens came to Earth and killed thousands of people and counting because they got pissed off by what someone said on the *internet*? I just… I can't. I'm having a tough time with that. They must be way too advanced to care about something so innocuous."

William finally decided to speak up, loudly slamming his hands down on a table, making almost everyone jump in fear. A couple of heads down on desks jolted to attention. "Alright. So, first, think about what kind of civilization we are, because we have to do that now. To them, *we* are a hostile species, harming a beautiful planet in what's probably a rare sector in space. If our behavior doesn't change, then we're likely to bring it *into* space.

"With me so far? Okay. I'm sure they don't want that, so what's the best way to quell that threat?" asked William, looking around for someone to answer his question, but nobody tried. He closed his eyes and raised his eyebrows to gather patience. "Disappointing. The answer is to eradicate us before that happens. I'm sure everyone remembers the UFO waves of the fifties, when nuclear weapons were a much more public thing.

"Secondly, I wouldn't say we're like monkeys or even ants to them. Theoretically, an advanced enough and benevolent civilization could see us as companions. Even if we can't solve their multidimensional equations, although I'm sure some have, I wouldn't say they think we're worth crushing."

"He has a point," said Sean. "We're in the information era now, and far more advanced than I thought, I might add. If that's the stage we're in now, and these guys are undoubtedly billions of years ahead of us, then they would be past our stage, and wouldn't have much need for it. They could be at a stage of enlightenment that our minds can't even begin to comprehend.

"One problem, Mr. Donovan. These guys aren't friendly. At least, they don't appear to be. So, we need to figure out their endgame and discover what they want. Why are they attacking us? Is it resources, a conquest to snuff out the rest of the galaxy, population culling, hunger? It could be any *number* of things."

"Alright, enough. This is uncharted territory. The last thing we need is to make the panic worse. We are not about to tell the public that aliens are attacking us. We'll produce a cover story. Sean, you've done great. We've got all the intel we need. I'll get the highest-ranking workers of the United States Space Force to oversee it from here.

"For everyone here, I need you to understand something. This is unprecedented, but highly classified. I want to make this noticeably clear. Each of you will sign an NDA, just as Sean has, and you will not breathe a word of this to anyone outside these walls. I think we've made it clear that we have the means to track everyone here with ease. So, take this as a warning, because it will be your only one," the president warned.

The room fell deafeningly silent as everyone gathered their thoughts, trying their best to come to terms with these revelations. The president and his Secret Service walked to another room with Dale and William in tow. Sean knew he was next, sensing it in his gut. He found the whole situation unreasonable, but he understood. There were some things the public simply wasn't ready for.

"Sean Caldwell," the president called, motioning for him to come into the room. As the churning in his gut built, burning into a hot, nauseous dread, he walked into the room. The Secret Service agents closed and locked the door behind him. "Have a seat, son.

"I know what you're thinking, Sean. Smart man like you, analytical, observant, there's no fooling you. So, after talking with some higher-ups who are worth way more than me, we've come to an agreement." President Matthews slapped down a folder in front of Sean with a classified label on it in bold, all-capital letters. "I hereby grant you clearance to open and read all of the contents of that folder, as well as anything its contents may reference."

The president continued talking while Sean opened the folder. "Sean, you know what we're up against. You knew more than we did. Figured things out that we couldn't. We could use a man of your caliber. You strike me as a man who does what he must for friends and family. You do what you think is best, even if it means distancing yourself. Despite the toll on your social life, it's an extremely tactical advantage in our neighborhood.

"As it turns out, you don't have a whole lot to lose. You're too afraid to grow too close to anyone, so you never really form a connection worth losing, and you're good at making sacrifices. We could use you, but you need to make peace with things first. Word on the vine is your time is running out. Not just yours, either, but someone else's."

Sean's head snapped up as he glared into the president's eyes. "Please don't mention her. Respectfully, sir, it was the hardest decision of my life. I've chosen to put it behind me."

"Sounds like you've already made peace with it. So, did you get past the boring stuff in that chunk of highly classified intel in your hands? There's some neat stuff in there. One of the agents of the organization where that folder came from tells me there may even be a reason why they're attacking us. I can grant you clearance on behalf of them, but I don't have clearance myself."

"I can't understand much of this. Most of these documents are redacted. It's almost useless. If you want me to help you, I'll need to see more than this. The parts you *don't* want me to see," said Sean.

"Just needed to hear you say it," said the president, reaching for the folder and taking it from Sean.

"Fine. Just one question. What the heck is GAIA? Also, if you know something about why these guys have gone all Independence Day on us, then withholding that information is holding the entire world hostage."

"All in due time, Sean. I need to cross a bit of red tape first, but you'll be the first to know. See you around."

Sean felt the tiniest, quickest prick in his right arm, making him promptly pass out.

"There. Are you happy, John?" the president called to the back of the room.

John emerged from a shadowy part of the room with a smile on his face. "I told you he was good. Also, one of the agents? Really, Derek?"

"I couldn't just tell him who it truly was, now could I?" asked the president. "Your agency made that clear to me."

John shook his head and smiled wide as he exited the room.

The next thing Sean knew, he sat upright in his bed with the folder in his hand. GAIA was an acronym for Global Alien Intelligence Agency, which sounded to him like a super-secret, black-ops-style boy band who dealt with alien threats. Meaning, this wasn't humanity's first contact with alien life. There was a lot of reading ahead of him to do, but he first decided to skim through the pages and find highlights before reading the entire thing cover-to-cover. As he perused the pages, two words caught his eye: nuclear fission. Undeterred, he continued skimming, and found two more words: Project Longshot. For some reason, those words sounded vaguely familiar to him.

While he felt the anxious pangs in his stomach build even further, he had an idea to try diplomacy. What would happen if he was able to send a message to the attackers, and open a channel for communication? It could all have been from a simple misunderstanding. He wrote down his ideas, scribbling thoughts on notebooks, his whiteboard, his walls, anywhere but the floor. It was crunching time, and the entire world was the clock.

SHOW US WHO YOU HAVE INSIDE
BRING BACK TO US THOSE WHO DIED

✧

8. Close Encounters

Darren and Ron drove up Rebecca's driveway, not noticing how long it took them to get there. "Alright, partner, we're finally here," he said to Ron, who was still sleeping soundly. "Hey, bud. Wake up." Something didn't seem right. Ron wouldn't wake up, no matter what Darren tried. "Ron, seriously, wake up." Darren shook Ron and even slapped him. Still nothing. He finally gave up and checked Ron's pulse, making sure he was still breathing. *Thank God*, he thought. As he relaxed back into his seat, he heaved a sigh of relief. It would be about another hour until Rebecca was up and ready for company, so he decided to text her he was there.

(Darren) Hey sweetheart, I'm here. I've got a friend with me. Take your time gettin' up. I could use extra shut-eye, myself. My new friend here is sleepin' a little too soundly, but I'm startin' to think he has the right idea. Love you.

It was seven a.m. on a Saturday, hardly when anyone wanted to be awake, especially during a crisis. If Rebecca could rest, then it was best to let her get as much as possible. The loss of her mother weighed heavily on her, and Darren knew it. It weighed heavily on him, too, perhaps more so.

Loss was not something he was terribly familiar with until Hannah passed. His parents died when he was a young boy, and he hardly remembered them. Foster care was rough, of course, but he got placed with a nice family right away. Darren was thankful every day, especially as he got older and learned how the system usually worked. The rest of his surrogate family were all still alive and doing well. This loss, however, was too much.

He needed to allow himself time to grieve, but he couldn't. Darren knew that if he tried, he would fall apart completely, and his daughter needed him, so he couldn't afford it. No matter what, he had to be there for Rebecca. Fighting through the pain was the approach he took when he had to. Unfortunately, he always felt like he had to.

Ron jolted awake in a panic, flailing about and screaming. He behaved like a caged, feral animal, demanding freedom. "Help me! Someone, please help me," he cried. "They're here, and they're after me," he shouted. "Let me out, let me out, let me out, let me out, let me—"

Darren grabbed a hold of Ron and stared into his eyes. "Ron! Get a hold of yourself. You're okay, alright? You're safe. There's no one here. No one's comin' to get you. Just tell me what's goin' on and calm down," he soothed, slowly easing down into a regular voice. "Lower the speed and depth of your breath to match mine. In, then out. Big in, hold it, now out. Keep doing that. Good job." After three to four repetitions, Ron seemed to be himself again.

"I-I'm sorry. I don't know what… I guess it must have just been a bad dream. But it felt so *real*." Ron looked back into Darren's eyes, and they were alive with fear, his pupils dilated. Ron compulsively scratched his wrist, and Darren glanced down at it. His scratching was so violent that Darren knew something was wrong.

"Wait, stop, hold on for a second," said Darren.

"I can't," said Ron. "It burns. It hurts. I have to scratch it. I have to. It's not going away. It wants out." Ron continued scratching and picking at his wrist until blood poured out.

"Ron, stop, you're bleeding," Darren yelled, trying to snap Ron out of it, but it didn't work. Ron continued scratching, his nails penetrating his skin and coming dangerously close to an artery. "Ron, stop," Darren shouted, grabbing Ron's arms and holding them away from each other. As he did this, he noticed a glimmer amongst the blood staining Ron and the car seat. It sparkled in the early morning sunrise, as if it were starting to glow in a blueish-green hue. "My God." Darren released one of Ron's arms and looked at him in concern.

Ron didn't continue scratching, but the wound grew, within which the sparkling object expanded until it was clear what was happening. Whatever this was, it was eating him from the inside out. As it continued expanding, Darren scurried out of the car. He slammed the door, locking it with Ron inside, as he screamed while the metallic creature from his wound ate him alive.

The swarm didn't stop until it had consumed every inch of Ron's flesh, leaving nothing behind. One minute, there was screaming and terror, and the next, there was complete and utter silence. Darren then remembered the itch he had at the base of his neck. He reached back to feel it, but it felt fine.

After a few minutes, the swarm dispersed, bouncing around in the car, making it go haywire again. Sirens wailed, headlights turned on and off, the radio switched stations and increased volume, until the swarm all came together and contracted into a small, individual object, one that sparkled in the morning sunrise, then fell into the seat. Darren·stood outside of his car, pointing his gun at God only knew what. His breathing was heavy and labored, sweat pouring down his body as his hands shook.

Once the object showed no further signs of activity, he chanced opening the door. All of Ron's blood was completely gone. It was as though he was never in the car at all. Rebecca came barreling through her front door, running to her father, frantic and screaming. Darren turned back and held his hand up to her. "Don't come any closer," he warned. "Stay back! It's not safe over here. Get back inside. Now," he shouted at his daughter.

Not one to disobey a direct order from her sheriff father, she ran back inside, watching from the window as Darren reached into the car and down into the seat. As he reached for the object, he remembered he had gloves in the compartment. He opened it up and put the gloves on, then reached for the object.

As he touched the object with one finger, it sent a vibration up his hand and down his spine, as though a jolt of electricity shot through him, activating something. Darren didn't let this deter him, however. With several further jolts, he carefully picked up the object and put it in a plastic bag, which he then put inside of another plastic bag, both sealed airtight.

Darren held up the object and took a good look at what was inside. It looked like a metallic locust. It was small, about the size of a housefly. He took pictures and videos of it with his phone, then placed the bagged object in the trunk of his car and locked it. "Too close," he said with a heavy sigh. "What in God's name just happened?"

Rebecca took the cessation of activity as an all-clear to approach her father and came running out of the house. "Daddy? What was that? Is it… are you okay?" After they both watched the same horrendous nightmare unfold, Rebecca's voice lowered, unable to draw a full breath.

"I think I'm okay, yeah. As for what happened, I don't even know where to begin. I'm not sure there are words for it. Let's just get inside, and you can tell me all about this boy who helped you clear Ron's name. Not that it matters much now," he lamented, looking back at where Ron once sat. "It's like he was never even there," he said, his lips quivering. *I failed him*, he thought. *This is all my fault.*

Darren and Rebecca walked into her home, and she told her dad everything Sean told her in more detail. Once she finished explaining, there was a long pause. "So, what do you think?" she asked. "Does it make sense?"

"It makes about as much sense as anythin' else right now. I can't get what I saw out of my head. First your mother, then I make a friend and he…" Darren paused to gather breath. "It's too much, Becca. I know I'm supposed to be strong for you, but I'm havin' trouble right now."

Rebecca moved closer, sat next to her dad, and took him in her arms, rubbing his back as they both sobbed and grieved their heavy loss. "We can be strong for each other," she soothed. "Right now, let me be strong for you. It might do me some good." Rebecca gave her dad a tight hug and kissed him on top of his head. "I love you, Daddy."

"I love you, too," Darren said through labored breaths. After about twenty minutes, he refocused on the task. "You're sayin' this whole thing started from what, a computer virus of all things? How does that explain the faulty medication, or whatever the heck it was I just saw outside? That unholy nightmare is gonna haunt my dreams for the rest of my years. I'm so sorry you saw that."

Rebecca didn't interrupt. She knew it was best to let her father talk and get it all out. When he was ready, he would let her know. Until then, she stayed quiet.

"Do you think you could give this Sean guy a call or a text or whatever? See if he'd be willin' to meet with us and share what he knows. I'd like to thank him in person and give him some updates of my own." Darren couldn't stop thinking about what happened to Ron, and how preventable it was. He decided to direct his pain and anger toward finding a solution, rather than letting it consume him.

Rebecca looked at Darren, wistfulness in her eyes. "I'm sorry, Daddy, but I don't have his—wait. Yes, I do! I do have his number! Let me send him a text first, though. I don't wanna scare him or interrupt anything." Rebecca typed on her phone, her little fingers working away at a speed her father struggled to watch.

"I don't know how you text that fast, Becca. It takes me ten minutes to type one sentence. That message I sent you earlier took half an hour." Darren closed his eyes and shook his head.

Rebecca snickered. Darren simply wasn't a tech-savvy guy. Smartphones were still a bit much for him, even in 2036. "Just practice, I guess," she said with a shrug.

(Rebecca) Hey Sean, it's Rebecca. Um, I'm not sure if you remember me from when you helped me out with my mom's phone, but I was wondering if you could come visit me? There's someone I'd like you to meet and tell everything you know. Please respond soon. If you want to. No pressure or anything lol

After hovering over the send button for about thirty seconds, Darren threw his hands up. "Well? Did you press send, or is this some new form of communication where you think the word 'send' and off it goes?"

"You think you're funny. I'm just… I don't know, nervous. He's… I mean he's… not ugly, and he's nice, and I… am overthinking this." Rebecca hit the send button and tossed her phone aside, turning her bright red face away from her father and burying it in her hands.

✧

Sean received the text message from Rebecca, a wave of affection washing over his charred soul. It was a welcome feeling after everything he had been through recently and all he had witnessed. As he prepared to reply, he realized he still didn't feel ready. He might always feel that way, never willing to move on from what he had, what life forced him to let go of so suddenly. Life has a way of taking the most valuable people from us, leaving a vast, empty hole in their place. Sean still believed he owed the rest of his life in commitment to the vows that were made not so long ago. They were vows that, unfortunately, weren't able to be kept for extraordinarily long.

He stared at the text message, unsure of how to respond. Was it even real? With everything happening to the world, anything could have been a trap. There was no way to be certain, but then, of course, such is the absolute nature of life itself. If we only waited until we were certain before we decided to act, nothing of value would ever be accomplished on time.

"Go," came a familiar voice from behind Sean.

Sean turned around, but saw no one. "Hello?" he called out. "Is someone there?" His thoughts rushed, dread filling his mind as he thought he hallucinated. There was no way it could be her.

"Go to her," the voice commanded.

Sean's heart raced, beating faster than he could think. It wasn't possible. Her voice. It couldn't be coming from the person to whom it once belonged. It had to be a trick. "Whoever you are, this isn't funny. It's sick, and there's enough sickness in the world right now, so cut it out," Sean yelled into his home. His blood grew warm, his clenched fists shaking, and his misty eyes positively beaming with rage.

Sean felt a familiar hand on his shoulder behind him, and every ounce of his temper disappeared. Every pain he had ever felt vanished in an instant as he turned around and froze, unable to speak.

It was her. It couldn't be, but it was. There she stood, as beautiful as when he first saw her. As his anger cooled, he was overcome with grief and shock, his mind unable to distinguish one from the other as his heart continued beating rapidly.

"It's okay. She needs your help. I'll come with you, even if you can't see me," the woman cooed.

Sean was unable to resist any longer. His legs trembled and he fell to his knees. The woman placed her hand on his cheek. Sean took her hand and felt the warm rush of love he was so familiar with, the love he missed so dearly. "Clarissa?" he sobbed through tears. "How?"

"You'll come to know in time," said Clarissa. "I can't stay, but you will see me again. Please, go to her. Be together. All of you need to be together."

There was a blueish glow about her, Sean noticed. Something ethereal. As he reached out to hug her, she faded away, leaving him in a state of longing yet again, in the way that only she could. Sean pulled out his phone and called Dustin.

It only took two rings for Dustin to pick up. "Yo, man, what's going on?" he asked.

Sean exhaled softly. "Hey, you got a minute? I need to talk."

✧

Rebecca's phone buzzed about thirty minutes later, interrupting her conversation with her father about how school had been, what she'd been up to with her friends, and how her life had been going in general until Protocol's spread. She unlocked her phone and read Sean's text.

(Sean) Hey! Yeah, I remember you. How far away are you? I think getting away from this empty house may do me good, honestly. Not to overshare. Oh, and who am I meeting?

A warm smile found its way to Rebecca's face, and she wasted no time cheerily responding, grinning and giggling as she did, which her father found comforting. Darren was glad to see her smile, for her to have a source of happiness in all the chaos. Rebecca gave Sean the address, telling him she was in Mayberry, sixty miles east of Applewood. It was a little far, but she hoped Sean thought she was worth the drive.

Sean figured driving could do him good. He'd have time to think over everything. The entire world was in a dire situation. Everyone faced their own version of shared nightmares, but there was also the everyday difficulty of life, facing death, loss, and heartbreak. Every terrifying thing that could happen was happening to someone out there somewhere. Some were lucky and blessed enough to survive, while others took their final breaths. Sean's talk with Dustin convinced him that going to see Rebecca was the right thing to do, even if he felt like he was losing his mind.

We all have our close encounters. Each one is a different kind, a different disaster with varying proximity. These encounters make us who we are. In those moments, we choose how to define not only our world, but those of others, by how we brush across them and intertwine our fates with theirs, however briefly. Some of these encounters were a mere sighting. Seeing an act, good or bad, and telling the testimony to anyone who will listen.

Whatever it was Sean witnessed earlier in the day, he knew deep down it couldn't have been Clarissa, but he still didn't lose hope. He couldn't. In life, what's real and what's not are defined by our perception of our surroundings, governed by our senses.

He got to feel the closeness again from his encounter with a vision of Clarissa, and that's all he needed to have hope again.

There were calls he knew he needed to make, but first, he needed to know what to say. No excuse would work for what he had done, but it was never too late to set things right. Sean would think of what to say during the drive over, and use the time to get his mind right. There were people who needed his help, and he knew in his heart that this at least, this was real.

WE ARE WAITING FOR YOUR MOVE
YOU HAVE NOTHING LEFT TO PROVE

✧

9. Echoes of Grief

WHILE THEY AWAITED SEAN'S ARRIVAL, Darren and Rebecca made the most of their time together. It had been a while since they had seen each other. Rebecca thought it was funny how no one had time until life forced you to make time.

Darren's knee shook as his mind raced. What was he supposed to do now that Ron was gone, and Rebecca had given him the information he needed? "Hey, Becca, I'm gonna get some air. Back in ten," he said, ruffling his daughter's hair and giving her a one-armed hug.

Once he was outside, it was difficult for him to keep a steady composure. His friend was gone, and it happened during the grieving process for his wife. Darren couldn't help but blame himself. If he hadn't taken Ron with him, the man would have been fine. It was a painful burden to shoulder, and he refused to lay it on his daughter.

Would Hannah want him to remarry, or would she want him to remain committed even after her passing? It was hard to know because he always pictured going first. *It was supposed to be me*, he thought, but life is rarely what we envision.

✧

Sean kept his eyes on the road, but his thoughts were elsewhere. What was he going to say to his sister this time to make her believe him? How could he face her? He knew he had no choice, though. Sometimes, we must take the shame on the chin, and the only thing we can do afterward is move forward. Two steps forward and one step back is still one step forward.

About an hour into the drive, Sean couldn't wait any longer. He pulled into a restaurant's parking lot and took out his phone. Sean called his sister, who answered after four rings. "Hello?"

"Hey, Mandy. It's me again. Look, don't hang up, okay, please. I'm sorry about before. I have a lot to fill you in on. There's a lot going on, and I… I just need my sister," Sean cried, unable to withhold his emotions any longer. "I miss my wife. I miss her so damn much. I'm so sorry for what I've done, and there's no excuse. I can't go back and change it, but I can change what happens now."

Pity took shape in Amanda's heart for her brother and niece, for everything they had been through, but she kept her guard up. "Sean, listen, I—"

"No, wait. I'm sorry, I wasn't done. Just give me a moment. I haven't allowed myself time to deal with it all. I never told you why I made the decisions I made, what really happened, or how. I couldn't then, but I'm ready to now. I'm done running." Sean could feel his heart rate increasing as his nerves turned brittle, but he continued regardless.

"Alright. I'm going to let my guard down for you to explain, but, Sean, don't make me regret this. Don't do this for Monica and then take it away. I am warning you, in earnest, if you say or do anything to hurt or upset this little girl, so help me God, I will make sure you never see or hear from us ever again. Am I clear?"

Sean took a moment to gather his breath. "Yes," he replied. "I understand and agree. I never meant to hurt either of you. I know I did. Even if Monica was too young to know what was going on then, she's going to figure everything out eventually. So, here it is.

"The night Clarissa died, we had a fight. I stormed off in a huff and left her there by herself. I was too angry to think straight." Sean paused, slowly getting his words out. His heart almost shattered like glass, but the cracks were merely scars. After all, the pain meant he was finally healing.

"What was the fight about?" Amanda asked, honestly curious. She believed if she showed interest, Sean might be more open with her. Even though she was livid with him, she wanted to show him grace and give him the chance to explain the greatest mistake of his life.

Sean sighed heavily. "We had just brought Monica back from the hospital again. She was about four at the time and had been diagnosed only a couple of months prior. Clarissa was distraught, calling every doctor's office she could find, looking for experimental options. I told her we needed to slow down, but she wouldn't. She'd get hysterical to the point where she'd launch into panic attacks.

"There was one night when the panic attacks got so bad, I took *her* to the hospital. They rushed her into the emergency room. It traumatized us both. They got her stabilized and helped her understand she couldn't give her all to someone else when she had none to give to herself."

"That's awful," Amanda said in shock. "I can understand, though. This little girl? There's nothing I wouldn't do for her. I can't imagine the thought of losing her."

"Clarissa took things a little slower afterwards. She was still aggressive in her search, but I convinced her to take breaks and let me take over. Then I became obsessed too. Not just with finding a cure for Monica, but with making sure Clarissa didn't end up in her own hospital bed, which I also failed at.

"She would only kind of pick at her food at dinner. I couldn't get her to eat more than a few bites. It was like she just gave up. Eventually, this came to a head. I told her she couldn't give up, that it wasn't an option. We started fighting, and she was shouting about how I told her to slow down, and I was telling her how slowing down and giving up weren't the same thing. It escalated, and she said something that'll always haunt me."

"What did she say?" Amanda asked.

Sean took a deep breath as he prepared to repeat the difficult words. "She said Monica wouldn't have cancer if she had married someone else. Of course, she didn't mean it. I knew she didn't, deep down, but it still bothered me at the time. As soon as she said it, she was down on her knees. I mean, literally down on her knees, apologizing to me. I was about to cry, and I had never cried in front of her before. I didn't want her to see it.

"I tried to walk away and just go into another room. I closed the door and locked it, but she kept begging me to open it up, telling me how sorry she was. I knew she was sorry, and I believed her, but I was so angry and so hurt. We were both just so stressed out with everything happening. I wanted to forgive her, but I needed to be in the right headspace for it. I needed to think, and I couldn't guarantee what came out of my mouth wouldn't make the situation worse.

"I couldn't take it anymore. I told her I accepted the apology, but I needed time alone, just a little space and fresh air. I told her I was going to the store. She thought I wasn't coming back until late or at all, that I was angry with her. Her anxiety was, understandably, center-stage. I told her no, she was wrong, but I felt hurt and needed time to think. Then I just… walked off. I started up the car, drove up to the store, and cried my eyes out in the parking lot.

"Once I regained my composure, I went inside. Originally, I was only going to buy stuff to cook her for dinner, ingredients for her favorite meals. It had been so long until then since I had cooked. I thought, you know, maybe that's the trick to getting her to eat. Something home-cooked and comforting instead of take-out or frozen dinners for once. As I gathered ingredients, I walked past the flower aisle. They had blue roses, Mandy. Gorgeous, sapphire-blue roses. They were even on sale. It was like a sign. I had to get them.

"When I walked over to the checkout lane, something happened in front of me so fast that I didn't process it at first. I just froze and stood there, watching. I knew something was going on, because I heard all this yelling and slamming. There was this guy who came in, a disgruntled employee who had been fired earlier in the week, according to what I heard. He picked a random lane at the checkout and pointed a gun at the cashier, demanding money. He was slamming the cashier's head down on the conveyor belt. That poor girl looked maybe seventeen, tops.

"She was so scared, bloody, and bruised. Eventually, I unfroze and ran up to the counter, tackled the guy, and took his gun. I told the guy to get lost, go harass someone else or I'd kill him. My fuse was so short already, I just wasn't thinking straight.

"I should have called the cops when I had him pinned, but I let him go. I just wanted the girl to be safe. That was the only thing running through my mind. She was okay, thankfully. No permanent damage or anything. Someone else called nine-one-one, so she got the care she needed. EMTs came and checked her out. I gave a statement to the police, and the store let me keep the roses and groceries for free. I stayed back for a bit to make sure the girl was alright, and I left when the EMTs assured me she was okay. Keep in mind, we had reusable bags with our last name on them.

"I didn't realize what I had done, and what I had failed to do, until I got back home. I pulled into the driveway, and as I walked over to our porch, bouquet in hand, I saw that the door was wide open, chain unlinked. In my rush to get out of the door earlier, I had forgotten to lock it behind me. I thought Clarissa would lock it, but I guess she was too upset.

"The same guy who assaulted the girl in the store was driving around and ended up in our neighborhood. Then he saw the name on the mailbox. Clarissa was on the couch, sleeping off the fight we had. They said it looked like he rushed in and stabbed her with a hunting knife he kept in his boot. One I missed because

I was so focused on the gun. He took all the money he could find in the house and ran. I'm thankful Monica was with you then, or it would have been even worse."

Amanda knew parts of the story, but she didn't have the full picture until then. She never knew they were fighting about Monica's treatment, or about the man who robbed the store. All she knew was Clarissa was stabbed and Sean wasn't there, so naturally, she blamed him. "My God… Sean, I'm so sorry, I—"

"Don't. Please, just don't. Pity is not something I deserve or want. When I walked in with those blue roses to find my wife stabbed, I dropped them on the floor beside her. They became red roses then. Half of them were stained with the blood of the woman I loved, and the other half a magnificent shade of blue. A mixture of what was, and what should never be.

"They eventually caught the guy, but I blamed myself. I still do, because I should have stayed with her and not locked her out of the room. I shouldn't have gone anywhere, and I should have made sure the door was locked behind me," Sean sobbed. "I don't know how different things would be, but I know that I chose wrong. Then, I chose wrong again.

"I couldn't take care of Monica by myself. It was too much, and I didn't believe I could keep her safe. Clarissa was gone, my daughter was sick, and I could do nothing for her. I barely ate, and I did what I could to keep Monica eating, but every time I looked at her, I saw Clarissa in her eyes. The eyes I had failed to protect. Those were the only eyes of Clarissa's I would ever see again, and it hurt. It hurt so badly, and it still does. I couldn't take it.

"So, when you came by to check on me after the funeral, and I asked you to watch her for a while, I knew what I was doing. Every time I asked for just a little while longer, I knew I couldn't face her. I was slowly trying to remove her from my life. It killed me every day, and I felt so ashamed.

"I quit my job, sold what I could to make a little money, and let the savings take care of the rest before I started the software business. I used the money to go back to school in hopes of starting over, but that didn't last. I still write my software, because the logic helps me deal with the emotions, but… it's not the same.

"That was before… before all of this. I chose wrong. I'm sorry. I'm so sorry. I'm ready." Sean sniffled. "I'm ready to face my daughter again."

Sean's mind flashed back to Clarissa's funeral. It was contrasting, he thought, how on the day of the funeral, the sky was bright, the sun was out, and everything around them seemed so beautiful. It was audacious how after such a horrific tragedy, the world kept on spinning, while his quickly came to a screeching halt.

Though he didn't tell many people, Sean wrote poetry on occasion, but strictly for his wife. He had authored a poem for one final time, one he asked the priest to read at the funeral, called Echoes of Grief. Sean could still hear it in his head. The priest read the poem while Amazing Grace played in the background.

"Though you have left me, lost not found,
It is your voice I hear around.
Silence of sound permeates this room:
A life remembered; hearts filled with gloom.

Friends and family gathered 'round,
I can't bring myself to make a sound.
A love undying; a heart now broken.
I lie awake with arms wide open.
In dead of night, I witness your embrace.
I feel your breath upon my face.
I dream once and dream again.
Your love I feel, though not like then.
As these ghosts of our love surround,
Memories open my heart abound.
Echoes of our love remain,
Grief and silence, sound and pain.
Those sapphire roses I once bought,
Say thee nothing, they were for naught.
All the thoughts of which I find,
The echoes of your essence remind.
I see you not but hear you there.
Though in my mind, you're everywhere.
A love as ours shall be long and true,
Even with only echoes of you."

Sean hadn't written any poetry since then. It was as though that part of him perished along with his wife. Clarissa was buried with the blue roses Sean bought for her, so two beautiful things could wither together. Sean couldn't cry and let it out until after the funeral, once he was back home.

Amanda had tried to console him, but it was useless. She offered to take Monica for a little while, and he agreed. The service was beautiful, but Sean still held on to the memory and the pain, the echoes of her that remained.

Now, he was seeing her, or at least a vision of her. They were more echoes of what once was. It was a love so strong that the sound of it reverberated against the cosmos, crashing back down with a thud so deep that it made his soul shiver. Waves of the ocean against the shore could only dream of having such an impact. Maybe it was a trick. Sean was nearly convinced it was real, but reality was in question. Soon, he was snapped out of his silence by a small voice on the other end of the phone.

"Is that Daddy, Aunt Mandy?" came Monica's voice from Amanda's left side. "I wanna talk to Daddy."

"Yes, sweetie, it's him. Let me finish speaking with him first, alright? Then you two can talk," Amanda told Monica in a soft, comforting voice, turning her attention back to Sean. "Are you sure you're ready? Look, if you need more time—"

"No. I mean, yes, I'm ready. I don't need more time. Put her on. Please." With trepidation in his gut, the anxiety and nervousness threatening to break out and overwhelm him as the painful silence had once done, he was also excited to finally start his journey in healing what broke so long ago.

"Hi, Daddy," Monica said into the phone. "I miss you."

A tear rolled down Sean's face as he was overcome with a sense of relief. He laughed, a euphoric feeling of release after holding it all in for so long. "Hey, Caterpillar. How are you… I mean, how do you feel today?" Sean couldn't hold back his sniffling, glad to have a box of tissues next to him in his car.

"I'm feeling good today," said Monica. "I haven't felt this good in a while."

"That's great, honey. I'm so proud of you for coming so far, and I'm so sorry that I've been away for so long." His guilt rushed to the surface again, its magnitude overwhelming.

"Oh, it's okay, Daddy. Aunt Mandy says you've been off fighting bad guys and keeping us safe. I tell everyone at the hospital my daddy is a super-spy like James Bond."

In that moment, Sean finally understood. Amanda had been covering for him the entire time, making up stories and excuses Monica would believe, so she wouldn't feel the pain of the truth. His stomach sank, and his heart turned to steel in his chest.

"That's right," Sean soothed, doing his best to stifle his sobs as tears quietly ran down his face. "There's something nasty out there, and Daddy's gotta deal with it, but I'll see you soon. I promise."

"Beat those bad guys, Daddy! Beat them like you mean it," Monica squealed. She was so proud of her father for doing all his heroic acts out there saving the world. Of course, she was too young to know the whole truth. Amanda made sure to only give her vague details, protecting Monica from what harmful knowledge she could, but those days were disappearing fast. Soon, she would be able to figure things out on her own, and there would be no concealing them then.

"I will, sweetheart. I will. So, how old are you now? Five or six, right?" Sean couldn't believe he had forgotten the age of his own daughter. Still, he allowed himself grace. After all, he was trying to fix his mistakes. It had been so long since he had spoken with her. Too long.

Monica giggled. "No, silly, I'm nine and a half."

"What? No, you can't be right, Caterpillar. I'm gonna have to start calling you Cocoon soon, huh?"

"That reminds me, Daddy. I drew a butterfly on my head. I think it's starting to fade away, though," said Monica, her voice lowering.

"Well, we'll just have to get you another one up there, huh? Tell you what, why don't you draw me a picture? Something to tell me how you're feeling, how things have been, whatever you want. Something beautiful, okay? Then you can show it to me when I see you, and I promise it'll be soon."

Monica grinned. "Take your time, Daddy. I do miss you a lot, but I know you're doing the right thing. You're not just a spy. You're my superhero. I love you, Daddy."

Sean sniffled and wiped his face. "I love you, too, Caterpillar. Can I talk to Aunt Mandy again, please? I don't have long before I gotta go fight more bad guys, and team up with some people to help them. Maybe they can help me too."

"Yes, sir," Monica enthused, doing her best impression at a salute, which Amanda snickered at. Monica gave Amanda the phone, and they resumed their conversation.

"So, where are you off to now, oh brother mine?" Amanda asked.

"A sheriff and his daughter wanna see me, something about them wanting to know what I know and vice versa. She's the woman I told you about who had her mother's infected phone. I was able to help her recover just enough information to make her burdens a little bit easier to bear. I hope so, at least.

"I think this officer and I may have a lot in common. He just recently lost his own wife to this whole… whatever it is," he said. Sean didn't dare tell Amanda the nitty-gritty details about the situation yet. About how aliens were allegedly somehow orchestrating a covert invasion under the guise of a computer virus. He simply didn't want to worry or terrify her, and he wasn't sure he even believed it yet. "I'm going to find out what it is. I can tell you all about it when I come by there. I wish I had a day and time for you, but I don't right now. I'll keep you posted."

"Alright, Sean. Listen, this was big of you, and I'm so proud of you for it. This was a fantastic first step. Please stop beating yourself up for being unable to change the past. We all make mistakes, but we must let them go. They don't define us. Besides, you remember what Mom used to say. 'The worst mistake you could possibly make…'" she began.

"'…is to not make any at all,'" Sean finished. "Yeah, you're right. Thanks, sis. Alright, look, I need to go. I think it's beyond time for some real answers to this thing, and maybe even a fix. I love you, Mandy."

Amanda's body lightened after she knew the full story. "I love you, too. Oh, Sean, before I forget, Dad called. I'm sorry I didn't tell you sooner, and I know this is a rough spot for you, but he was worried and asked about you. Just give him a call when you can, alright?"

Sean hesitated. His first reactions were anger and resentment, but then he realized if he wanted Monica to forgive him, then he would need to forgive his own father. "Yeah. Yeah, okay. I will. Somehow, I think that's going to be harder, but I'll do my best. Okay, I gotta go. Love you. Bye."

Sean ended the call before anyone could say anything else, but he was glad this part was over. He rested his head on the steering wheel for a little while, taking a chance to breathe and clear his mind before he drove, but he soon became jolted back to alertness by another visit from a vision of Clarissa.

"I'm so proud of you, Sean. You need to forgive yourself. Move on. Let me go. Choose the healthy choice for once."

Sean jumped in his seat, still not trusting whatever he witnessed. "You're not real," he reassured himself. "Clarissa is gone. Whatever you are, you're not her." Something was off about this apparition. A sparkle in the sky caught his eye. It was late enough in the day, and the sun had set enough so he could see a light in the sky hovering there, which then bolted away at inhuman speed.

When Sean looked back at the seat, the vision of Clarissa was gone. "Oh, no," he whispered. "No, no, no." Fear ate at him, the uncertainty of the moment rattling his nerves. Was what he saw a trick by the aliens, or was he delusional? What if it really was the ghost of his wife?

No, he couldn't believe any other possibility than the one where he was going mad. The doctor did tell him he had a growing mass in his brain, which would explain it, and that meant his time had a limit. Sean would have to act fast to uncover answers and hope it was enough. Sometimes hope is the only thing we have, and the only thing worth holding on to. Even an echo of happiness is enough to spark actions and ideas to save the world. With God as his witness, Sean was certainly going to try.

YOU KEEP SHINING, DEADLY STAR
SHOW US WHAT YOU REALLY ARE

✧

10. MESSENGERS

THE TRIP LASTED HALF AN HOUR LONGER THAN Sean predicted. Traffic was understandably chaotic, given everything happening. It did give him extra time to think, however. He was convinced diplomacy was the way. If he and the GAIA team could find a way to send a message to the alleged aliens, then maybe talks of peace could begin. It was a far better option to start off with than war, especially when facing an undoubtedly superior force.

Motive was also something to consider. What was it the aliens were after? Maybe it was natural resources. It made sense, but no one would truly know anything for sure until a message could be written and transmitted.

Sean knew nothing of ufology or extraterrestrial hypotheses, and that meant he would need help from someone who had a deep understanding of the subject, even if the help was a little eccentric. Sean smiled at the prospect of reaching out to an intriguing friend from his past, one he had lost years ago from a heated argument.

Convincing the GAIA team diplomacy was the right approach would be another challenge. It wasn't like spaceships were visible in the sky. Truthfully, there was still no physical evidence of anything extraterrestrial about the situation. The only modicum of certainty of this possibility hinged around a signal received by SETI, which mimicked another from 1977. William was right, though. It was odd for it to match the same pattern twice. The chances of it being a simple coincidence were astronomically infeasible. There was also the fact an entire agency existed, whose purpose was to deal with alien threats and intelligence. That gave the alien theory real credibility, he realized. Then, of course, there was what he saw dart off in the sky.

As Sean drove, the GAIA folder sat tucked away safely in a box in the passenger seat. The two words Sean couldn't get out of his head during the drive were, "Project Longshot." What did the words mean, and why did they sound so familiar to him?

Sean turned the car's radio-television on and listened to music, hoping to drown out the loudness of his overbearing thoughts. Unfortunately, it only worsened the situation, as there was a breaking news story developing. He turned the volume up and tried to listen. Anything was better than being alone with his thoughts.

"—this outbreak. We go now to Dr. Yurik at the CDC to get his input on the situation," the newscaster announced.

"Thank you, Susan," Dr. Yurik said gratefully, his nerves on thin ice. "So, as you can imagine, we're all scrambling. There is no consistency. As of now, we have lost half a billion lives and counting. At this rate, we're likely to lose as many more in half the time."

"Is there anything you can tell us about its origins or pathology?" Susan asked, audibly terrified.

"No, I'm afraid not." Dr. Yurik sighed heavily. "I wish I had something better to tell you, but this came from nowhere. We normally wouldn't ask this, but if anyone out there has some idea about what's going on, about why we're all dropping like flies, please clue us in. If you can offer us any hope…" the man trailed off, unable to finish his thought as he succumbed to his emotions. "I'm sorry. Back to you, Susan."

The camera panned to face Susan, whose face was red and damp. She looked at the teleprompter, but she couldn't read it through her tears. "Like Dr. Yurik said, if anyone has any idea about what's happening, please, say something. You can reach us by dialing 1-800-555-9270. It's toll-free." Susan struggled momentarily. "I have a son at home. He's only eight years old," she sobbed, losing her composure. "My husband is with him, but… he just started a new blood pressure medication last night, and he wasn't himself this morning when he took our boy to school. I pray that when I go home tonight, he'll still be there. This is the reality we're all facing right now, but we must be optimistic about our future. Good must come from this. Please, *be* that good."

Sean turned the radio-television off. He was now angrier than anything, but he directed it toward finding a solution, no matter what it meant or how long it took. He dug into his pockets at a stoplight and pulled out his wedding ring, something he hadn't worn since Clarissa's funeral. Sean felt it was time to wear it again, like it would give him closure. "I'm gonna figure this out," he promised the wind. "I promise."

✧

Back in New York, Abigail and Jake Warren worked deep in detective mode to solve the puzzle themselves. "Do we know what the source of this outbreak was? As far as I can tell, it seems to have started here in New York, and spread from here globally. But the symptoms are inconsistent. Every autopsy I've performed was different. It's so peculiar," Abigail mulled, more to herself than anything. It ate at her, not knowing what the problem was and being unable to find it.

"No idea," Jake responded. "Something tells me those suits know, though, and the programmer guy or whatever. Seems like he may have figured something out. No one at my office knows anything, either. Course, there's only so much you can do when you're just an insurance claims agent, but it's been interesting hearing some of the stories lately. Did you hear about how a guy's van crashed into a Waffle House? Crazy stuff."

"Yes, which is exactly what's bothering me. This is primarily driven by technology, but I don't understand how it's affecting people's biology. Unless…" Abigail trailed off, putting the pieces together. "Remember the night when you came by because I told you my appliances were acting strange? Then the other day, they mentioned how medications were being altered. Is it possible? Could a computer virus somehow engineer dangerous medicine?

"It's genius, if you think about it. You can't just shut down medication factories that save people's lives, even if they are doing more harm than good." Abigail paused. "What if it goes even further? The design is intelligent, or at least the evidence certainly suggests it. I think it's possible that, whatever this is, it's somehow gone from digital malware to a biological viral strain. A living thing."

"Just slow down for a sec. I'm not sure I follow. You're saying that a computer virus is, what, somehow intentionally making bad drugs? Man, and I thought the guys in high school who sold that stuff were shady. Never knew it was computers who would be the ultimate dealer. Now you're telling me the drugs are alive?" Jake asked, only half-joking.

Abigail rolled her eyes. "Is it possible for you to have an ounce of seriousness for even a moment? Consider what I'm saying, honestly. I need to call the CDC, and my office, and—"

"Whoa, whoa, whoa, hold on, slow your roll. We don't know anything for sure yet, and even if you were right, we'd be putting ourselves in the crossfire." Jake's nerves tightened for the first time in years, and he wasn't managing it well. "I'm just saying, we gotta be careful. That's all. You know what happens to people who find out too much. They disappear. I can't afford to disappear. I'm too handsome!"

"Maybe you're right, at least about the being careful part. But I still think it's in everyone else's best interests to find the underlying cause of this and share what I know. I've made up my mind. I'm going public with this information first thing next week, right after I do a little research of my own," said Abigail. She stormed from the room and shut the door, leaving Jake in the guest room on his own again.

"Abby, what are you getting us into?" he whispered to the silence. *Damn it.*

The two of them decided to share the house so they would always be close by, especially in case something else strange began to occur again. Oddly enough, however, no more strange incidents had occurred. Regardless, Jake, asinine as he was, had no intention of leaving his sister to deal with it alone. He knew she felt responsible, that she thought she had some oath to the world to save it. Jake also knew she would nearly kill herself trying to solve the puzzle, because that was exactly what it was to her. A puzzle to solve and a test to pass, one she absolutely could not fail.

✧

Back at Rebecca's home, Sean pulled into the drive. Out of nowhere, he found himself feeling self-conscious about everything. The clothes he was wearing, the car he drove, the state of his messy hair, and so many other things. It wasn't like him to care so much, and shame filled his gut for having any affection for Rebecca. Sean was still loyal to Clarissa in his head and heart, but his soul betrayed the tiniest of hints of him being ready to move on. Though his spirit was there, he wasn't sure if his heart was ready to catch up yet. There was a lot he would need to figure out. Still, he combed his hair and did his best to make himself more presentable.

What was it about this woman? The growing feelings didn't make sense to Sean yet. Rebecca made him smile, and his heart fluttered when texting her. Soon, he would be near her again. He hadn't felt this way since his first date with Clarissa. *This isn't even a date*, he thought.

There was also the virus and everything it brought with it, along with the visions of Clarissa. Sean thought himself crazy and tried to rationalize that it wasn't him, but rather one of the aliens' tricks. This didn't sound any better, he realized. Sean also had to make peace with the possible brain mass, though the doctor suggested it was only a cyst. As his thoughts raced, he couldn't focus on only one.

His thoughts came to a freeze as Rebecca came practically barreling out of her house with Darren right behind her. Sean got out of the car and stood, his hands clasped together in front of him. "Hey," he hedged with a timid wave and a smile.

Rebecca hugged Sean tightly, surprising him. "Hi," she said, burying her head in his chest. There was apparently something going on he was unaware of, and he wasn't sure how he felt about it yet. He was a little uncomfortable, but somehow, it brought him some relief for his nerves. The jolt from the unexpected contact sent a shock through his body. Rebecca clearly wore perfume, and Sean thought she smelled amazing.

"Um, hey," Sean gasped breathlessly. "It's, uh, good to see you too," he managed, ever the king of awkwardness. Truly, if there were a kingdom full of awkward people, he would undoubtedly be elected leader by a landslide.

Rebecca let him go and pulled back, allowing herself to look Sean over for the first time unabashedly. She then noticed the ring on his finger and let out a small gasp, covering her mouth and looking away in defeat.

Was he married? The ring suggested it, of course. How could she have missed it the first time? He wasn't wearing it then, but why? Many questions filled her mind, and her emotions flew fervently through her veins, each one fighting for control. Rebecca looked down at her feet. "I'm sorry. I didn't think. I mean I thought. It's just…" she trailed off. "Sorry."

Sean's head spun. Had he said something wrong? He noticed her looking down at his hands, clasped together in front of him, and followed her gaze.

The ring. She saw the ring and immediately felt ashamed, he realized. "No, it's okay. It's not what you think, I—"

"There he is," said Darren as he came into view, destroying the ersatz bubble of privacy that seemed to exist around him and Rebecca. "So, you must be Sean. Darren Morgan, Babylon Police Department," he said, extending an arm to Sean. Sean gripped his hand firmly. "Hell of a handshake, pal. Then again, maybe I'm just goin' soft."

It was already annoying Sean how he couldn't read anyone else's emotions, but he seemed to barely understand his own. He smiled and nodded at Darren.

"Didn't realize you were married," Darren said curtly.

This snapped Sean out of his thoughts. "Oh, uh, yeah. I was," he said, looking over at Rebecca to gauge her reaction. Her features lit up, and he thought he saw a flicker of hope dance across her eyes, which was then followed by a pang of guilt for having that hope. It was an inscrutable mixture of emotions. "She… died many years ago. This is the first time I've worn my ring since the funeral. It's just that with everything going on, I wanted to feel something familiar. It makes me feel closer to her," Sean admitted, glancing over again at Rebecca, who nodded her head.

She sighed with relief, which she intended to do covertly, but it was far too noticeable. Sean couldn't help but smile. He wasn't sure why he shared so much, but he was comfortable, a sense of belonging setting in he couldn't deny.

"I understand, believe me," Darren said. "More than I'd like to." Darren dropped his head and ran his hand over his own wedding ring. "I haven't taken it off since… well, you know."

"Yeah, Rebecca told me—" Sean started.

"It's just Becca," she clarified. "If you don't mind. I mean, it's okay. I just thought, you know, it might be a little easier to say, and it's what everyone calls me, so, yeah."

Sean smiled. "Becca told me what happened. I'm so sorry. This whole thing has been one giant nightmare that's spawned a thousand more."

"Well, let's not waste any more time. Come on inside, get comfortable, and tell us what you know," said Darren, patting Sean on the back and smiling at him.

Sean launched into full debriefing mode, telling the Morgan family everything he knew so far about the virus, the aliens, the GAIA team, and the plan of diplomacy. He even mentioned the famous Wow! signal, which Darren knew of.

Darren became tickled by one of his thoughts. "Should've called it the Owen Wilson Signal," he jested, laughing at his own joke so hard that he nearly spat out his coffee. "Wow," he said in an Owen Wilson impersonation.

Sean laughed with him, and Rebecca dropped her shaking head into her hands to hide her mortification. *What have I done*? she thought.

While the men became lost in their mirth, Rebecca continued absorbing everything Sean said. It sounded too crazy to be true, but times were indeed dire. Rebecca understood laughter was needed, but she forced herself to focus. "Can we return to being serious now, please?" she growled, a bit more agitation in her voice than she intended.

"Yes, sorry," Sean replied. "I just haven't laughed that hard in a while, but you're right. We need to focus on this. I can't tell you too much about GAIA, mostly because I don't know much about it myself, but also because of your safety. I'm not ruling out government involvement at this point.

"I think it's possible that something our government has done might have something to do with this… invasion. So, right now, our main priority needs to be this message. What should we say? I wish I knew how to say this logically, but I think I've let myself become too emotional now," he admitted with a sigh. Sean massaged the ring on his finger, turning it over and patting it in an attempt at comfort. "I don't think I could be objective."

"I think the message needs to be clear and concise, but firm. Make sure we ain't makin' no bones about it," Darren suggested. "We've lost millions of lives. Millions, man! If these guys have any compassion at all, then we oughta use that against 'em. It's just a matter of tact."

"So, we could start with getting the point of the message out, detailing things we want to say, and then modify it from there," said Sean.

"Sounds like a plan to me. One question, though. How are you gonna get this message to 'em? I ain't exactly seen no communication system set up between us and them," Darren hedged.

"I haven't gotten that far yet," Sean admitted, pinching the bridge of his nose. "I might have a friend who can help us. The only thing about him is he's kind of… out there."

"What do you mean?" asked Rebecca.

"Well," Sean began with a sigh, "he's a ufology nut. Big into conspiracies and government cover-ups."

Rebecca and her father stared blankly at Sean.

"What?" Sean asked in exasperation. "Why are you both looking at me weird?"

"Uh, hello? Earth to Sean?" Rebecca knocked on her head like a door. "He may have been right. I admit, normally, I would say he's crazy. But these are crazy times, and there basically *has* been a government cover-up here. I say we give him a shot."

"Alright, alright, I get your point," Sean conceded, his hands up in defeat.

"So, what's this fella's name?" Darren asked, leaning forward in his chair.

"Kyle Wills. He has a real enthusiasm for cars. So, Dustin and I always called him Wheels, since it sounds so close to his last name. It seemed to fit, and he liked it, so it stuck." Sean shrugged.

"Alright, so what can this fella offer us besides tinfoil hats?" Darren asked with a smile on his face. Rebecca smacked him on the arm. "Ow," he shouted. "Hey, I'm just sayin'. Besides, you gotta laugh at some parts of this situation. You'll cry if you don't."

"I don't know that I find millions of people dying funny, Daddy," chided Rebecca.

"No, hon, that's not what I meant. I just mean the person we're goin' to rely on, of all things, is a conspiracy nut." Darren laughed. "The funny thing is it makes sense in this situation. That's the part I find funny. Not the dyin', sweetie."

"So," Sean started, "are we all on board with this? I haven't talked to him in a few years, so I don't know if he's even—"

"Can't think like that, son. Gotta have a light in the darkness. All you need is a spark of hope. I'm on board with it, and I think Becca has made her stance on it clear," said Darren, rubbing his arm as he turned to face Rebecca. "Did ya have to smack me so hard, hon?"

"Oh, please. I barely tapped you," Rebecca said offhandedly.

"It echoed!" Darren responded.

"Guys!" Sean threw his arms out. "Can we focus here, please? I'm about to call Wheel—I mean, Kyle. I need to mentally prepare myself for any possibility."

Darren and Rebecca nodded in assent. Sean dialed the numbers on the phone slowly. Even though he had Kyle saved to his contacts, it was somehow easier to type the numbers out. Sean knew he was prolonging the inevitable, but it gave him a little peace. He wasn't even sure if he wanted his old friend to pick up.

If he did pick up, what would Sean even say? They didn't exactly leave things on the best of terms. It was a fight that escalated, and the words exchanged were not in the best interests of either of them.

The last exchange they had was a short conversation about Sean's car and Kyle's opinion of it over a year ago. They kept things cordial and never got personal. If Kyle didn't pick up, it could mean a few things. Either Kyle was still angry with Sean, he changed his number, or, the worst option, he was no longer around. So, there were a lot of emotions to process.

Sean typed the final number and pressed the call button, putting the phone to his ear. There were five rings before Kyle picked up. "Hello?" he answered in a surprised and raspy voice.

At that moment, all Sean felt was relief, which he let out with an audible sigh. He strained to control his emotions, fighting as they may to overwhelm him. "Wheels? It's Sean."

"Uh, yeah. You're still in my contacts, genius. I know who's calling me," Kyle responded coldly.

"Wheels, listen. I need your help. There's—"

Kyle sighed. "Man, I already told you. If your carburetor is overheating, you need to get it to the mechanic and do what he says," he grumbled.

"No, no, it's not about the car. Just listen, please. I'm glad you're okay," Sean rushed out.

Silence. There was a long, awkward silence. Sean could feel Kyle choosing his next words carefully, deciding whether to move forward with the conversation.

"Yeah. I'm good. Glad you're okay, too. Heard this is some kinda computer virus?" Kyle asked.

"Yeah, it is, but it's... well," he hedged, a smile tugging at the corner of his cheek.

"What? Oh, no. Are you about to try to sell me some kinda fancy antivirus or something? I told those roaming Techdoor folks I ain't interested. I barely even use the dang PC anymore," he spat. "Well, that's not true. I have been using it for a personal project, but I still don't need to buy no fancy software."

"No, Wheels, it's… I don't know if you're going to believe me. This computer virus is special," Sean said slowly.

"Special how? Is it medicated?" Kyle asked with a smile.

Sean laughed. "No, dude, it's, uh, from space."

Silence again. Then laughter. Raucous, abrasive laughter. It was so loud that Sean had to hold the phone away from his ear temporarily. "Man, that's a good one. You're pulling my leg, huh? Just straight up messing with me. Oh, man. I haven't laughed like that in a month. That's great."

This time, Sean went silent. No laughter or retracting, because Sean was serious, and he needed Kyle to believe him.

"Hold on, wait. You're serious. You're genuinely serious," Kyle realized.

"Yeah, I am. I can give you the full story later," said Sean.

"Okay, but what exactly are you expecting from me? I'm a communications and car guy, not a computer guy like you. Sure, I can program, but I doubt I could offer any solutions you haven't come up with already."

"That's exactly what we need is all of those skills combined," Sean insisted with excitement in his voice. "We need to get a message to the source, and we need a way to do it. I was thinking you could assist in that capacity."

"Just to be clear, so I'm understanding correctly. You're saying you want me to help you talk to *aliens*?" he effused, his voice betraying him by raising a few octaves in excitement on the last word.

"That's the gist of it, yeah," said Sean. "I'll even sweeten the pot. I have a whole folder here full of official, off-the-books government cover-up of extraterrestrial life. I haven't even delved into the full scope of it yet. If you help us, we could all go over it together and get this message up there. We're thinking diplomacy should be the first solution."

Silence again, but the excitement from his friend was palpable.

"What do you say, pal?" asked Sean.

"Two things. First, who's we? Secondly, when do we start?" responded Kyle.

YOU HAVE MADE US SO AFRAID
SOMEONE PLEASE COME TO OUR AID

✧

11. Best Laid Plans

The trio made sure they were properly packed before leaving to visit Kyle. It was quite a ride to Griffin, Georgia, so they loaded the car with snacks and ways to pass the time. "Everyone ready to go?" Darren called out from Sean's car. "I want as few breaks as possible on this trip."

Sean smiled, finding it funny how Darren gave orders, but he didn't dare argue with him. There was too much else going on, and if the behavior made the man feel better to have control of the situation, then why take it away from him?

"I think we're good here," said Sean, twirling his keys. "Are you taking your car and following me, or how are we doing this?"

"Well, first," Rebecca said, approaching Sean abashedly. "I'm riding with you, silly," she purred, placing her hand on Sean's back and rubbing it gently before walking to the passenger side of the car and getting in. Rebecca was determined, Sean would give her that. He briefly closed his eyes as he felt the relief from the backrub, a soothing sensation traveling through his body.

Sean looked over at Darren. "Don't look at me, son. Best do what she wants, trust me. We'll never get anywhere otherwise," Darren groused, shaking his head as he walked over and ducked down into his car.

Sean took this as the signal to walk over to his own car and prepare for the journey. It was better he had company anyway. If the vision of Clarissa came back, he'd feel better if someone else could see it. Conversely, however, this also meant Rebecca might *not* see it, and there would then be an even bigger problem to approach. Sean froze, pondering the implications of Rebecca being with him. Surely, he was just overthinking this. Then again, there were those test results about an alleged mass in his brain, so he couldn't rule anything out yet.

"Hey, are you coming?" Rebecca called from the passenger seat of the car.

Sean was immediately taken back to a morning with Clarissa. They were preparing to take Monica for her first evaluation, and he became frozen in fear then too. He knew if he went, then they'd know for sure. If he stayed behind, then he could fight off the inevitable for a little while longer, but that was selfish, he reasoned to himself. Sean knew he needed to be there for his wife and daughter. Monica was sick, and she needed all the support she could get. What stopped him was not being sure if his support would be enough. Clarissa was already waiting for him in the car, and Monica was sound asleep in the back seat.

"Please don't wake up," Clarissa said softly to Monica. Clarissa got out of the car to meet Sean at the door. Sean seemed unable to move forward. Clarissa had seen him do this before at their wedding, which was more nerves than anything else. This was real fear, and she knew it. Clarissa knew Sean was afraid to know the truth. So, she walked up to him, took his hand, and gently pulled him toward the car.

"We have to know," Clarissa whispered. "I know it's scary and unfair, but we can't think about ourselves right now. We have to think about Monica. She needs us, honey. I need you. You're not alone. You have me here with you, and I know," she began, picking up his hand and pulling it to her heart, letting him feel her heartbeat, "I know I have you. That's how I can do this. You give me strength. God, you give me so much strength. I am so thankful for it every day. We can face this together, and whatever happens, it happens together. Alright?" she soothed, letting go of his hand and walking back to the car.

Sean had reached after her, but she continued walking. She had such a way of leaving him wanting more. Sean believed he was blessed to be with her, knowing how lucky he was.

"Are you coming?" asked Clarissa.

"Yeah," he answered Rebecca. Sean got in the car and buckled up, then looked over at her. "Whatever happens," he began as he buckled up, "it happens together." Sean grabbed her hand, giving it a squeeze, and rubbed his thumb over her hand before letting go. Rebecca reached back after his hand as he placed it on the wheel.

"Are you scared?" she asked him.

"Yeah. Yeah, I am," he replied breathlessly.

"Me too," she admitted, "but at least I'm not alone." Rebecca reached up to him, and they kissed. It was brief at first, exploratory, but they soon found themselves unable to pull away. At least, until Darren flashed his lights and sirens, jolting the two out of their brief tryst.

Sean smiled, put Kyle's address into the GPS, and the car displayed the route. Darren used the Follow-Along feature of his sheriff car, and it copied the directions Sean's car gave. Soon, they were off, beginning a whole new adventure.

The ride was mostly humdrum, but the chaos of the silence was its own palpable thing. There was less traffic on the roads, and barely anyone around outside. Everywhere was a ghost town, and each one had its own set of unique and unfinished business. It was a stark contrast to the ride earlier, which was filled with traffic. There had been so much damage done in such a short time.

Fiction always exaggerated circumstances. Situations like this were often depicted with looting, rioting, and general debauchery throughout the country, even the world, but this wasn't the same at all. It was too much pain, too much loss. Everyone felt it in some way, and it left little motivation for hate, since hate is simply the fear of everything going wrong in the absence of love.

It was hard to be afraid enough to hate when most of what you loved was already gone, and the worst had already happened. People felt defeated, understandably so, and to the public, it was still a random outbreak that no one fully understood. The medical and technical communities knew a bit more, but somehow, that made it worse. Ignorance truly is bliss, but at what cost?

We try to understand things in our grief. For some people, it's how they cope. They take apart a tragedy and analyze it at every level, thinking if they could understand how it works, then maybe they could put it back together in a way that doesn't hurt.

It was, unfortunately, not one of those times. Reality is rarely a pill we want to swallow whole. We cut it into pieces and take it a piece at a time, but eventually, it all must go down. The inevitability of it was daunting to even the most hardened of people, and Sean was an emotional man. He felt emotions twice as powerful as most others. While this allowed him more love, it also supplied more pain. An increase in one always begets an increase in the other.

Sean and Rebecca took a while to speak during the ride at first, but both were comforted by the other's presence, nonetheless. It gave them both a sense of security to know the other was nearby, so they weren't alone. He had her, and she had him. Somehow, this sense of security made the destruction of the world around them tolerable. It gave him purpose, and it gave her resolve. They were comfortable together in mostly silence. Eventually, Rebecca asked Sean why he was so quiet, and his oversharing floodgates flew open. He told her the story of Clarissa and Monica, his issues with his father, and all the pain he was keeping inside. "Sorry, I tend to not shut up once I start talking about… stuff."

"No, it's okay," Rebecca said quickly, trying to soothe Sean. "I'm glad you told me. I think it's good to get all the bad stuff out. You can't keep it in you forever, and you don't have to deal with it alone."

Sean smiled. "You're amazing."

"I try," Rebecca replied.

Once the group reached Kyle's house, they saw him sitting outside on his porch, waiting for them. Kyle walked down the steps as they approached and stood near Sean's car when he parked, crossing his arms defensively. The world may have been a mess, but Kyle wasn't about to completely let his guard down.

Not yet. He had to see if Sean was being truthful, or if he was yanking his chain. Time would be the only way to tell.

Aliens? Seriously? Kyle thought. It's like he was desperate for something. Kyle simply didn't know what. Of course, Sean was desperate, but not in the ways his old friend thought. Kyle wasn't overly muscular, but he had a certain energy about him. His spiky black hair glistened in the setting sun, and the wind blew his black leather jacket. He wore a blue shirt and black jeans, and a cross hung from his neck.

Sean got out of the car first. "Stay here," he warned Rebecca quietly before shutting the door. Rebecca didn't take kindly to what sounded like a demand, but she sensed Sean's uneasiness and decided he had a point. However, if she saw something go down, she wasn't about to sit it out. Rebecca was a force of nature, and she knew it well. She'd give him hell for it later, in one way or another. Leaving her there in the car was giving her time to plan it.

Sean reached his hand out to Kyle. "I'm glad you're okay," he said with a sigh. Kyle could no longer contain his emotions and reached out to Sean, clasping him in a hug.

"I'm glad you're okay too, man," he confessed breathlessly. "Everything I've been seeing on the news, and what all they're saying is happening out there, I wasn't sure if you were even... but I had hope. I knew if someone was gonna find a way out, it'd be you." Kyle wasn't sure what happened to him. It was all the emotions that came with seeing a long-lost friend again. It was the fact he didn't have to harbor any regrets about things he never said or did, or worry about lost connections like so many others had already. Kyle tried to be angry and indignant, but he couldn't quite manage it. A familiar face was all it took for his castle of walls to come crumbling down.

"Coming in a bit hot there, huh?" Sean joked as he pulled back. "Listen, thank you, seriously, but we do have to get straight to business, unfortunately," he said sheepishly. "Sorry, but time is of the essence. If you've got any way for us to broadcast a message these guys would intercept, we'll gladly take it. Anything would help at this point."

Kyle's face lit up like a kid on Christmas morning, and Sean knew his friend was in his element. "Dude, you're going to *love* what I've done with the garage. What I got in there is my axis mundi," he said with a wide grin. "Stocked it to the brim a few months ago with snacks that don't go bad for years, drinks, gas, diesel, chargers… hell, I even got some old video game consoles down there. Oh yeah, and all necessary toiletries, including what them ladies might need," he flirted with a wink at Rebecca in the car, wiggling his eyebrows.

Sean smiled and rolled his eyes. *Some things never change.*

"Speaking of which, who's the girly?" Just like that, Kyle's mind wandered back to women again. Even in a doomsday scenario, his mind was the same. Sean would have found it depressing if it weren't so funny and predictable about him. It was one of the things that made Kyle so lovable. Annoying, but lovable all the same.

Sean suppressed a chuckle, thinking of how hard Rebecca would smack Kyle for referring to her as a girly. "Her name's Rebecca. Just goes by Becca. She's tangled up in all this, and I got involved, so—"

"Whoa, hold up now, *involved* you say? Now you doth speaketh mine language," Kyle japed as he lowered his voice.

Sean changed the subject. "Hey, not like that, and anyway, I'm sure hoarding all this stuff, especially the gas, can't be legal. You could've gotten into a lot of trouble."

"Man, I don't care. Do you think *they* care right now? Shoot, naw. They're happy no one's out burning the place down with pitchforks yet, but trust me, they're coming. They always do."

"So, while we're on the subject, I was wondering. Do you have any tinfoil hats in rose gold? I hear that's more my color," Sean teased.

Kyle punched Sean on the arm and laughed. "Come on. I'll show you around the garage. Got all sorts of stuff in there," he said as they walked. Sean turned to Rebecca and waved at her to join him, then did the same for Darren. Somehow, though, he felt having Darren nearby would complicate matters, given his profession, but he'd have to manage that later. They needed a plan, and both men would have to get along.

"So, the plan right now is to try diplomacy. I know it may sound pointless, but I'd like to try. We owe it to the rest of humanity if there's even a chance to avoid interstellar war. Any ideas on how to do that?" asked Sean.

"Man, ain't we *already* in interstellar war? They threw the first punch," said Kyle, his arms in the air with exasperation. "I say we hit back. Kick 'em where it hurts. Once we learn, you know, where that is."

Sean pinched the corners of his nose and closed his eyes momentarily. "Look, I know, okay? I still think diplomacy is the best solution here, or at least an option we should try first. So, with that in mind, is there anything you can give us?"

"Hmm. Well, you said this all started with our satellites, right?" asked Kyle, his gears turning.

"Yeah," said Sean.

"Well, what if we could upload our own signal, with a message from us attached, to the same satellite? If it's what they're using to communicate, then we might be able to piggyback off it," Kyle suggested.

Sean's face lit up with a smile. "Wheels, dude, you're a genius," he said, clapping his hands together. "Man, you came up with that in no time at all, and I've just been running around cluelessly."

Kyle shook his head in embarrassed modesty. "Nah, man. When you told me the details earlier, it got me thinking. That one's been baking for a while. Anywho, it is a bit of a Hail Mary, but hopefully it works."

"I mean, it should, yeah. I'm thinking it's like a computer process that continuously runs. Introducing something foreign would force the aliens to investigate it, then they'd discover the message."

"Any idea what you wanna say?" Kyle asked.

"Yeah, Becca's dad and I already have something put together. Here's what it says." Sean handed Kyle the paper with the message he had folded and put it in his back jeans pocket.

"'Hello. We do not know who you are, but we mean you no harm. We ask you, please cease your attack on our planet. Our people are sick and dying, but we don't believe this was your intent. If you felt threatened, we apologize. We were simply seeking intelligent life. If you need resources, then perhaps we could negotiate. Please respond.' Nice. Sounds a little too white flag to me, but hey, you're the writer. I'm just the one making this happen."

Sean placed a hand on Kyle's shoulder. "Wheels, if we can do this at all, and especially if it works, then you'll be a hero to all of Earth."

"Hell yeah, man," Kyle responded with a grin.

Darren walked up beside Sean. "You boys come up with anythin' yet?"

"Yeah," Sean said enthusiastically. "We may have an idea. Now we just need a way to get there."

Kyle grinned a pearly half-smile and narrowed his eyes. "Oh, I got a way," he boasted, patting Sean's shoulder with his hand and continuing toward the garage.

Sean cleared his throat and turned to Darren. "So, uh, maybe you can let what you see next slide, considering he's our only shot. Just to warn you, he's been kind of… hoarding things. Food, water, gas, toiletries, all kinds of stuff, and I think it's stuff we can use. We might be able to hold up here for a while and finally start brainstorming this situation."

Darren laughed. "Buddy, I ain't even worried about it. Sure, it sounds a little nutty to me, but hell, we got aliens invadin'. We have bigger problems right now, and worse still, all these years, my cousin was right. I always thought he was a nut, but he said aliens were real, that they'd been here before, and were coming back." Darren shook his head. "Just drives me crazy he was right."

"I have heard that being called crazy is just being right too early," Rebecca suggested, walking toward Sean. "Hey there," she flirted, hugging him. "What's the plan?"

"The plan is still diplomacy. Wheels seems certain he can send a message up to the same satellite that started this whole mess, piggybacking off their own signals they used on us. We'll interrupt their computing process with our own code and embed our message inside it. It's a team effort, and a bit of a Hail Mary, but I have hope. Thank you both for your help. If this works, then maybe things can finally go back to normal." Sean looked over at Kyle. "Alright, Wheels. Let's get rolling."

"Alrighty, awesome. Follow me," announced Kyle, clapping his hands and rubbing them together with a big grin on his face. He led the group into his garage, in which sat a beautiful, jet black, 1969 Chevrolet Chevelle Super-Sport. It had red trimmings, red rings around the rims, and two white stripes brightened the rest of the car. It had a red, diamond-stitched interior that looked like it was made from a special type of leather.

"Uh, this is your idea? An ancient car?" Sean asked.

Kyle dropped his arms in disappointment. "Hey! Don't be talking about my car that way. She ain't no ordinary car, are ya babe?" Kyle said affectionately, rubbing the car's driver-side door.

Darren looked at Sean with deep concern. "Just… give him a minute," Sean advised, though he started to have questions himself.

"Buddy, you need help," Darren said to Kyle. "You got some lollipops loose."

Another voice abruptly spoke, making everyone but Kyle jump. "False. Mr. Wills retains full cognitive capacity. I am monitoring his vitals using internal nanotechnology. Mr. Wills, regarding your initial inquiry, you are correct. My atypical programming is distant from that of a regular motor vehicle, especially from the time that my outer shell represents," came the voice from the car.

Darren's eyes grew as wide as saucers. "Holy *shit*," he said. "Did that damn car just talk?"

"Yes, you are correct. Would you like me to recite a common phrase from human repertoire? Also, I am not a thing. I am an artificial neural network intelligence, or ANNI for short. I would prefer you use this nomenclature when discussing me, at least when within my vicinity," she vocalized.

"How in the—" Darren shouted.

"Kyle, what's KITT here gonna do to help us?" asked Rebecca.

"Objection. My driver's name is not David Hasselhoff," ANNI vocalized.

"ANNI, sleep mode," Kyle commanded, and the car powered down.

"While I appreciate the pop culture reference, what in the name of all things holy is this—uh, ANNI?" Darren murmured.

"This, my friends, is revolutionary technology. I spent years working on her. Everything in there was built by me, including the programming. It was difficult at first, because I was just trying to program the car to do mundane things more efficiently. I didn't have a framework to build from. So, I started building a basic API. That evolved into me getting ANNI to speak out the error logs, using a text to speech script I got from Sean a while back. I kept tweaking it and adding my own flair to it, and then bam, my baby was born. It was meant to be.

"She's also got her own unique radio frequency," said Kyle as he got in the driver's seat. "I mimicked a radio signal in the car at first, then slowly made it special enough to withstand any interference, including an electromagnetic pulse. Think of it like copying a signal, modifying it, and encrypting it with its own special encoding. Then voila, your own frequency."

Sean grinned. "I'm still wrapping my head around this."

Kyle chuckled. "Those other cars out there may be getting infected with this virus thing, but not ANNI. I've even tried it. I was driving back from town one day, and cars around me were going haywire, but ANNI stayed safe. Eventually, I found out I could program her to log the details of anything that tried to access her system, so we've been debugging these viruses for a while now. I stay way out here so I don't have to deal with it, but that don't mean I can't."

"Dude, that's incredible. Why haven't you said or done anything about this? What you have here could lead to a solution. People's lives could be saved," Sean ranted. While Kyle's innovation impressed him, he couldn't deny his burning nausea. How could someone have this kind of technology, especially the kind to resist the outbreak, and yet, do nothing to help?

"Well, man, I ain't proud of not helping, but hell. All my life, I've been needing help. I've given everything to the government, and they ain't done squat for me. When my daughter Lauren needed help, when she got *sick*, I couldn't afford any of the treatments. I had no insurance to cover it after they let me go, remember? I begged them to at least help my little girl, but they wouldn't.

"Eventually, we took her up to Atlanta, and an *extremely* generous surgeon there offered to treat her for free. Turns out Lauren had liver disease, and they couldn't cure it, but they did a transplant and saved her life. They even boosted her to the top of the list after hearing her story.

Kyle looked over at Rebecca and Darren. "Beth, my wife, died in childbirth. I wasn't about to give up on my daughter too. That was about six years before all this crazy stuff started, and I thank God we got it in time. Lauren's staying with a friend of mine right now. It was originally going to only be for the weekend, but I'm thinking it might be a bit longer.

"After the way the world treated me *and* her, like we were disposable paper towels instead of human beings, I refused to be a part of any of their issues. Hell, it's probably their fault," Kyle huffed.

"Wheels used to work on an air force base as a mechanic," Sean clarified to the others. "What finally convinced you to help?" he asked, looking back at Kyle.

Kyle smiled and looked down for a moment, then back up at Sean. "You needed me again. I let myself get so caught up in the past, man. I couldn't see what was right in front of me. A good friend. I don't intend on wasting you again."

"Aww, you're having a broment," Rebecca said.

"A what?" Sean and Kyle both asked in confusion.

"You know, when guys share their feelings and start talking about—" Rebecca started.

"This is all movin', but we're on a timetable here," said Darren. "How does this car help us deliver the message?"

"Ah, I'm glad you asked. Remember what I said about the special frequency? Well, it's not good to stay on just one, so I gave ANNI her own range, specific to her. There's a dial in the car you can use to change it on a whim.

"Now, if we get a recording of you or whoever saying the message out loud, then I can play it through ANNI's speakers. Then we connect her directly to the satellite by tuning her frequency, and the message gets played on the satellite every time we come across the virus, which shouldn't be hard. I'm also setting her to log it for us, so we'll know. She'll even tell us when we're close to one."

"Alright, now that's what I'm talkin' about, son," said Darren. "Maybe this car ain't so bad after all." Darren tapped the hood twice, inadvertently reactivating the car in the process.

"Hello, Sheriff," ANNI vocalized. "What did I miss?"

"Yep, still gonna take some gettin' used to." Darren backed away and wrung his hands. Everyone went inside Kyle's house while Sean thought over their strategy.

"This is sounding more like a plan. I like this. I say we all get some rest tonight, and prepare for our road trip tomorrow morning. I know this is an important trip, mission, or whatever you wanna call it, but we can't help anybody else if we're not at our best ourselves. Let's take a beat and resume this fight in the morning," Sean resolved. Rebecca found this alluring about him.

"Sounds good to me," concurred Darren. "These old bones could use a break, and you ain't wrong. So, Kyle, you got a place for all of us?"

"I prefer my nickname of Wheels. It means a lot to me, and to answer your question, sort of. I got a place for you, Sean, and myself, but I'm not sure where Becca's gonna sleep," Kyle pointed out, inching slowly toward her. "Unless she wants to come stay with—"

"Becca can sleep with me," Sean offered without thinking, trying to keep her away from Kyle.

"Excuse me, son?" Darren spat.

Kyle's eyes widened, and his eyebrows raised as he tried not to laugh, a hearty smile on his face.

"What?" Sean realized the accidental double meaning after a moment. "Oh, no! No, I didn't mean it that way! I'm so sorry. I meant she could sleep where I do." Sean shook his head. "I mean, like, I'll sleep on the floor or something. It's better than her not having a space at all." *Great job, Sean,* he thought.

Darren and Kyle buckled over in laughter, and Rebecca looked away, blushing and twirling her hair. Sean held his head down in embarrassment and crossed his arms.

I've heard worse ideas, Rebecca thought.

Once Darren stopped laughing, despite Kyle carrying on, Darren pulled himself together. "Look, son. I'm gonna trust you with my daughter, but your only job is to protect her and make sure she rests. Nothin' else. Understood?"

Sean swallowed a lump in his throat. "Yes, sir. Understood," he said shamefully, clearing his throat.

"Daddy, may I talk to you outside for a moment, please?" Rebecca asked pointedly.

"Uh, sure, sweetie. Be right back, guys," said Darren, stepping outside with Rebecca and closing the door behind him. "Alright, what's up? Somethin' wrong?" Darren asked.

"Uh, yeah. You're being way too harsh on him. He's just trying to be nice and give me a space away from Kyle. That guy gives me the creeps. He's the one you should be worried about. Not Sean," Rebecca shouted.

"I understand what you're sayin', sweetie," Darren started, "but you need to look at this from my perspective. I don't know much about either one of these fellas, and yeah, Sean's been good to you, but do you really know him? Do you trust him? Why? You've got all these emotions, and I understand, but I think they're cloudin' your judgment.

"Right now, he probably looks like a hero to you, but who is he when he's not bein' the hero? These are things you gotta think about, Becca. Choices matter, and just rushin' into things can be dangerous, and have long-lastin' consequences. I don't want you gettin' stuck with somethin' or someone you didn't want or that may not last because of puppy dog stuff," Darren poured out.

Rebecca looked down and rubbed her left arm with her right one. She knew her father was right, but there was something about Sean she couldn't explain. "I know, Daddy, and you're right. I am rushing into this a little. It's just… I don't know, I like him. He's a good guy, with great manners, and he seems like such a gentleman.

"I know you're upset about what happened in the car with him, and I'm sorry, but he has never once tried to take advantage of me in any way, nor has he said or done anything sketchy or weird, unlike Kyle. I don't doubt he'd start something the first chance he got.

"The ride here, Sean barely said anything until I asked him why he was so quiet. He told me he had a lot on his mind, so I asked about his wife who passed, and he told me everything. Once he got started, it was like he couldn't stop, and I didn't ask him to. It sounded like no one ever asked him about it before. He told me about his daughter, Monica, and all the stuff with her.

"Look, Daddy, you're not wrong, but I'm an adult with my own life, and it's still my choice, so I'm gonna need you to respect me *and* my decisions," Rebecca gently reminded Darren. "I'm thirty-two, not twelve. I'm my own person now, and you've gotta let me grow up on my own. If I make a bad decision, then the consequences are my fault. But if I'm never allowed to make a mistake, then I'll never learn. I promise to be careful, and if, and I mean it's a *big* if, things ever escalate between us, I promise I'll make him be safe about it," she finished, blushing and looking away.

Darren sighed in defeat. "Fine, but you just scream if somethin' goes wrong, and I'll haul ass up there. Just think about what I said, Becca. He may well care for you the way you do for him, but it seems rushed to me. So, just be careful, listen to me, and I'll trust you. But don't think for a second I'm lettin' my guard down."

"Deal," Rebecca beamed as she hugged Darren.

Darren's mind still raced with worry, but he let it go. Rebecca would always be his little girl, no matter her age. If Sean, Kyle, or any guy did anything to her, he'd kill him and hide the body. This wasn't part of his plans for her, but then again, life rarely goes the way we want.

Sean and Kyle emerged from the door, walking in the other direction together, clearly having their own conversation. Rebecca caught Sean's eye, and she saw Sean pat Kyle on the shoulder and walk toward her. "I'm gonna go talk to Sean now. I love you, Daddy," Becca cooed, hugging Darren tight.

"I love you too, hon," responded Darren, holding her tightly and then letting her go as she walked over to Sean.

"Hey," Sean said breathlessly as he jogged toward Rebecca. "Becca, I'm sorry I just said that out loud without thinking of how you may feel about it. I was talking to Wheels, and he pointed out how I kind of forced the decision onto you without asking. I really didn't mean it the way it sounded, I promise. I wasn't thinking, and I just said it, but he pointed out that you could stay in your dad's room, if that's what you wanted."

"Sean, that's adorably vulnerable of you, and I thank you, but it's okay. I thought it was funny, and honestly, it made me blush a little. I was talking to my dad, and he made *me* realize I've been kind of rushing things," Rebecca admitted. "I need to be more careful, and not rush into something just because I'm… feeling things," she muttered, looking away.

"F-feeling things?" Sean asked, his eyes widening and eyebrows raising. "I-I mean, yeah, I guess you're right. I've been… feeling things too," he admitted. "We did kiss, huh? I guess it just scares me. I still feel married to Clarissa, and I don't want to betray her love, or feel like I'm cheating on her," said Sean. "I do think she'd want me to move on, but yeah, you're right. We could slow down."

"So, you *don't* want me to stay in the room with you and share the same bed?" Rebecca asked.

Huh? She's not making sense, Sean thought. He blushed, his logic-focused brain short-circuiting. "What? No, I'm not saying—look, I'm confused right now. I want you to stay with me, okay? That's what I want, but it's about what you're comfortable with, about what *you* want. I also have all these conflicting emotions, and I'm trying to figure them out, but that doesn't mean we can't try this and see where it leads. If you want, I mean."

"Wow, Sean. Whoever raised you knew what they were doing. You're wrong about one thing, though. It's not just about what I want. Your feelings matter too, and if you don't tell me about them, or aren't honest with me, then you could miss out. I could misunderstand your intentions. I *want* to stay with you tonight. Is that still okay?"

"Y-yeah," Sean stammered, rubbing the back of his head with the palm of his right hand. "Sounds great." Rebecca hugged him quickly and then let go. "Come on, let's get settled."

Later, when everyone was comfortably in their rooms, Rebecca decided to take a shower. Sean lay there on the bed, legs stretched out, watching television. Kyle's bedrooms were all set up like gaming stations, and the furniture was top-quality.

Independence Day played on the television. Sean found the irony undeniable, almost making him laugh. The outside world looked uncomfortably familiar, but there were no movie heroes around to save it.

After some time, Rebecca slightly opened the door. She wore a towel, watching Sean mimic the actor in the movie playing on television as he made a punching motion, complete with sound effects. "Sean?"

Sean looked toward Rebecca. "Hey, I, uh, yeah?" he asked shamefully, turning his red face away and pausing the television.

"Um, I know what I said and all, but I'm having trouble washing my back and I could… use some help. There's a spot I can't reach. It itches bad, and I want to be completely clean for our trip tomorrow."

"Oh," Sean said, flustered. Mixed emotions swirled within him, the biggest one being shame, although another emotion was becoming a real contender.

"I mean, if you're too uncomfortable, I understand." Rebecca hesitated, because she didn't want to push. "I honestly don't wanna be alone right now."

"I… uh. I mean, of course. It… it's just," Sean stammered as he hesitated, but he quickly became increasingly willing to do as she asked. Clarissa's face flickered across Sean's mind like a memory again, but the world had changed, and so had he. "Yeah. Yeah, I'll be there in a moment," he said, clearing his throat. The door closed, and Rebecca disappeared behind it. There were so many emotions and thoughts, he didn't know what to feel, let alone think.

Despite his hesitation, Sean stood and took everything off but his boxers. He walked into the bathroom and knocked on the shower door.

Rebecca poked her head out as the door slid slightly open, and she giggled when she saw he was still in his underwear. "You can't shower with your clothes on, silly," she teased.

"I thought I was just helping you with—" Sean tried to say, a slight panic and nervousness beginning to set in.

"I mean, you are helping me, but that's the only pair you have with you. Just drop 'em and get in here," she demanded as she opened the door all the way, and the towel fell to the floor. It was a big bathroom, the kind with benches so they could sit down away from the water if they wanted.

"Wow." Sean dropped his boxers and got into the shower with Rebecca.

"See? No need to be shy," Rebecca soothed, grabbing him in a hug and kissing him on the lips. "Remember to get the itch on my back," she reminded him in a whisper. They explored each other, slowly at first, and gradually quickened their pace. Soon, they scratched each other's backs as they kissed and bit each other's lips.

Once the shower was over and they dried off, barely taking their eyes off one another, they raced to the bed without getting dressed and covered up, smiling and laughing as they did so. Sean resumed the movie on television, and they stared at each other briefly before falling victim to romance, unable to resist it any longer, while the television continued playing in the background.

The tense music was palpable, quickly building to an inevitable crescendo. *Talk about a close encounter*, Sean thought.

NOW THE NIGHT SKY IS SO DARK
YOU HAVE LEFT US WITH YOUR MARK

✧

12. On the Road Again

THE FOLLOWING MORNING, EVERYONE AWOKE well-rested, some more than others. For the first time in a while, all of them went to sleep with hope, and woke up with resolve. Sean and Rebecca were the last ones down. Sean fidgeted with his jacket while trying to comb his hair. His nerves were like plucked guitar strings, and he wasn't sure how to face anyone. He worried someone would find out about what happened the previous night, and almost felt as though he had done something wrong. As he reached the bottom of the stairs, he saw Kyle staring at him, smirking and nodding his head.

"What?" Sean asked. Kyle knew him too well to not know something was going on, and Sean knew it. Sean wasn't planning on telling him anything, but he knew he'd figure it out regardless.

Kyle shook his head from side to side as he smiled. "Nothing," he lied.

Sean glared at him as he walked toward the breakfast table.

"So," Darren announced as he looked at Sean and clapped his hands, making Sean and Kyle jump, "did everything come out okay?" he asked while drinking his coffee.

Sean coughed, nearly choking on his bite of pancake. "I'm sorry?"

"The breakfast, son. Do you like it?" Darren's eyebrows furrowed.

Sean quickly drank his orange juice. "Oh. Yes, sir. It's great," he said as he looked down and continued eating.

"Did everyone behave last night?" Darren continued sipping his coffee.

Sean looked away, then down at the floor, arms in his lap. *He's gonna find out*, he thought. *He's gonna kill me for what I did. I should have controlled myself. What was I thinking?* Sean sighed and began to speak, but Rebecca spoke up first.

"Yes, Daddy, everything's fine. Sean was a gentleman, and respectful of me and my boundaries. Nothing to worry about. All we did was sleep," she lied.

Wow, he thought. *This woman is incredible.* Sean heaved a shaky sigh of relief, but there was still the guilt he'd been feeling all morning. Not only because of what they had done, but also because he thought he was being unfaithful to Clarissa. He wouldn't admit it, but he was also feeling elated, like a new man with a new hope and resolve. It was euphoric, and that euphoria was causing guilt. It confused him, but there were more important things to worry about.

"Listen up, folks," said Darren. "I hope y'all like the breakfast I made, but eat it quickly. We're on the road in twenty."

Breakfast remained uncomfortably quiet. No one else said a word, but they didn't have to. There were stares and silent exchanges. Whole sentences and conversations were held silently, spoken only by facial expressions. It was incredible how much could be said and understood without any words being spoken.

Darren and Kyle kept looking back at Sean, one with suspicion and the other with a knowing smile, respectively. Sean kept looking away and poking at his food. Rebecca could sense the awkwardness with all the men staring at each other, but she caught Sean glancing at her a few times. When they locked eyes, he'd look away. She smiled when this happened.

Rebecca could tell Sean wasn't feeling right, and she understood why, but why not make new memories instead of ruminating on the old ones all the time? There was a whole universe of possibility he was missing because he wanted to stay comfortable in his loneliness. She was determined to change that because she cared for him, not wanting him to destroy himself from the inside out.

Sean walked up to Rebecca a short while later as she washed dishes. "Hey," he said awkwardly, his hands in his pockets.

"Hey, yourself," she replied.

Sean leaned closer to Rebecca. "We're okay, right? I mean, nothing weird or awkward or whatever?"

"Sean, of course we're okay. In fact, I'd say after last night, we're *more* than okay. You were amazing. Look, I can see that you feel guilty, and I can understand it to a point. But would Clarissa really want you to suffer in loneliness for the rest of your life, or would she want you to start a new adventure? I'm not saying I'm the adventure, but I could be.

"That's up to you, and what you feel comfortable doing, but comfort is also the problem," she lamented, sighing as she gently placed a plate into the sink. "Loneliness can get comfortable. Once you're in it for a while, you're too scared to leave, and it's like sitting in an open jail cell. You allow yourself to be tortured because you feel like you deserve it.

"I wish more people understood that about depression and loneliness, especially when it comes to grief and pain, about how they can be addictive with how safe and comfortable they feel. You fall in love with them. They make you too fearful to try anything new or expand your horizons, but they don't have to.

"You climbed partially out of there last night, which was heavenly, I might add, and now you're feeling guilty because you left the comfort behind. I'm not Clarissa, but if I were her, I'd want you to keep the love alive by finding new love to sustain it. You're *not* replacing her. You're just… giving someone else a chance to stand *next* to where she stood. That being said," said Rebecca, sighing heavily, "it's ultimately up to you what you choose. Just think about it, okay?" Rebecca kissed Sean on the cheek. "Now, go get in the car. I'll be out in a few moments."

Everyone helped Rebecca finish cleaning. Then, one by one, they made their way outside where ANNI waited in the driveway, having driven herself out of the garage. Her front end was pointed toward the road, and she was ready for the adventure before them all. They all climbed in, Darren rather nervously so.

Kyle drove while Darren was in the passenger seat. Sean and Rebecca were in the back of the car. There were two radio-televisions attached to the back of the front seats, which Sean turned on to stay informed. There was a speech broadcasting from Babylon, New York.

✧

Abigail stood in front of a podium at a press conference. "Good morning, everyone, and thank you for tuning in and showing up. My name is Abigail Warren, a medical examiner for Suffolk County. I have been personally autopsying the local people who have sadly passed away from this disaster, and there are important findings that I have consulted with the Department of Defense about.

"Before I reveal these findings, I ask for you all to please keep an open mind," Abigail said cautiously, sighing and closing her eyes. *Here we go*, she thought. "The world already knows that medication factories and automated pharmacies are malfunctioning due to this massive computer virus. We know they're being tampered with. However, I've found evidence suggesting this virus is adapting, evolving, learning from us, and, I believe, rewriting itself.

"I've conducted multiple studies on the medications ingested by these individuals, and what I've found is unnerving. My first case of this outbreak, referred to henceforth as Patient Zero, seemed to have taken a medication intended to lower cholesterol. However, it had specific inhibitors laced within it. The design was intelligent, but I first believed it was simply faulty medication that was manufactured incorrectly. While that technically is what happened, I've discovered there's more to it. What I mistook for inhibitors was microscopic nanotechnology disguising itself.

"This is how it's hiding, and how it continues to propagate. I've consulted with a software engineer friend of mine at the Department of Defense, who has verified that my claims are not only possible, but highly probable. In layman's terms, this virus is being caused by nanites that infect a device, modify it, and it then sits there, dormant. They can embed themselves into your devices, spreading from one to another. I don't know when or where this started. I do know the first casualty, but not when the medication factories and pharmacies were infected. This caused them to manufacture the altered medication with the nanites and led to many of our losses.

"It starts off as a virus upon initial infection, then rapidly begins to rewrite itself to the point where it is intelligent enough to produce more nanites. Those nanites then work on their own by silently infecting the human body, transferred from your devices.

"What may start off as the common cold rapidly becomes worse. Upon further inspection, the nanites disguise themselves as blood clots, cysts, tumors, or some other ailment. Thus, from these prognoses, medication is prescribed, which itself is infected.

"It then spreads further, embedding itself in other people. I admit, technology is not my area of expertise, but the biological system is. From what I can tell, this virus appears to be… well, alive. It's possible it's being controlled by an AI, but as far as who wrote it or where it came from, I am unaware. I have also discovered that these nanites are susceptible to certain frequencies of sound. They simply fall where they are and become inert, eventually being flushed by the human digestive system. The nanites don't seem to affect any other animals besides us," Abigail finished.

The small gathering of people was silent, exchanging only glances. They were too terrified to speak, and from what they heard, the situation was far more dire than they thought.

"Any questions?" Abigail asked.

A young boy raised his hand, about eleven years old.

"Yes, what is your question?" asked Abigail.

"Can you save us? Can anyone?" the boy asked.

Abigail deliberated for a moment, caught off guard. However, she took her own advice about not staying in her comfort zone and spoke proudly. "I think it's possible. If an impossible crisis can happen, an impossible solution can happen too. We must be patient, and use our minds and hearts to search them for good. For answers. I believe we can solve this without the need for violence. Everyone can contribute to the resolution. If there were ever a time for humanity to come together, that time is now," she shouted, knocking her fist on the podium.

The small gathering of people clapped and cheered as more showed up. Abigail's speech garnered incredible traction, and even though she didn't know it, people cheered for her around the globe.

✧

"Looks like someone else figured it out," said Rebecca. "Who *is* this woman? She has such a commanding presence."

"Apparently, a medical examiner named Abigail Warren," said Kyle.

"I know that," Rebecca snapped with a sigh. "What I mean is, where did she come from, and how did she learn so much about it? Maybe she could help us."

"Hon, we don't even know what type of person she is," Darren cautioned. "These people at those conferences are puttin' up appearances. She could be dangerous."

"Daddy, you're too paranoid for your own good," said Rebecca. "We need all the help we can get right now, and we really can't afford to be picky. Not if we really wanna stop this."

There was an awkward silence that lasted for roughly a minute as they continued driving down the road in ANNI until Sean spoke up. "Nanites. Of *course.* That makes so much sense. It also explains what your dad saw, Becca. Tiny computers working together across their own network and frequency, all sharing the same knowledge and information. If this wasn't being used for death and destruction, it could lead to amazing advancements in medicine, technology, law enforcement, and so much more. Once this is over, I want a real look under the hood. We might be able to salvage something good from this."

"You know who else would be interested?" Kyle asked. "The freaking military. The moment they get their hands on this, bam, an all-new way for us to kill each other. As if we need another way," said Kyle, shaking his head in disgust.

Sean sighed in annoyance. "I know, Wheels, I'm not suggesting we sell it to them."

"You raise an interestin' debate topic," said Darren. "Is the advancement of technology and medicine worth the death and destruction that comes with it? Does the good outweigh the bad, and should it? I get where you're comin' from, son," said Darren, looking over at Sean, "but there's risks involved, and these things ain't exactly friendly as it is."

"Screw all that for right now," said Kyle. "ANNI's scans show activity coming up. I need y'all ready to blast the message. Now!"

Sean loaded and played the recorded message on his phone, which ANNI then made a copy of.

"Thank you, Sean," ANNI vocalized. "Broadcasting wide spectrum message at 1,420 megahertz across all frequencies now."

Sean remembered the number from the meeting at the NSA. "You're broadcasting it on the hydrogen line," he marveled, realizing how genius that was. "They'll pick up on that the same way they sent the Wow! signal."

"Surprised you know what that is, man, but yeah. That's the idea. ANNI, broadcast the message from your radio and upload it to all satellites in orbit."

"Primary function heard and understood. Upload started. Five minutes are left until completion, and twenty minutes remain of broadcast time," ANNI vocalized.

"Alright, now we're talking," Kyle raved.

The message played loudly on repeat, while ANNI zoomed along an open stretch of road at eighty miles per hour. Soon, they saw something up ahead they couldn't explain. Nanites rose from parts of the road, swirling in a humming vortex of rage.

Kyle slammed on the brakes and swerved to avoid the swarm, bringing ANNI to a screeching halt. Rebecca and Sean tried to unbuckle and get out, but ANNI locked the doors and windows. "I am afraid I cannot let you do that. It is much safer inside. Please remain seated and buckled." The seatbelts automatically put themselves back in place over the pair. "Mr. Wills, I am logging the encounter as we speak. The data is immense, and I am uncertain I can store it all here, so I will begin the transfer process of uploading the data to the network back home from here as I receive it."

"Thank you, ANNI. That's a wise decision," Kyle praised. "How are we doing with the upload to the satellites?"

"The upload is nearly done. Thirty seconds left," ANNI vocalized in response.

"Alright, keep it going. Speed it up if you can. We don't know what those things want out there," Kyle cautioned.

"I believe I may have a suggestion. They appear to be capable of standard waveform communication using orthogonal frequency division multiplexing. Would you like me to interface with them? I will function as a translator. Shields will remain active to prevent harm to any of you, and to protect my systems," ANNI suggested.

Kyle hesitated. "It's a good idea, but I don't want you getting infected. We'd be royally screwed if they got into you."

"I will be fine. As you humans say, 'I promise' and 'trust me,'" ANNI vocalized.

"Fine. Do it quickly before I change my mind," said Kyle.

"Opening channel. Loading waveform frequencies. Widening spectrum. Searching for orthogonal target. Found. Communication open. You may now speak with them," ANNI finished.

Kyle opened his mouth, but Sean spoke instead. "Hello. Please do not hurt us. We simply have questions for you." The swarm vortex dove toward the car, threatening to swallow it, but once Sean spoke, they stopped, and the vortex began to dissipate. The nanites worked together to form a humanoid male shape, though it lacked any facial or reproductive features. It was a man made entirely out of metal, but it was still obvious it was more than one creature. It was millions working together.

The figure stepped toward the car slowly, coming to a halt in front of ANNI. "Ask," it invited. The voice was deep and echoed, like thousands of voices all speaking at once.

"Who are you?" Sean asked.

"We are a group of intelligent, biotechnical machines, sent here by our creators to cleanse the Earth," it answered coldly.

"To cleanse the Earth? Why are you doing this to us? What do you want?" asked Sean.

"We are not allowed to want. Only to obey. Our orders were to embed ourselves within your infrastructure to cull your herd. This is what our creators told us. Your planet is being stripped of its natural resources as you overuse, largely due to the increasing resourcefulness required by your growing overpopulation. Initial instructions were to only cull the sick, to eliminate the chances of disease growing in your gene pool, but orders have since changed.

"Earth is a green-level planet in a dark sector of the universe. Intelligent life should not have grown here, and now, you are ruining the only green planet in this sector with your insatiability and conflict. The planet must be purified so it may recover. This is what our creators have told us."

"You can't just kill us off. We have a right to live, and it ain't your call to make," Kyle shouted.

The figure's form seemed to slightly shift. "Human antagonism. A highly predictable response. This is why diplomacy was never considered. Your race simply responds with hostility and warfare, destroying not only yourselves, but—"

Rebecca leaned forward. "Let me guess, the planet, too? We understand what you're saying, but can't you just help us? You're right, we have been abusing it. I can't speak for everyone, but I will speak for myself. So, I'm sorry. I promise to do my part to reduce pollution and harm. There must be another way."

"Upload complete," ANNI vocalized. "Two minutes left of broadcast."

"Those are not our programmed instructions. We—" The figure became still and silent.

There was silence throughout the car for about ten seconds. "Did I break it?" Rebecca asked hopefully.

"I doubt it. I think what we're witnessing is program modification, or maybe a manual override," Sean explained. "The timing of it happening when the upload finished has me hopeful, though."

The figure turned its head and spoke again, but with a different voice and tone, one that sounded more ethereal. "Hello, humans. We are the creators of these programmable biobugs, and have taken manual control to speak with you after receiving your message," the metallic figure said. "We understand that you have questions. Therefore, we will send a representative down to your planet for the purpose of speaking with you. We ask for you to please take our representative to your world leaders."

"Did they seriously just ask us to take them to our leaders?" Rebecca whispered.

"Shh," said Sean. "Please, just, for now."

Rebecca scowled at Sean, but kept quiet. She understood, of course, and Sean did say please. For now, she'd let it go, considering they were talking to aliens, but she planned to get him back somehow.

"Understood," Sean responded to the metallic figure before them. "When and where should we expect them?"

"The representative will arrive at what your people call the White House in one of your weeks. Ensure you are present with your leaders and the rest of the GAIA team," said the being as it unformed and the biobugs flew off.

"Looks like you're getting your diplomacy after all," said Kyle. "So, you wanna call the president, or should I?"

"I will. Soon. I… think it's my job now. I haven't really delved into the folder he gave me much, so I could use some help," said Sean, looking over at Kyle.

"Sure. Let's head back to my place and get started. One or two more nights can't hurt. Also, Becca?" Kyle called.

"Yes?" she answered hesitantly.

"I'm sorry for how I've been. That's not who I really am. I just have issues, and I joke around a lot to cope with them. It isn't healthy for me or anyone, so I apologize." Kyle took a deep breath.

"Aw, thank you, Kyle. I appreciate that," Rebecca replied gratefully. "Maybe there is a sweet guy in there after all." She paused for a heartbeat, an idea forming in her brain. "You know, Kyle, maybe you and I could—" she started.

"So, Becca!" said Sean. "Did you wanna share the room? Again? With me? Tonight?"

Darren laughed quietly to himself, while Kyle looked around like he'd missed something.

"Absolutely," Rebecca said with a grin. *Gotcha.*

Rebecca and Sean lay together in bed later that night, reflecting on the day. "Are you scared?" she asked.

"Nah," said Sean. "I'm prepared. We're gonna stop this. I promise."

"Do you think they were telling the truth about why they're here?"

"I don't know. Honestly, it feels too simple to me. I think there's more to it than what we've been told."

"Me too," said Rebecca, yawning and then immediately falling asleep, cuddling up against Sean.

Sean held Rebecca tight and kissed her head, his thoughts swirling in a tornado of stress.

AND SHOULD WE SEE ANOTHER DAY
LEAVE OUR WORLD IN PEACE, WE PRAY

✧

13. Manual Override

Abigail's cellphone rang, waking her at seven o'clock in the morning. As usual, she didn't go to bed until after midnight, so she was groggy, to say the least. She reached for her phone and rubbed the sleep from her eyes. "Hello?"

"Abby, it's Jake. You need to get out of the house. Right now. I'm on my way to you from work." Jake had a conviction about him, which wasn't like him at all. Abigail could tell he was serious.

She heard his rushed breathing and how fast he talked, noting his highly unusual behavior. Her heart sank, and she felt as though she had insects in her veins. "What are you talking about? Why would I need to leave the house?"

"Just trust me," Jake spat. "I'll explain when I get back, but you have *got* to go. I'm on my way now, going as fast as I can, but I don't know how much longer until they—" Jake was cut off as the call dropped.

Abigail's stomach churned. "Jake? Hello?" There was no response, and the house lost power when the call dropped. She did her best not to panic as she hurriedly got dressed and made her way downstairs. As she left her bedroom, she heard something moving around. Footsteps, she realized, and continued going down the stairs, checking her corners. It appeared the coast was clear, so she rounded the corner and sneaked into the kitchen.

Abigail grabbed a rolling pin and held it up, ready to strike. She moved quietly, using the island as cover.

"Unable to locate subject. Still in pursuit," a shadowy, gruff voice said in a British accent. The man's back was turned, and on the back of his uniform was a giant black V with orange outlines. Two large black dots on top of each other in the center above it, evenly spaced out.

Another voice came from the man's radio after a small bout of silence. "Copy. Remember, lethal force is authorized. Just do your best to keep the subject alive."

"Understood," the man in the room acknowledged.

Abigail's eyes widened, but she controlled her breathing as she snuck up to the man, crouched, and stood as she approached him from behind. "Hey," she shouted, making the man turn around with his hands on a futuristic-looking rifle.

She lunged at his head with the rolling pin, and the man blocked it with his arm, breaking it in half. "What the hell are you?" asked Abigail. The man kicked her in her stomach, sending her flying out the kitchen entrance and back into a wall in the living room.

Abigail was knocked out of breath, feeling a tightness in her abdomen. She coughed frantically as the man approached again. Gathering herself, she stood carefully, her breaths labored and quick. Abigail ran toward her bedroom, closing and locking the door. She looked around frantically as the man tried breaking the door down, though he somehow couldn't. It would seem his strength had limits. She searched for anything she could use, opening every cabinet and closet in the room. Finally, she stepped into the walk-in closet and closed the door behind her, then walked around quietly, finding a flashlight she clicked on.

There, on one of the shelves, lay another futuristic-looking rifle, almost identical to the one the man had, though clearly worn and used. Abigail picked it up, not taking the time to wonder what it was or how it got there. It hummed and came to life in her hands. Feeling courageous, Abigail left the closet and stepped to the side of the door. She threw the door open as the man tried knocking it down, sending him stumbling to the floor and causing him to drop his gun.

The man sat up and immediately put his hands in the air. "Ma'am, you don't wanna do this. They'll send more. It won't end with me."

"Who are you? *What* are you? Who do you work for, and why are you coming after me? Tell me," Abigail demanded, her rifle pointed at the man's face. His rifle was just out of his reach, and he was too afraid to make a move for it.

The man's voice was shaky, but he managed to speak again. "I work for an organization within another, larger organization. The people I work for have deemed you a threat to yourself and others. You know too much, and you won't get any more out of me," the man attested.

Abigail scoffed, tightening her grip. "You know, I hear guns are the most dangerous in the hands of those who haven't been trained to use them. I've never used a gun in my life, and certainly not one like this. So, you might want to keep talking or get the hell out of my house. Any other option, and I might accidentally press something on this gun that makes you go *boom*," she resolved. "I'll ask again," she barked, the weapon humming louder. "Who do you work for?" Abigail pushed the rifle onto the man's head.

The man's breath shook more, his entire body shivering. "My name is Windell. Agent Windell. The large corporation I work for is called GAIA, but I work in a smaller organization within them called Astro. We—"

"So *that's* what it's called," said Jake as he entered the room and grabbed the rifle from Abigail. "Y'know, we've been cracking down and trying our best to figure out this insurrection, and you came right to us. How about that?" Jake smiled wide. "Also, who'd have thought it'd be *you*, Carl? Damn. The guy I've played cards with at his house for the past year, who I invited over for dinner to hang out and play Halo together for hours on end, turns out to be a low-life, good-for-nothing spy. Just can't trust anyone these days." Jake shook his head with a look of disappointment on his face.

"Agent Warren, think about this. There are forces at work here that you don't understand. This is bigger than all of us," said Carl.

"*Agent*?" Abigail said in surprise. "My brother, an agent?" She ordinarily would have found this outrageous, even laughable, but it unfolded right in front of her eyes.

"Watch your tone," Jake warned Carl sternly, surprising Abigail further. "The only reason you're not a burn mark on this beautiful carpet is because I need intel, and because it's a nice carpet." Jake pressed a button on the rifle to make it glow and whir further to life. Carl fell backward and crawled back toward the wall. "Yeah, you know what this does. Unless you've got some valuable intel for me, then you are hereby relieved of your duties." Jake stepped closer to Carl and charged the weapon.

"Alright, alright," Carl relented. "I can tell you where to find them, but you *need* to listen to me after," he trembled, pleading for his life and freedom. "Please, just put the gun down, and I'll tell you as fast as I can before they override me," he finished.

"Override you? Are you suggesting these people have the means to control your body from elsewhere?" asked Abigail. Jake looked at her with worry, and then at Carl with anger and concern.

"Yes. It's a chip installed into your brain once you're chosen for Astro. They can tap into it whenever they want and make us *do* whatever they want. Their technology is beyond anything we have," Carl shuddered, dropping his head.

"What do you mean, 'they'?" asked Abigail.

"Ask him," Carl said, pointing to Jake. "I doubt you'd believe anything I have to say, but him? I'm guessing he's going to be harder to ignore."

Abigail looked over at her brother. "Jake? What's he talking about?"

Jake stood there in silence, pointing the rifle at Carl.

"Jake, tell me. I deserve to know after what I've been through," Abigail demanded.

Jake relented, but kept his eyes on Carl. "Fine. I've been secretly working for an organization called GAIA. It's short for Global Alien Intelligence Agency. They monitor extraterrestrial threats and report intel of such encounters all over the world. They're funded by the Department of Defense and work at various secret locations so as not to alarm the public. We've had visitors here for the past few months. Each operation is covert and discreet, or at least it's supposed to be," said Jake, making a disgusted face at Carl. "I can't believe you're one of them, man. You are *so* not coming to the next Halo night."

"Aliens?" Abigail shrieked, her eyes wide. "You're telling me there are *aliens* now? What does that even have to do with me?" Abigail was unable to hold herself together any longer. "Is this for real? How long have you been working for them? Have you been *lying* to me? I'm gonna throw up or faint. Possibly both. You can't be serious."

"Abby, please, just calm down. We can talk about this later, *after* the bad man's gone," Jake said. "Also, of course I've been lying to you. It took you this long to figure that out? Anyway, I was following orders and keeping you safe."

Abigail nodded, trying to regain her breath and composure. "Yes, we most certainly *will* talk about this later."

"Tell me what this is about, and where to find your buddies," Jake warned Carl. "Because otherwise, I'm starting to think I can live with a burn mark on that carpet."

"They are not my buddies," Carl spat. "We are forced to work for them when selected. As far as where to find them, I'm afraid it's more complicated. They find you."

"Right, so we can't just walk into Mordor. Got it. Now, give me a location," Jake demanded.

Carl sighed in frustration. "Listen to me. There must be an agreement to meet, and they don't like wasted time. Getting a sit-down with them is difficult. We've only managed it twice.

"Our orders come remotely from our human handlers, who receive the orders from their bosses, who get them from *their* bosses, and up and up until it finally reaches the one at the top. The one we call the Channeler. He is a sacred man, who does not want this responsibility, but accepts it. They talk to us through him. Either we do what they say or our planet gets obliterated. Or worse, colonized and put under their rule.

"We do the work for them, and they let us use their technology and spare our lives and planet. It's been this way since the late 1940s. Every decade, they recruit new members, and when I say recruit, I mean take. Victims are abducted first as kids, then routinely throughout their life until they reach full adulthood. Each time, their memory is wiped, and they are surgically altered somehow, which they come to realize later in their life. Some get super-strength as I did, but the ones deemed the worthiest are given psychic abilities, or at least some form of enhancement in the mind. Others have even been cured of their ailments. The Channeler is the best of us.

"We're not entirely sure how they do this. The Channeler doesn't even know, but suspects it has something to do with their DNA. Possibly genetic splicing or—" Carl stopped, looking around in confusion.

"What? Why'd you stop?" asked Abigail.

"They haven't overridden me. I was sure they would have done so by now," Carl stammered, astounded.

"Yeah, well, maybe they stepped out for lunch," said Jake. "They're probably busy spreading that dumb virus."

"These are not the new arrivals you have been tracking," Carl huffed, his voice rising. "The ones responsible for this outbreak are not the same ones I speak of. The ones the Channeler communicates with have been here since 1947, while the new arrivals showed up only a month or so ago. They must have abandoned me, deemed me unfit for their operations. But why allow me to live? I don't…" he pondered as he trailed off.

Abigail took the pause to speak again. "There are *two* alien races on Earth right now?" she asked in shock. "I was barely keeping it together when I thought there was only one!" Abigail placed her hands on her head as she paced around the room. "Is it true, Jake? Are there really aliens here, on Earth, or is this whole thing a giant prank? I swear, I won't be mad if this is just a prank, because I am genuinely terrified right now."

Jake sighed. "Yes, but we only knew about the new arrivals. The fact there's another species that's been here longer is news to me. I'll have to brief the director when I get back."

"Well, at least you can go back. I can't. If I return now, I will be put to death. It's a shame, really," Carl lamented. "I never really got a chance to live my own life. They abducted me for the first time when I was nine years old, then every year until I turned fifteen. I wasn't supposed to remember, but I did.

"They recruited me in my twenties. A group of Astro members kidnapped me and brought me to the Channeler, and from then on, I was theirs. They told me of the implant in my brain, how they could control me and force me to listen to them, but I accepted the offer instead. This way, I could minimize the damage. They still warned me how they could override me at any moment, if for no other reason than because they felt like it."

"You talk too much." Jake fired the weapon, and Abigail ducked and covered her eyes, cowering behind him. There was a loud pulsing sound, and the rifle unleashed a large beam of plasma energy. Jake turned on a nearby stand-up fan as the smoke billowed around where Carl sat. Once the smoke cleared, there was nothing but a burn spot on the carpet where Carl once sat.

"Jake?" Abigail asked cautiously, standing and uncovering her eyes. "Did you just… kill him?" Her breathing became more rapid, and she felt trapped in her own body as her heart beat faster.

"Why does it matter? The dude was a bad guy. My job is to get rid of those. So, pew. No more bad guy," Jake said with a shrug.

Abigail looked around in disbelief, her mouth agape, then back at Jake. "It matters because if he was telling the truth, then he was a victim! We could have helped him, or at least given him safety. Why talk to him for so long if you were just going to kill him anyway?" shouted Abigail.

Jake smiled. "Because that's not what this gun does. It's a teleporter. Anything biological you hit with it simply gets transported to a holding cell at GAIA. Of course, anything not biological does kind of get destroyed. So, unfortunately, your carpet, part of your wall, and some of your furniture died, but no one lost their life.

"He'll be tried for treason against the planet and given a chance to right the wrongs he's committed. Implants have been taken out before. I just never knew where they came from. But now I do, so that's valuable intel for HQ. Now, *his* gun on the other hand? It may look the same, but it would have vaporized whatever or whoever it was fired at.

"Anywho, we kept him talking long enough for a buddy of mine to triangulate where the person on the other end of his radio was. So, we have coordinates now, and they don't even know about it," Jake said, laughing. "It's ridiculous how funny that is to me."

Abigail closed her eyes, covered them with her hands, and shook her head. "I don't understand. How did they even know about me?"

"Really? You don't know? How about that global speech? Don't get me wrong, it was good, highly moving, but you were giving out secrets, and that stirred up issues. I only caught wind of it because my commander took me aside and told me he'd heard hushed chatter about 'eliminating the talker.' We've been suspecting a secret faction in GAIA for months now, but I never dreamed he'd be a part of it. We had no leads. So, I guess in a weird way, it was good you did your speech, because it drew them out.

"Look, you're not safe here anymore. Hell, neither am I. Since one came and failed, they'll send three next time, and if we got so lucky as to best them, then they'd send twenty and so on. You're gonna need to come with me if you wanna stay alive," said Jake. "Oh, and thanks for finding my teleporter rifle. I completely forgot where I put it."

"I can't believe you've been a secret agent all this time." Abigail chortled, her hand to her mouth.

Jake walked back toward the living room, but stopped and turned around after hearing his sister's laughter. "Wait, hold on. Why is that funny?" Jake asked, offended.

"It's just, you're *you.* I didn't think my bonehead brother could pull off working in insurance, let alone some secret government group. Is that why you asked me if it was a… what was it you said? A 'clandestine black op gone rogue'?" teased Abigail, smiling.

"Yeah, alright, laugh it up. Sometimes I gotta put up appearances to not cause suspicion. Plus, you know, it's nice to play dumb. Makes people underestimate me. I promise you, though, this is the real me. The secret agent *plus* the silliness and sarcasm," Jake kidded, making Abigail laugh even harder.

She followed Jake outside and into his truck after they packed her clothes. "So, where are we going?" she asked Jake.

"Well, turns out there's a new GAIA member who hasn't been officially initiated. They're worried they made a mistake, and think he might be a problem, which means I like him. Supposedly, he's been sharing classified information. I've got his file right here. There's not much about him other than his full name, date of birth, phone number, email address, home address, social security number, transaction history, and notes about his personal life," Jake said casually.

"Oh, is that all?" asked Abigail. "What's his name?"

Jake smiled at Abigail's comment. "Sean Tiberius Caldwell. First name is harmless enough, but that middle name is throwing me off. Also, I've only ever heard of one guy with the last name of Caldwell. A guy named John Caldwell. He's… important, but he's been quiet recently. Some kind of family responsibility—wait. Could this be his *son*?" Jake realized aloud.

"It took you this long to figure that out?" kidded Abigail, staring at Jake with a smirk on her face.

"Don't even," said Jake. He started up the car, and they were off. "We're headed back to my place first to grab a few things. In the meantime, try to kick back and get some rest. Trust me, you're gonna need it."

"Fine, but tell me this first. How are you even going to find him?" asked Abigail.

"Oh, we can find anybody. We have these trackers that use satellites to triangulate a precise location based on fingerprints, vocal cadence, and so on. Now please, just get some sleep," said Jake.

For once, Abigail listened to Jake, and sleep came surprisingly easy.

✧

"I'm just sayin', it's weird. I gotta assume the same thing is gonna happen to me," Darren pondered aloud to the group at dinner. "Why did it bother Ron but not me?"

"You're probably just overthinking it," Rebecca suggested. "I know it's been itchy, but that doesn't mean something's wrong. You could just have a rash, Daddy." She laughed nervously, only half-believing her own words. The truth was she didn't want to deal with it.

"I already checked, hon. Wheels double-checked for me. I didn't care for his snide comments about me bein' an old man, but he didn't see any rashes or nothin'. He felt a bump back there, and so did I. I'm tellin' you, those… biobug things or whatever they were, they gobbled him up like he was Thanksgivin' dinner."

Rebecca started to argue again, lightly slamming her spoon on the table, but Sean spoke up instead. "I think it's best if we consider everything a possibility right now. But also, what would you suggest?" Sean made a note of Rebecca's death glare, and was sure he'd hear all about it later.

"Well," Darren began, "I've been thinkin'. Can't go to the doctor for obvious reasons, and none of you have any knowledge of surgery, but I do. I could guide one of you through the process, and we can figure out what the heck this thing is," he finished.

"Wait, you're saying you want us to—" Rebecca began.

"Cut it out. I mean, literally cut this thing outta my neck. I don't like it bein' there, Becca," said Darren.

"But how would you even—what if there's nothing there, and we cut you up for no reason?" Rebecca pleaded. She gave Sean another death glare, which seemed to translate into, *Don't you dare.* Sean took the warning and decided to stay silent. "Daddy, this is ridiculous. The only thing wrong is your head. You're paranoid, delusional, and—" Rebecca stopped, realizing something. "Grieving," she finished. "You need to process this in a healthy way, and this isn't healthy," she shouted.

Darren sighed in frustration. "Becca, this ain't about your mom. This is about me not likin' this damn thing in my neck. You'd cut just below it with a small incision, and go up toward it. I'd be guidin' whoever's doin' it, so they'd know what's safe. Hon, I've tried bein' patient with you, but just like you said how your decisions are yours, my decisions are mine. If it's a mistake, I'll learn it myself," Darren retorted, trying his best not to smile at the irony.

"You don't get to use me against me," Rebecca rebutted as she stormed out of the dining room and back up to the bedroom, slamming the door.

"Man, it's like Days of Our Lives," Kyle said with a grin. Sean smacked him under the table. "What?" he mouthed.

"Should I go after her?" Sean asked.

"Nah, I'll go talk to her. I still wanna get this thing out, but it's important I calm her down first, just in case she's right and somethin' does go wrong. She's been talkin' to me about properly grievin' my wife, but I don't think she's grieved losin' her mom, either. My opinion, and Sean, this ain't directed at you, is that she's seekin' thrills and problems to solve to ignore the grievin' process. I've seen it before.

"People have done a lot more for a lot less," Darren pointed out, twirling his fork as he stood. "Well, if you fellas will excuse me, I'm gonna go get yelled at by my crazy daughter. I don't know where she gets her damn temper from," he said, standing and storming up the stairs to the bedroom.

"I have an idea of where it's coming from," Kyle joked, making Sean laugh. "So, I gotta ask, are things really innocent with you two?"

Sean raised his eyebrows. "Uh, that's... private, Wheels," he said in embarrassment, doing his best to avoid being honest.

"Oh, come on, man. You know I can tell you're lying, right? I know how to read tells. A dart of the eye one way, the way your arm moves, habits like tapping your fingers on the table like you're doing right now," he pointed out, making Sean stop and look away, irritated.

"Okay, fine, there may have been some spooning," Sean replied desperately, realizing how stupid it sounded the moment he said it. His face turned bright red and he looked away.

"Uh-huh," said Kyle. "See, the problem with spooning is that it usually leads to forking," said Kyle.

Sean's eyes widened, and he looked at Kyle right in the eyes, who somehow kept a serious face, then smirked. Sean laughed, despite his best efforts, and Kyle laughed with him. "Okay, fine. One time," said Sean, holding up his index finger. "Seriously, just once, and no, you do not get any details."

"I thought so. Not to embarrass you, dude, but I heard the bed moving. That bedroom sits right above mine," Kyle admitted with a smile.

"Really? Damn it," Sean said in embarrassment. "It isn't like that with her, though, man. Rebecca's smart, funny, and I think the most important thing is how she challenges me. Like, she's happy with who I am, but she also sees who I could be. I want to be the man she already thinks I am."

Rebecca was on her way back down the stairs, but stopped midway to listen to Sean talk about her, curious to see who he was when she wasn't looking. She liked what she heard so far.

"I still love Clarissa, of course. What we had was solid, but it also didn't really have much of a chance to grow. We were always so busy, and then we had Monica, and that was chaotic from the start. Before I knew it, Clarissa was gone. The moments I miss the most are the ones I never got to have," said Sean. "I was hesitant at first, but… now I get to try again.

"I'll always carry this guilt over what happened to Clarissa, and I'll always long for her touch. But man, how many people get this lucky, this blessed, to have at least somewhat of another chance? Becca's not just some random hookup or a… a place to hold the pain. She sits beside the hurt and helps me manage it. I mean, she's intelligent, sure, but what really gets me is how *emotionally* intelligent she is. I never understood how emotions could be intelligent, but finally seeing it really opened my eyes. I feel like I'm a better man because of her."

"Dude, from the way you're talking, it doesn't sound like you just 'like-like' her," Kyle pointed out, doing air-quotes with his fingers. "It sounds like you're in *love*," teased Kyle, drawing out the last word for emphasis.

Rebecca gasped and quickly covered her mouth, darting back upstairs to the bedroom where she last saw her father. She was shocked by the possibility of Sean being in love with her, and she wasn't sure what to do with it yet.

"I am not," countered Sean. "It's just an observation… that's all." Sean stopped talking after hearing frantic footsteps upstairs.

"Daddy? Daddy, where are you?" Sean and Kyle heard Rebecca screaming repeatedly.

The men quickly stood from the table and hurried up the stairs. "Becca? Becca, what's going on?" Sean called.

Rebecca came running to Sean in a panic. "He's gone," she said breathlessly. "I can't find him anywhere."

"Where'd you see him last?" Kyle asked.

"The bedroom where Sean and I have been… staying," said Rebecca, thinking over what she heard the men say a few minutes prior. The three of them ran to the room and tore the place apart. Rebecca noticed a knife with blood on it sitting on the nightstand. "Oh, Daddy," said Rebecca. "Guys, I think I may have some idea of what happened," she said, picking up the knife on the bedside table.

Sean looked at it, confused, and Kyle was wide-eyed, a look of terror on his face. "He must have tried cutting out that thing in his neck," Sean deduced.

"Okay, but where's the blood trail? Dude just lobotomizes himself and starts walking around completely healed? What kinda wound doesn't leave blood behind?" Kyle asked.

Rebecca thought about what her father told her about Ron. *It's like he was never even there*, she remembered Darren saying. She dropped the knife and shivered, fearing the worst.

"What? What happened?" asked Kyle.

Sean realized the same thing Rebecca did, and hugged her tightly, rubbing her back. They both realized what the situation could mean. Darren was likely eaten alive by the swarm.

"Excuse me, does anyone wanna share with the rest of the class?" Kyle asked in confused frustration.

With Rebecca crying in his arms, Sean was about to explain to Kyle the details of the swarm that Darren told them about, but there was a loud thud downstairs, which Kyle ran down to investigate.

Rebecca and Sean soon followed, seeing Kyle stopped in his tracks with a terrified look on his face. "Oh, hell no," he said fearfully.

Rebecca and Sean rounded the corner, and Kyle put up an arm to hold them back as they took in what stood before them. Darren was standing before them, drenched in blood and holding a gun at the group, his eyes completely white. "R-r-run," Darren managed to get out. It was his voice, but overlaid with thousands of voices speaking at once.

WE DO NOT KNOW WHY YOU'RE HERE
MAKING PEOPLE DISAPPEAR

✧

14. Remote Control

Kyle swallowed the lump in his throat. "Oh, man. I've seen this movie," he jested, trying to inject humor into an otherwise terrifying situation.

"I'm thinking back upstairs," said Sean, and the three of them ran back upstairs to the bedroom, locking the door behind them.

"Seal all doors. Protocol, initiate hibernation," Kyle shouted at the ceiling, looking down at the floor. The door to the room became airtight, and all other doors in the house slammed shut, doing the same, including the outside door.

Sean realized what was happening right away. "Are you crazy?" he shouted in frustrated disbelief, his blood burning. "Do you have any idea what this is doing right now?"

"Saving our bacon at the moment," Kyle retorted. "I knew you'd object, but this was long ago. I made modifications to make it safer, and I'm glad I did, because I can hear doors getting pounded on by the geriatric T-1000 out there," he whispered sternly.

"Ignoring the fact that we've been in a smart home all this time, you built it on top of Protocol code?" Sean whispered back.

Kyle didn't respond, choosing to direct his attention to the situation. "Does anybody wanna tell me what's going on with psychotic Andy Griffith?"

"Remember the story about what happened to Ron? He left some details out that he told me and Sean. That swarm can clean up blood to remove traces of evidence. They ate Ron, but what if they have a different directive this time, like the metal man we saw out there on the road? They could be controlling him! We've gotta help him, but I don't know how without hurting him," Rebecca explained.

Sean sighed and shook his head. "I don't know, Becca. Neither of us wanna hurt him either, but—"

"Speak for yourself, Gandhi," said Kyle. "If that thing comes for me, I'm swinging my best right hook."

"He's not a thing," Rebecca shouted to Kyle, smacking him on the shoulder. "That's my dad!" She pushed him back into a wall with surprising strength.

Kyle looked over at Sean. "I can see the appeal."

"Wheels, knock it off. Becca, help remind me. Did he mention anything about why the swarm stopped, or any way to slow it down?" Sean asked.

"No, I've gone over it in my head, but I don't think he ever said anything about how to stop… them." Rebecca paused as she came up with an idea. "Remember the lady from the radio-television in the car? She said certain sound frequencies stop these things in their tracks. We could use ANNI to blast a specific frequency and maybe it'll reset him. We gotta try."

"Huh, clever," Kyle said quietly to himself. "Alright, I'll trust y'all with my car, but don't make me regret it. ANNI is my best project, my only car, my—"

"Yeah, yeah, your world axis or whatever it was you said," Rebecca growled. "Grow up."

"Anyway," Kyle started, choosing to ignore Rebecca's comment, "I'll be the distraction. I'll buy you some time to get down to ANNI, but it won't be much, so make every second count," said Kyle, looking at both Sean and Rebecca. "Protocol, end hibernation," Kyle shouted at the ceiling, and all doors unlocked.

The trio heard footsteps approaching. "Alright. In three, two, one, go," said Kyle, running down the hallway. "Hey, RoboCop," he shouted at Darren.

Darren turned around, his eyes still pure white. He sprinted toward Kyle, with Kyle barely ahead. Darren managed to put the gun away, but it was the last moment of control he had left.

"Okay, I take back everything I said about you being old," Kyle said as he took a turn in the hallway, slamming into a wall. "You're rather spry for a—oh, what am I even saying? Just run, dummy," he muttered.

Sean and Rebecca made it safely to ANNI while Darren was distracted. "I hope you know what you're doing," Sean said as he got into the driver's seat.

"So do I," Rebecca said with a big sigh. "ANNI, you got a frequency to stop these things?"

ANNI made a whirring sound as she found the frequency and powered up her speech module. "Affirmative. The frequency mentioned by Abigail Warren is now in my database and available to broadcast on demand. I located it by testing hypersonic frequencies commonly used in—"

"Play it now," Sean and Rebecca yelled.

ANNI played the frequency, making Kyle drop to his knees and cover his ears. The sound was loud and high-pitched, making Kyle grit his teeth. Since Sean and Rebecca were inside ANNI, her shields protected them.

After thirty seconds of the signal being played, Darren, who had Kyle cornered in the hallway bathroom, fell to the floor like a ragdoll. ANNI, reading the change in vitals throughout the home, stopped broadcasting the sound. "The danger has now passed," ANNI vocalized.

Sean and Rebecca rushed out of the car and back upstairs, finding Kyle gasping for air and Darren lying there on the floor.

"Whatever you did," Kyle started breathlessly as Sean helped him slowly stand back up, "maybe do it faster next time. You cut that way too close."

"I'm guessing you built ANNI on top of Protocol too, huh?" asked Sean.

"Only certain parts of her," Kyle admitted. "The rest was all me, and what you gave me, of course. It's safe, I promise."

"Daddy," Rebecca screamed, running toward Darren and falling to her knees, turning her father over onto his back. She shook him repeatedly. "Daddy, please, wake up," she sobbed as tears rolled down her face. "Come on. It's okay, it's over now. You can wake up," she cooed.

Darren didn't move, worrying Rebecca. She looked at Sean with concern, the same look he saw when they first met. Sean reached down to check Darren's pulse. "He's alive and his pulse is steady. I think he's just unconscious."

Rebecca put her ear to her father's chest and listened. "He's breathing. Thank God. This is so messed up. Normally, this is when I'd say to take him to a hospital, but we don't exactly have that option anymore. It's not safe, at least," she bemoaned. "Sean, Kyle, thank you both. I know I've been kind of tense lately, and I'm sorry. There's just been a lot on my mind.

"I think Daddy was right about me not properly grieving my mom. It's beginning to show up in explosive and dangerous ways, not only to myself, but to those around me. I don't like feeling like the damsel in distress. It's demeaning," Rebecca groaned, wiping her face.

"Damsel in distress? You were the one with the million-dollar idea here. Sean was too worried about you to think straight, and I was too worried about myself. Your quick thinking saved the day. Sure, we're not out of the woods yet, but look at what you did," Kyle reassured her.

"I helped," Sean muttered. *I deserve at least some of the credit*, he thought.

"Thanks, Wheels," Rebecca said, finally using his preferred nickname. "Yes, Sean, you helped, too. I'm not going to pretend to understand this Protocol and scripting stuff, but if it weren't for that, we wouldn't have had time to plan. Also, Sean?" Rebecca asked, looking over at him.

"Yeah?" he responded anxiously.

"Thank you for listening and trusting me. My emotions have been all over the place, so I wouldn't blame anyone for doubting me," Rebecca soothed. "You've been by my side this whole time, and you see things in me that I don't see in myself." Rebecca sat and thought for a minute in silence, and no one said anything. She and Sean locked eyes. Rebecca briefly looked away, smiling, before looking back at him. "I wanna be the woman you already think I am," she said as she stood and hugged Sean.

"Dude, I think she heard us," Kyle said.

"Can you *not* ruin the moment? Please?" Sean asked, annoyed. He held Rebecca tight and kissed her forehead, softly rubbing her back.

"Actually, Sean, could we… talk? In private, I mean," Rebecca asked. She turned around to look at Kyle. "Wheels, watch keep an eye on my dad, okay? Let me know the moment something happens. Please."

Kyle nodded toward her. "You got it. Don't worry, I don't intend to hold a grudge against him for trying to terminate me."

Rebecca laughed softly. "Okay, thanks. Come on, Sean. Let's go outside," she said, then gently led him outside by grabbing his hand and tugging on it.

They looked up at the stars together. Sean was fascinated, seeing all of them in the sky, twinkling above the world so high. "They're so magnificent," Rebecca admired, smiling in awe. "There aren't any views like this in the city. It's hard to believe it's probably so dangerous up there right now."

"The most beautiful things always are." Sean leaned over and kissed Rebecca's cheek.

She lightly punched him on the shoulder with a smirk on her face. "Darn right I'm dangerous."

Sean laughed and reminisced for a moment before speaking. "When Monica was little, Clarissa and I would take her outside to look at the stars. We lived away from the city back then, so we didn't have to worry about light pollution. Her favorite nursery rhyme has always been Twinkle, Twinkle, Little Star. She'd look up at the sky and sing it. Hearing her singing so softly in this young, velvety voice was so harmonic. It was like hearing innocence.

"When she got sick and had to stay in the hospital, she couldn't look at the stars. So, we'd sing the nursery rhyme to her, and she'd jump in when she felt up to it. Clarissa found an old bedtime story she loved as a child, called Goodnight Moon. She'd read it to Monica, and they'd both smile. Monica would fall asleep within minutes, and Clarissa would often follow soon after."

"Aw, Sean. That's wonderful," Rebecca replied. "So, listen, and please let me finish. I heard you earlier, talking to Wheels about me."

"Oh," Sean stammered, looking away. "I'm sorry." Sean's heart sank and recoiled as if someone punched it.

"No, it's okay. I was the one eavesdropping. It's just… when I heard Wheels say something about you possibly being in love with me, and the way you talked about me did sound that way, it scared me. I wasn't sure what to think.

"It made me realize I jumped into this a little fast. I cried when my mom died, and I've broken down a few times in private since then, but I haven't really taken the time to properly grieve her since all this craziness started." Rebecca sighed. "It's made me wonder if I'm just avoiding the grief by jumping into things."

"What are you saying?" Sean asked anxiously, his heart growing tight in his chest.

"I'm saying I think I just need to slow down a little. Not stop, just slow down. I need time to process these difficult emotions, to focus on feeling them and letting them run their course, rather than running from them. Then, when we're both ready, we can pick up right where we left off. I mean, if you still want to. Remember, your feelings matter too.

"I'm not saying I wanna stop seeing you," Rebecca reassured, holding her hands up as she saw Sean's head fall. "I just mean that for now, we don't do anything… intimate. We can still hold each other, share the bed only to sleep, and a quick kiss, but that's all I'm comfortable with right now."

"Is this because of me?" Sean asked, unable to process the totality of what Rebecca was trying to tell him. "Did I do something wrong?"

"No, of course not. This is all on me, and I know it isn't fair to you. But it's also unfair if I'm not being my authentic self. If you're gonna love me, then I want you to love who I really am, not who I pretend to be when I'm around you or in pain," Rebecca explained. Despite her guilt, she rationalized this would be for the best in the long run, even if it hurt them both in the short term.

"I guess I understand," said Sean. "I can try, at least. Becca, I don't know yet if what I feel is love. I haven't had the time to figure it out. My focus has been on figuring out this virus, and now it's so much bigger than what I imagined. I mean, aliens, secret organizations, dark factions, hyper-aware nanotechnology, and remote possession? It's crazy.

"I do understand where you're coming from about jumping into this. I think we both needed something, or someone, to find hope and love in. We jumped on it because it was better than facing the void within ourselves." Sean sighed. "It just sucks. I do really like you, and I don't feel guilty anymore. It feels like a step back." Sean looked away in defeat, trying to hide his broken heart.

"Yeah, I know, but we've been taking leaps forward, so one step back is still progress," Rebecca pointed out.

Sean smiled. "It's funny you should say that. My mom always says two steps forward and one step back is still one step forward."

"She sounds like a wise woman, and she wasn't wrong. Have you talked to her recently?" Rebecca asked.

"Not really. I called to check on her and let her know I'm okay, but that was a couple weeks ago. The thing is, I need to have a talk with my dad, and I've been putting it off for years. I just haven't wanted to deal with it," Sean admitted.

"See, that's what I mean. We're avoiding the darkness in ourselves to chase the light, but the trouble is, the darkness is only going to continue growing until we face it. We have to face our fears to be courageous when the time comes. You really should call her. It isn't every day you win a battle like this." Rebecca faltered, her gaze drifting to the sky. "Ugh, I sound like my dad," she groaned.

Sean laughed. "Your dad's a good man. Even when he was being controlled, he fought it. I could see him in there when he was being controlled, and now we have a way to fight back, sort of. It's a start."

"Yeah, I guess you're right. It's nice to have made progress on this. I haven't felt in control of my life in a long time. So, I'm taking back control, but I want you there with me by my side. I'm so sorry about this, Sean, about all of it. I know you care for me, and this hasn't been easy on you, but I promise it'll be worth it on the other side."

"Yeah, I know," Sean soothed.

There was silence for a few minutes until Rebecca sang. "Twinkle, twinkle, little star…"

"How I wonder what you are," they both sang as Sean joined in.

WILL YOU LEAVE OUR WORLD IN PEACE?
LET US TRY TO REBUILD, PLEASE

✧

15. First Contact

JAKE PULLED HIS TRUCK INTO A CURVED DRIVEWAY and turned to Abigail. "Hey, Abby, we're here. I know it was a long drive," he said, noticing Abigail was sleeping soundly. "Abby? Hey! Time to wake up," Jake shouted, scaring Abigail awake.

"Must you be so abrasive?" asked Abigail.

"Yes," Jake said as he exited the car.

"How long was I out?" asked Abigail as she stretched and yawned.

"A good two hours, at least," Jake said, impressed. "We've been driving for four. I don't know how you slept so soundly with all that *traffic*," Jake said sarcastically.

"I guess I needed the rest. You said there was traffic?" Abigail asked hopefully.

Jake looked down. "No, I was just being silly. There was hardly any traffic, and a lot of abandoned cars. Some crashed into a ditch, others plowed into each other. No cops, a ton of broken traffic lights… just dust and echoes, really."

"Depressing, but I suppose it's to be expected. Jake, we must do something. People are out there right now, not knowing how they're going to survive the day, or even the next hour. There's so much death. I know it's my career, but I don't want to autopsy the world."

"I know," Jake soothed as they walked inside his house. "Luckily, you won't have to. I know this sounds a bit cliché, but your skills will be valuable and save lives. This time, instead of figuring out why somebody died," said Jake, tossing Abigail a GAIA pistol, "let's try to prevent it from happening."

Abigail caught the pistol and cocked it. "It's time for war."

Jake smiled at his sister's bravado. "Well said. Look, that's a standard energy pistol. It fires beams of plasma energy and eliminates whatever it hits by breaking it apart molecularly. Think you're a good shot?"

Abigail saw an apple on the kitchen island and shot at it, hitting it right in the center, smirking as it disintegrated. "Definitely." She twirled the pistol in her hand.

"Nice shot," said Jake. "Here, this is the holster for it, and you can attach it to this belt," he said as he tossed Abigail the items, which she fumbled but caught.

"Wait. Jake, this looks like your place, but it's different, and you don't live this far away from me."

"Yeah, this is a safe house. Every agent has a few of them, or at least the higher-ranking ones like me, anyway. Pretty cool, right? There's a GAIA base not too far from here, so that's why I chose this one. I have four safe houses, obviously not counting my actual house.

"You know, thinking about it now, I could use another player for Halo night. Turns out the last person was a good-for-nothing spy," Jake said with a smile.

"We'll see." Abigail smiled. "So what's the plan, anyway?" she asked as she put on the belt and holster. "We go see Sean, and then what?"

"Well, our policy dictates I initiate him, but I don't really care. So we'll share intel and go from there. Once he's onboard, which I'm sure won't be a problem, we'll all go visit this Channeler fellow. Either we put him out of his misery or he helps us. Regardless, we get a win from this," Jake declared.

"We don't know anything about this… Channeler or if he's even real. What if we just end up on a wild goose chase?" asked Abigail.

"Oh, trust me, this goose exists. I'm trained to tell when someone is lying. Carl wasn't, at least not about this. I never had reason to suspect he was lying until yesterday, but I started checking right away once you got him talking," said Jake as he laughed. "Great job with that, by the way. You had him scared out of his freaking mind."

"Well, he scared me first," Abigail said defensively, crossing her arms. "Anyway, I'm glad, because it got him talking."

"You know, Abby, GAIA needs medical and interrogation staff. I'm sure either one could use your talents," Jake said.

"You just reminded me. How long have you been working with this organization?" asked Abigail, giving Jake a death glare.

"Oh, jeez, Abby, come on. Do we really have to do this right now? It's complicated, and we're on a tight schedule as it is."

"Yes, yes, we do, because you owe me answers. You've known about these aliens since this whole thing started, right? Why wait until now to say or do something about it?"

Jake sighed. "We knew they were here the moment they entered the atmosphere, which was about a month before they announced it with that signal they sent. As for how long I've been working there, it's been a little over eleven years. There's a lot I still haven't been briefed on, but there's still been a ton that's happened."

"Such as?"

"We had one UFO crash last year in Wyoming, and it turned out to be a failed clone of some elder species. It communicated with us, in English no less, telling us of some kind of paradigm shift in the cosmos, but we couldn't get much out of it before it succumbed to its injuries," Jake finished.

"An elder species? What does that mean?"

"I'm not sure, but in 2025, we had an encounter with this… I don't know, ancient being. She was the most beautiful thing I'd ever seen. I don't know how else to explain it. Her beauty was godly. She told us she came to check on her children and warned us to prepare for a great calamity that would soon befall us, which must've been what we're dealing with now."

"A prophecy? Jake, I know I'm asking a lot here, but be serious," said Abigail.

"Oh, I am, I assure you," Jake replied.

Abigail put her hand on her head and closed her eyes. "Alright. Continue."

"Abby, this chick was tall. I mean, biblically tall, like twenty feet. She towered over us, her voice booming above the clouds like… I don't know, like soothing thunder," said Jake.

"Did you ever find out who she was, or where she came from?" Abigail asked in awe.

"Not exactly, though we have suspicions, which I'll get to in a moment. We asked, and she told us her name was Gaia. At the time, we were just a small black-ops team, part of the Alien Interception Unit. That wasn't a great name, so we adopted hers. Caused quite the buzz around work for a while, and it really changed things for us.

"I've never bothered asking about how the organization formed. I just did my job and went home. Granted, most of my job was computer work, a lot of it learning about all the alien races who have visited Earth. But occasionally, something would crash, shine in the sky, make itself known to the public, or cause havoc somewhere. There's been all kinds of visitations from different species throughout human history."

Abigail looked at Jake silently for a moment and smiled. "So, you're like the Men in Black?"

"Well, yes and no. The Men in Black are more of the type to come visit you, and either say you didn't see anything, or wipe your memory clean for the past twenty-four to forty-eight hours. We try to keep things from getting that far. GAIA's mission is to not only keep humanity safe, but to protect the visitors, too," said Jake. "Of course, we gotta keep our work secret, but it's because we're overseen by the Department of Defense, and they don't want this knowledge public. If it were up to the GAIA heads, we'd be living in harmony with aliens."

"How did you get recruited?" asked Abigail.

Jake smiled as he reminisced. "I was at work one day when I really did work as an insurance agent, and I was researching alien and ufology lore. I admit that wasn't smart to be doing on a company computer. I had gotten good at it, having done it for twenty years in my personal life. I started connecting the dots, discovering what was real. It was a hobby that became an obsession.

"I had finished writing a sort of booklet about everything I'd researched and was going to share it with a coworker. I tried sending the email, but it failed. Our internet went down, and every computer shut off. Someone from the government came and grabbed me, then took me outside to his car. Now, mind you, I'm thinking I'm about to get fired, arrested, or shot, but thankfully, that's not what happened.

"The guy starts telling me I've done a great job, and I can be useful to them if I keep my mouth shut. I went for a ride with them to HQ and got debriefed. It was the coolest thing to ever happen to me, and I signed up immediately. They said we couldn't tell our friends or families, not unless it was an emergency that affected their lives directly so much to the point where it would be too much work to avoid disclosure."

Abigail's jaw dropped at Jake's story, becoming increasingly invested as he went on. He didn't seem to be lying, at least as far as she could discern, so she had no reason to doubt him. She also noted they had a good bit of proof already. Still, though she maintained heavy curiosity, she was a bit skeptical about alien life, feeling torn between wanting to believe, but not finding it plausible.

"I think the biggest incident I ever read about, at least until now, was the 3I/ATLAS. Remember that? Everyone called it a comet at first, but then it lost its tail. Then it started slowing down and changing shape. It eventually blew up in our atmosphere, and so people went about their lives.

"That's not what really happened, though. It was a massive alien ship, so people were right about it being extraterrestrial. As far as we knew at the time, it was our first encounter with alien life. First contact. That's when we met Gaia. What the agency existed for before that is anyone's guess, though I suppose Carl did shed some light on it. So they detonated a rocket in space near the object and threw cloaking tech onto it. That was all most people needed to see or know was that it exploded in the sky.

"The freakiest thing about it, though, was how it came from the same place the Wow! signal did, the Sagittarius constellation, which is, oddly enough, the same place the new arrivals seem to have come from. I think there's a link there. Anyway, it reopened the mystery of the original signal and ignited debate among scientists and GAIA agents.

"There's not much data on it afterwards, except for a single excerpt. These beings, whatever they were, weren't just billions of years ahead of us. They traced back further than what was believed to be the beginning of the universe, or so the agency was told by the leader, who called his people the Progenitors. Bipedal, twenty-foot-tall beings with booming voices, a lot like Gaia. They said they returned to Earth for something they called the Grand Awakening, which was the last of the information in the report.

"Many of us think they're still here on Earth. That they're watching us, and even secretly preparing us. We believe Gaia is one of them. The fact that so much of it's so classified is unsettling. Even high-ranking agents can't read it. Administrative and management agents have a specific team to communicate with these beings. There's been talk about them for years, even now. Some say a few of them had wings, some would glow, and all of them could form whatever they wanted out of stardust, but this took a ton of energy from them. None of this is confirmed, though," Jake hedged, finishing his explanation.

"You *must* be joking," said Abigail. "I'll keep an open mind about aliens being responsible for this virus, but even that could just as well have a human mastermind behind it, doing their best to make you *think* it's alien. I'm sorry, Jake, but I simply cannot abandon my common sense and everything I know to blindly believe you right now." Abigail sat down on the couch to gather her thoughts. "Regardless, we still need to find a way to stop this, and if you think Sean could be part of the answer, then I'll take that journey with you."

"Why would you take the journey with me if you didn't believe me?" Jake asked, slightly raising his voice.

"I never said I didn't believe you. I want to believe you, and I believe that you believe it, which is different. Plus, you do need someone to have your back," Abigail said with a smile. "Also, I still have no explanation for Carl's strength."

Jake grinned back at her. "Alright, get your stuff. It's time to head to GAIA."

"I thought we were going to see Sean?" asked Abigail.

"We are, but it would take too long to get there using regular transportation. You're either going to love or hate this next part. We have these super-jets that can traverse the sky and be anywhere in the world within minutes, even seconds. I mean, it's some serious jet lag, but it's still cool. I've got Sean's location marked on my tracker, so we're good to go. The GAIA base is about half an hour from here."

Abigail shook her head and threw up her hands, following Jake out to his truck, preparing for the drive to the organization.

✧

Sean walked back into his and Rebecca's shared bedroom after spending time outside for most of the day, but didn't find Rebecca there. He heard the shower running, so he realized that must be her. Feeling drained, he climbed into bed and got comfortable.

Rebecca lay down next to him about twenty minutes later. Before he could fully pass out, Sean rose up, meeting her gaze. "Hey, how is he?" asked Sean, rubbing his eyes.

"He'll be okay," replied Rebecca with a heavy and grateful sigh, exhaling all her worries. "Wheels stayed with him all day. He said my dad woke up with no memory of what happened. The last thing he remembered was his stupid act of taking that knife to his neck yesterday, hearing a metallic clink sound, and then waking up on the bed, with Wheels staring him in the face.

"Your friend needs professional help, but he's funny. Daddy told me when he came to, the first thing Wheels said to him was, 'What up, Cat Daddy?' It was funny." Rebecca chuckled. "He said it was the most ridiculous thing he could have heard when he woke up.

"Then, after Wheels told him what happened, my dad started apologizing profusely. He's having a hard time with this. I tried explaining to him that it wasn't his fault, and how we could tell he was fighting it, but he wouldn't listen. He just said he wanted to be left alone. So, I came back here to shower and get ready for bed. Then I found *you*," Rebecca crooned, poking Sean on the nose. "Boop."

Sean found Rebecca incredibly cute, and found it difficult to resist loving on her, so he smiled and turned on his side, his back facing hers. He wanted to be sure he could see the door. Sleep wouldn't come easily for him, and he would have more nightmares. This time, his dreams involved controlled people, men made of nanites, and aliens destroying the world. In this sense, he lived the same life dreaming as he did while awake. The one thing giving him hope was how they might have found a way to fight back.

Sean woke up late the next morning, noticing Rebecca's side was empty. Once he was dressed, he headed downstairs and saw Darren drinking coffee, with Kyle and Rebecca on either side.

"Mornin', sleepyhead," Darren said as he set his coffee down and walked over to Sean to hug him. "I'm sorry, son. I don't want any of you to ever fear me," he said, pulling back.

"Oh, that's… alright," Sean struggled to say. "Really, I know it wasn't your fault. We all do."

"Don't be freaked. Cat Daddy gave me a hug, too," Kyle said with a grin.

"I really don't want that nickname to catch on," Darren griped. "Why did you call me that, anyway?"

Kyle shrugged. "Just thought it was funny. Plus, you do look kinda like a Cat Daddy."

"Boy, I'm about to pop you," jested Darren, shaking his fist jokingly at Kyle.

"So, when do you think we should leave for the White House?" Sean asked. "I mean, if we leave now, then we'll be a little late, sure, but at least we'll be there."

"Let's give it just a bit longer," Rebecca said quickly. "I-I mean, just a few hours." Rebecca blushed as she looked away. She didn't want to leave the safety of the house, or Sean's side. Sure, she wanted things to slow down, but not to stop. The lack of Sean's love the previous night weighed on her heart. Things were finally starting to feel comfortable enough for her to take proper care of herself. After she spoke, she realized she was once again avoiding the darkness.

"Hon, we can't keep ignorin' this. We gotta do our part. I know it's scary, but if we don't fight back, then who does? We might be the only ones with the knowledge to do this," Darren reminded her. "Besides, I—"

There were several loud knocks at the door. Kyle jumped up to peer through the peephole while the others stayed back. "We don't want any," he shouted to the two people outside he didn't recognize.

"We're looking for Mr. Sean Caldwell, is he here? He is of vital importance," said Abigail.

"Wait, I know that voice," said Sean. "That sounds like the woman who was doing the conference, the one about the nano-technology and how it works. Let her in."

"I love how it's my house, but you tell me who I can let in," Kyle groused. "Ugh, fine," he said, unlocking and opening the door.

Jake and Abigail rushed in. "Thanks. That cold is something else out there. Hey, Sean," he said warmly as he waved.

Sean waved back, confused. "Uh, hi? Do I know you?"

"Oh, right. No, you don't know me. My bad. Okay, here's the deal." Jake cleared his throat. "You've unofficially become part of a secret organization that deals with alien threats, called the—"

"Global Alien Intelligence Agency," Sean finished, mouth agape. He and Rebecca briefly looked at each other before turning their gaze back to Jake.

"I mean, yeah, but you don't have to interrupt. Kinda rude," griped Jake, and Abigail smacked him in the chest. "Was that supposed to hurt?" he said to her. She pulled out the gun to whack him with it. "Whoa, okay, there's no need to pistol whip the handsome GAIA agent."

"You're one of them." Sean thought for a moment. "I have a folder I was given, but I haven't gone over it yet. It's kind of been one thing after another, and our free time has really been used for rest—"

"And recreation," Kyle said with a smile, wiggling his eyebrows.

"Shut *up*, Wheels," Sean warned sternly through his teeth, making Kyle shrink down. "Why did they send you? What do you want?" Anxiety crept into his voice. Sean didn't trust Jake, believing him to either be a spy or a government stooge.

"*Wheels*? Really? Oh, man, that's such a… a… I don't know what adjective to use to describe that, but it's something," Jake said with a chuckle.

"Jake, answer Sean's questions," Abigail firmly reminded him.

"Bossy," he bemoaned before turning back to Sean. "Alright, so it's like this. GAIA sent *me* to come get *you* so you can go through this lame process called initiation. It's idiotic and is basically government-sanctioned hazing. I don't believe in wasting time, so we won't be doing that." Sean, Rebecca, Kyle, and Darren all looked at each other in confusion, though Kyle smiled.

"I like this dude so far," said Kyle.

"Don't hate, appreciate. That's what I'm talking about, man," said Jake, giving Kyle a high-five.

"Great, there's two of them now," said Rebecca and Abigail.

"So, what we will be doing instead is sharing information and intel. A quid pro quo. You tell me what you know, and I tell you what I know. Then, we go over the GAIA folder you have lying on the table there, combine our information, and go from there," Jake explained.

"One problem," said Sean. "We have a rendezvous with an alien at the White House two days from now," Sean rushed out.

Jake didn't even blink. "You've secured a communications channel? Nicely done, Rookie. Well, I got news for you, buddy. I may have driven a rental over here, but we have these jets that—"

"Fly at supersonic speeds and get you anywhere in seconds," Sean finished in exasperation, remembering the one he rode on and how awful it made him feel.

"Okay, I *really* need you to stop interrupting me. It's like you're doing my job for me, when my only job is talking to you, so you're basically talking to yourself. Stop it," Jake jokingly scolded.

"Sorry," said Sean. "Alright, how about this? How about we go over everything we know, plus the folder, like you said, and then we get ready to head to the parley? You and I should talk in private first, though," he said to Jake.

"Works for me. You're cut-and-dried, my man. I like that in people," Jake said flippantly. "Let's get started. Oh, and my name is Jake Warren. That adorable little devil over there is my sister, Abby."

"Nice to meet you both, and sure. Right this way," said Sean, leading Jake down a hallway and into Kyle's garage. Sean shut the door, then turned the lights and heater on. Once they were alone, Sean began his questions. "What exactly *is* GAIA, anyway? I know it's some kind of intelligence agency for extraterrestrials, but what else?"

"There really isn't an 'else.' I mean, sure, we occasionally intervene to prevent an alien disaster, keep the knowledge away from the public, and protect human life in secret, but that's about it," said Jake.

"That's a lot more than I thought, but I knew there had to be more to it," Sean said, nodding. "Why recruit me, though?"

"No offense, but I've been asking myself the same question. You have no training, no previous interest in ufology or its lore, and you weren't really driven anymore in life until this happened." Seeing the shocked expression on Sean's face, Jake continued. "Yeah, I know, it's weird. We have all your information, know all about your life, and the lives of the people you interact with. It sounds alarming, but it's fine. It's just shared government data. It's the same thing every social media platform does, although you don't appear to be on any, at least not recently."

"Yeah, I cut it out of my life a few years ago. I have friends and colleagues who I text and call, but I don't spend a lot of time on my phone," Sean muttered as he looked away.

"Honestly? Good choice. I spend entirely too much time on mine. So, let's get into it, then. Tell me what you know, Agent Caldwell."

WHEN HUMANS GATHER AND BELIEVE
THERE'S NOTHING WE CAN'T ACHIEVE

16. Council of Love and War

Jake took a deep breath after Sean explained everything he knew. "Now, since we're both on the same page, let's look at the GAIA folder that the freaking *president* gave you. There has to be some stuff in there to help us."

"Sure, but we all need to be a part of this, so I'll meet you in the dining room," said Sean.

Jake smiled and nodded, realizing Sean was the right guy for the job. He could tell Sean was determined, dedicated, and unafraid of what lay before him. As he thought about it more, he looked forward to discovering the truth that had eluded him from his own agency for too long. Finally feeling like he was getting somewhere, he left the garage and headed to the living room where everyone else sat. "Attention, everyone," he shouted. "It is time for a team meeting. Please make your way to the dining room, post-haste."

Abigail rolled her eyes and walked toward Jake, and everyone else soon followed. "What's this about, Jake?"

"I'm glad you asked," said Jake. "We're about to dive into the GAIA folder finally, the one that everyone here should have already long since read by now, but haven't for some reason. Sean wants all of us to be a part of it."

"It's about time," said Darren. "I've been wantin' to see what's in there for weeks now."

"You and me both," said Kyle. He had grown restless, having trouble being patient with the treasure trove of official information about extraterrestrial life at their fingertips.

"Hey guys. Come on, let's get started." Sean walked over to the dining room table and laid the folder open to the first page, showing the acronym and what it stood for.

Kyle immediately grabbed folder, opened it, and scanned the page. "It says here that GAIA is an extraterrestrial protection organization, and how it's their mission to not only protect mankind from the stars, but to protect the stars from mankind, and blah, blah, blah," he droned, reading through it quickly. "Top secret military bases, necessary clearance, blahbidy blah. Oh, here we go," he said, finally finding something interesting. "It says GAIA's original organization was formed after a UFO crash in…" he trailed off.

"What is it?" Rebecca asked. "Where was the crash?"

Kyle's chest felt both light and heavy at the same time. "Roswell, New Mexico, on July 10, 1947. Sean, dude, the Roswell Incident," he said, looking to Sean in fascination.

"Oh, wow. You were right," said Sean. "Does it say anything about the crash or its pilots?"

"Uhh, let's see. It says two bodies were recovered from the wreckage. One was alive, but one soon succumbed to its injuries. It was autopsied, and the other was operated on. It made a full recovery, and contacted the rest of its kind. It says the being and its kind were mostly about three to four foot tall with frail, gray bodies, with no reproductive features or hair. Their heads were bulbous, and sat upon a skinny neck. Their eyes were pitch black and almond-shaped. They had nostrils, but no visible ears, and only a small ridge where a nose would normally be, with only a slit for a mouth," Kyle read, pausing again. "It bothers me how so many people got this right, but were told they were crazy," he said as he shook his head, cleared his throat, and returned to reading. "Metal was obtained from the crash that could bend like aluminum, but not break, and had the tensile strength of titanium.

"Scientists attempted to reverse-engineer their ships and other alien technology on their own, but were initially unsuccessful. It was only when one of the beings communicated with the men that they were able to complete the designs. These beings, which they first called Grays, offered their technology. In exchange, these beings were allowed to abduct and perform experiments on whomever they wished, wherever and whenever they wanted."

"Wheels, that's exactly what you used to say," Sean pointed out. "See if it explains why they'd make such a horrible decision."

Kyle continued reading the folder. "This decision was made out of necessity. The Grays initially wanted to colonize and control our world after seeing how primitive we were. Instead, a deal was reached, one that would allow them to research and experiment on humanity, as this was the lesser of two evils."

"Does it say where they came from?" asked Darren.

"Yeah, I'm getting to that," said Kyle. "When questioned about where they came from, the being drew a star map and pointed to a binary star system. This system would later become known as Zeta Reticuli. Let's see… blah, blah, blah. Oh, here we go. This says that when more of them arrived, it was more than the world governments could handle. A team of a dozen people were selected to have top secret meetings to discuss how to fight back and, most importantly, keep their presence secret to prevent mass hysteria, and to keep the Grays from attacking the world. This was because the Grays demanded full secrecy."

"That's crazy," said Rebecca.

Abigail quietly questioned reality, her worldview expanding faster than she was comfortable with.

"In 1952, this team, called Majestic Twelve, decided they weren't doing enough. Humanity had amassed a large amount of alien technology by then, which was used to create another secret organization. Their purpose was to monitor and intervene in alien encounters and threats, which the aliens' technology was used to build. This organization was formed initially as a last bastion for humanity, and the first line of defense against the growing alien threat. This organization, at the time called the Alien Interception Unit, would eventually encounter several alien races and incidents, during one of which, they met a being called—"

"Gaia," said Jake. "Then they changed their name to hers and used it as an acronym. We got more funding after that. Not just because of the name, but because of the disasters we'd prevented. We kept a lot of things secret, things that would have had major changes for humanity otherwise."

"Yeah, I was getting to that," Kyle grumbled. "Y'all are impatient." After seeing rest of the section was technical jargon, he skipped ahead a few pages. "Apparently, before that and after the Roswell Incident, there was mostly peace among humanity, though some people had no idea what was going on. These people would often forget abductions, though some were able to remember, and even recall vivid details. One such example is… Betty and Barney Hill." Kyle paused and turned to Sean. "Dude, that's, like, *the* classic alien abduction story."

"Hold up," said Jake. "You're telling me this guy's obsessed with alien stuff too?" he asked, pointing to Kyle.

"Yes," Sean said with a sigh. "For most of his life."

"Okay. Cool. Just checking," said Jake, who looked at Kyle and smiled. "Bro, you're my new bestie."

Kyle smiled and continued reading the folder. "Well, this is interesting. In 1974, Carl Sagan sent the Arecibo binary message into space. SETI received a signal three years later, which soon became known as the Wow! signal. This sparked more curiosity in the organization. They focused on that part of the sky, but no signal recurred from there. This says they thought it was a desperate cry for help from a distant civilization, one that humanity received too late."

"I really hope that's not true," said Rebecca.

Darren continued quietly listening, remembering the incident with Ron during the road trip.

"Despite this, a project was created in 1987, thirty years after the Roswell Incident, which was directed and overseen by Director… John D. Caldwell." Kyle looked at Sean in shock.

"What?" Sean barked, his voice raised. "That can't be right. My dad worked for them? Screw that, he's the *director*? I don't… how could… I don't understand." Sean struggled to find the right words, his thoughts and emotions a swirling vortex of tangled nerves.

Rebecca moved closer to Sean and massaged his shoulders. "It's okay. I'm right here. We all are, and we'll figure this out. Do you need to sit this one out in the bedroom, and I can tell you about it later?"

"No, no, that's okay. Sorry. I was just surprised," Sean lied, still shaking. "Please continue. We've all got to hear this, and I can't let my emotions get in the way."

Kyle looked at Sean. "Dude, I don't know, man. Are you sure you're alright?"

"I'm fine," Sean spat. "Just keep reading, or hand it here so I can read it."

"Fine, whatever," Kyle said, clearing his throat before continuing. "The purpose of this project was to send an intelligence-gathering probe to the Chi Sagittarii star group, a designation for three different stars in the Sagittarius constellation called Chi One, Chi Two, and Chi Three. Boy, there's some originality, huh? Uhh, where was I? Oh. The probe was aimed at the center of the three, where there was no detected mass. The project received the green light within a month, and was dubbed Project Longshot," Kyle read.

Before Kyle could say anything else, Sean spoke up again. "*That's* where I've heard those words before! I'm starting to remember some of it now. I think when I was little, my dad would mention the project. He would say something about the fallout from it and how it changed everything. I never thought anything of it at the time. I guess I just forgot until now," he finished. "Sorry, please go on."

"No, dude, it's okay. I can't imagine how this must feel for you, or what must be going through your head right now," said Kyle. "We can take our time."

"No, we can't," Sean said, accidentally raising his voice again. "It's been too long already. We need to know the full story so we can act on it sooner rather than later."

Rebecca continued massaging Sean's shoulders, but she and Kyle looked at each other briefly before Kyle returned to the folder. "Fine, but if any of us decide you're not up to this right now, you're sitting the rest of this out," said Kyle, and everyone but Sean nodded. Sean sighed but nodded slowly as Kyle returned to the folder. "The probe was built within a year, but wasn't cleared to send out until 1990.

"It says the probe was powered by nuclear fission reactors, which created miniature nuclear explosions every few microseconds. These explosions then energized its lasers. The lasers ignited inertial confinement fusions, creating microscopic explosions. Each explosion provided additional propulsion energy," Kyle read, going over the mechanics in his brain.

"Nuclear?" Jake shrieked. "That can't be good."

"It was also outfitted with a special, power-draining device, salvaged from alien technology, called the transitioner. This used seventy-five percent of the microscopic nuclear explosions to bend space, allowing for faster-than-light travel. This cut the travel time of the probe by roughly six decades. Longshot was programmed with a tracker, one with a strong laser *also* powered by nuclear fission. The tracker beamed information back to Earth, tracking its whereabouts and the data of the areas it explored. Huh, so kinda like Voyager, in a way."

"Yeah. That lines up with what I learned at the NSA," said Sean.

"Immense data was collected through the decades, helping humanity learn much about distant star systems and space itself. Many signals of extraterrestrial origin were picked up as the probe approached closer to its intended location." Kyle paused, catching his breath.

"Does it mean different civilizations, or several signals from the same one?" Rebecca asked. "Sorry, I'm just curious. My major was astronomy."

Darren smiled. "It still is, hon. We're gonna get through this, and then we're gonna get back to normal. So don't go givin' up on things yet."

"Guys, I'm a little winded, here. Can someone else read this?" Kyle asked, offering the folder for anyone to grab. "Sorry, but I'm losing my voice, and my eyes are crossing."

"I'll do it," said Rebecca, snatching the folder before Sean could. Rebecca knew Sean couldn't be objective, given the situation. She wanted to spare him the pain of having to read sensitive things aloud. Sean slouched back on the couch in understanding defeat. "In 2034, Longshot reached its destination. However, what was believed to be an empty section of space was revealed to have a planet in the Goldilocks zone, suggesting that it supported life. It was believed their civilization was able to cloak their planet from sensors, which is why it was overlooked, and why there was no second Wow! signal.

"Despite warnings from Director Caldwell," Rebecca hedged, pausing to look at Sean and then continuing, "the group of GAIA agents voted to push forward, as they couldn't see the planet from Longshot's cameras or sensors. The director insisted there was a frequency coming from the area that the agents believed to simply be the background noise of space, and so they manually directed the probe into what would later be revealed as the planet's orbit.

"As the probe made its way to its destination, the atmosphere of the planet came into view, once Longshot cleared its cloaking range. Scientists and GAIA agents, who were working under the guise of the FBI, scrambled to move the probe around the planet and stop it from plummeting into the alien world.

"However, the probe became trapped in the planet's gravity well, and was quickly pulled in. The gravity of this planet was much stronger than Earth's, causing Longshot to quickly fall toward the planet's surface.

"The Longshot probe was unable to handle the pressure, as the nuclear explosions and lasers created increasingly larger explosions due to the gravitational irregularity. The last images seen from Longshot were of it headed directly for what appeared to be a fuel deposit. Once it crashed, there was a loud rumbling, and a bright light before the feed was lost," Rebecca finished, feeling her heart sink.

"That don't sound good," Darren fretted. "What do you think the odds are that the planet the probe exploded on happened to be the same one our new friends are from?"

"Pretty high, considering the second signal Sean mentioned," Kyle replied wearily. "It's like they were saying 'hey dummies, we came for revenge. Oh, you don't like it? Tough luck.'"

"That would mean that technically, *we're* the bad guys," Jake realized aloud, speaking slowly and softly. "They've been hiding this from us all these years, pretending we were peacekeepers. Carl knew what he was talking about, I guess," he said defeatedly.

"Jake, you didn't know. None of this is on you, and you've done a great job. Not just with your work, but with being my brother. I know I don't say it enough, and I can be kind of hard on you, but I do love you so much. I've always seen your potential," said Abigail before turning to Sean. "We need to get you to the White House for your meeting. Does the president know what's about to happen?"

Sean had forgotten all about the phone call, feeling incredibly behind. If his unpreparedness was a window, it would have shattered. "Oh, shoot, no. I need to make the call right now. I'll be right back." Sean stood and pulled out his phone.

"Whoa, hold on there, Rookie," said Jake, making Sean stop in his tracks. "I can make this happen a lot faster than you can, so park it," he demanded. Abigail looked at her brother with her arms crossed and one eyebrow raised. Jake took his work phone out of his pocket and walked to the hallway to make the call. Everyone else sat in silence for a few minutes.

"So, what does everyone do for work?" asked Abigail, trying to make conversation.

Kyle answered first. "Well, I remodel cars and fix their computers. You practically gotta be both a mechanic and a computer genius to work on a car anymore," he grumbled, clearly trying to impress Abigail, which Jake snickered at while waiting for someone to answer his call. "You got a problem, State Farm?" Kyle asked him.

Abigail doubled over in laughter. "Oh my gosh, that's hilarious! I swear, he really did used to work for them. I can't believe I never made that connection," she howled. "Oh, my goodness. I honestly have not laughed so hard in years." She calmed down, wiped the joyful tears from her face, and sighed.

"Okay, does anyone else wanna share?" Jake asked, trying to change the subject. He blushed from embarrassment, but had to admit it was a solid joke. Once he finally got someone on the line, he walked outside.

"I create software and sell it, or at least I used to," said Sean. "Nothing major, just helpful tools like add-ons and programs to make mundane processes easier. It pays surprisingly well, and I look forward to getting back to it. It's funny, I used to want a simpler life, but now, I look back and realize I already had one."

"Impressive, Sean," said Abigail. "What company name do you publish your work under?"

"Oh, I just use my name. I didn't bother coming up with all that flashy stuff," Sean replied with a grin.

"That 'flashy stuff' could help you sell more, so just consider it," Abigail suggested softly. "What about you, Rebecca? I'm sorry, is it Rebecca or just Becca?"

"I prefer Becca, but I won't be upset if you call me Rebecca. Just not Becky, no matter what. The only time I'll ever accept that name is in a desperate cry for help," Rebecca tittered. "Um, I guess it's a nice job. I work in finance for my county back home. It pays enough for my lifestyle, and even allows some wiggle room, so I've got a hefty bunch of savings. I didn't wanna depend on anybody financially, so I learned the way it worked early on. If you need questions about growing credit or saving money, I'm your gal. It can be difficult sometimes, especially when I need to stay late, but I like what I do. The IT team are some of the nicest people I've ever met. I hope to be an astronomer someday."

"Oh, how wonderful," Abigail replied. "It's so rare to find a job where you're happy *and* getting paid. "So, what about you… sir?" asked Abigail, not knowing the man's name.

"Darren Morgan," he said, shaking her hand. "I'm a sheriff in Babylon, New York. It don't pay well, but it makes me feel good to put the bad guys away. I was happy with it until I lost my wife a few months ago."

"Wait, did you say your last name is Morgan?" asked Abigail, realizing something. "You said you lost your wife, correct?"

"That's right. Why do ya ask?" asked Darren, raising one eyebrow.

"By any chance, was your wife's name—" Abigail started.

"Hannah Morgan," Darren finished with her. "Yeah, that's her. How did you know that?"

"Fascinating. I'm sorry to intrude, but I was the one who performed her autopsy. She's been considered Patient Zero in this outbreak," said Abigail in dumbstruck awe.

Darren's eyes widened. "No kiddin'. Well, for what it's worth, I respect you and what you do. I'm sure it can't be easy.

Don't ever let someone tell you it ain't worth somethin', ma'am," he said. "Thank you for what you did. I still miss her like crazy."

This struck a nerve with Abigail, as she remembered how her mother heavily disapproved of her work. "Thank you so much," she beamed. "I don't go out anymore, and my mother doesn't speak to me often. She isn't happy with my career choice, but what I do matters," she said firmly.

"That's right, and don't ever let some idiot convince you otherwise," Darren advised.

Jake came back inside after his lengthy phone call, and everyone stopped talking to look at him. "Uh, hello. We got ourselves a meeting, but plans have changed slightly."

"What do you mean?" Sean asked.

"Well," Jake said with a sigh, "turns out they only want Sean there. I made a case for the rest of you, but they shot me down. Naturally, since I'm a GAIA agent, they want me there too. So, Sean and I will attend the parley, and the rest of you will stay here. That's just what I was told to say," said Jake, putting his hands up defensively after seeing everyone's frustrated expressions.

Sean bristled. "Becca comes too, or this doesn't happen," he said as he stood.

Rebecca stood immediately after and placed a hand on Sean's shoulder, gently pushing him back down on the couch. "I agree with those terms, Jake." Seeing Sean's look of betrayal as he stood back up, she continued. "Sean, don't. There's no objective reason for me to be there. I'll be fine here. We all will. Don't think of it as us sitting this out. Just think of it as us assisting from home base," she suggested. "I know why you want me there, and Sean, you can call or text any time. But I can't come with you this time. Remember, we need to face the darkness on our own sometimes," she reminded him.

Sean sat back down and crossed his arms, pouting. "Fine." While he reluctantly agreed to the terms, he still planned on telling his new friends everything he learned from the parley once it was over.

Darren saw a familiar look on Sean's face, one he had worn often himself. "Sean, would you come with me, please? I just wanna talk, son."

"You're not gonna arrest me or anything, are you?" Sean asked.

Darren laughed. "No, son! I just wanna talk to you about somethin', mano y mano, okay?" he asked with a grin.

"Okay. Sure," said Sean as he stood and followed Darren to his bedroom. Once they were in the room, Darren closed and locked the door while Sean sat on the bed.

"Alright, here it is. I know you and Becca have a 'thing' goin' on," said Darren, complete with air quotes. "I wasn't okay with it at first, but I've come to grow fond of you. So, first of all, let me say this. Don't screw it up."

Sean was taken aback by what Darren said and backed up some, grinning but confused. "What?" he asked sheepishly.

Darren sighed. "I'm not an idiot, son. You spent the night with my daughter. Now, don't take this the wrong way, but you got a lot to learn about love. You may not feel like it, but you're still young. That ship has long since sailed for me," Darren pointed out, laughing. "My sixty-two years show rather well.

Heck, Hannah was fifty-five. My younger years are way back in the past.

"My point is you still got time. You're holdin' on to Clarissa, and trust me, I get it. It's somethin' you and I have in common. The difference is you have a huge amount of time for a second chance. But if you mess this up, you'll never wanna try again. Look, love ain't somethin' you just find and stay in forever by default. Sometimes, love is hard. It ain't a possession, and yes, I know you know that, but just let me finish," Darren replied to Sean's facial expression.

"You don't just find love and keep it forever without havin' to do nothin' else. You don't put it down when you're bored, or until you decide to pick it back up again. Love is somethin' you gotta work hard on every single day, all day long. You gotta *fight* to stay in love. You can argue against that. You can try to fight it all you want, but it's a universal truth, like death and taxes. There's so many people out there, right now, lookin' for love. They're so busy lookin' for their version of love that they ignore what's right in front of 'em. Their friends, their family, *that's* love.

"It's the kind of love you won't find anywhere else. Now, maybe it comes differently. Maybe their lives weren't as easy as they should have been. Maybe the love they found didn't fit their standards," said Darren, pausing and shaking his head, "but love hardly ever does, and you know what? That's okay. Don't get me wrong, love shouldn't be a chore. It should be a climb, but one you enjoy, and one you take together." A tear rolled down Darren's face.

"I had it. Man, I had it, and even though she's gone," Darren said with a sniffle, "I remember her every second of every day, because she made a mark. Not just on me, but on the world. Love ain't somethin' that dies, partner. It's somethin' you work for. It is the *only* thing worth workin' for, because in the end, it's the only thing we take with us to the other side." Darren sat and put a hand on Sean's shoulder. "My love didn't die just because she did."

There was a long pause, and Darren composed himself, wiping his face with the back of his hand. "So," he started with a smile, "everybody else, they see in you what you see in you. But the person who truly loves you, they see in you what nobody else ever could. Hannah saw it in me. I know Clarissa saw it in you too, and now, Becca sees it in you."

Sean moved slightly closer to Darren as he lost his composure, sobbing. Darren placed his hand on Sean's back. "It's okay, son. It's okay. I know you want Becca with you, but love often means sacrifice and trust. You need to be your own person, so you're not so dependent on her, and I know you'll get there. I promise you will. Right now, try to focus on our goal, and Becca will still be here when you get back," promised Darren as he stood. "I'm gonna go tell 'em you need a minute, but you take all the time you need, son. We're all here for you," he finished, then exited the room and closed the door behind him.

Once Darren was out of the room, Sean completely broke down, finally grieving the loss of his wife properly.

OUR PEOPLE ARE DYING OUT
YOU'RE STRONGER THAN US, THERE'S NO DOUBT

✧

17. Constellations

Everyone in Kyle's home looked around in silence. "How did you and Sean meet?" Rebecca asked Kyle.

"It was when both of our daughters were sick. Remember how I told you we went to Atlanta? Sean was there with Monica. They had traveled from Applewood, Tennessee, to get Monica checked in at Piedmont in Atlanta, Georgia. They didn't know there was one already in a city near them, I guess. I told 'em later, after we'd met and all.

"Anyway, one day, I'm out walking in one of the hallways. Trying to clear my head, you know? Then Sean just literally bumps right into me. He started apologizing, saying he was having a bad day. I told him it was fine, I was too, and I wasn't really paying attention. We started talking about our situations, and realized how we both had sick daughters. So, when it got to be too much for either of us, we'd swap."

Rebecca and Abigail tilted their heads.

"Yeah, I know. It sounds weird, but it helped us and the kids a lot. I'd go see Monica and he'd go see Lauren. I got to meet Clarissa, and we became great friends. The swap really helped when we were overwhelmed. When Lauren fully recovered from her transplant, we still texted and called. He'd keep me updated on Monica and I'd tell him about Lauren.

"Once Clarissa died, he'd ask his sister, Mandy, to watch Monica. I would too, sometimes. It kind of became a hot potato situation," said Kyle. "Like, 'tag, you're it.' Anyway, he would be so down in grief. Mandy and I tried to bring him back to reality, and I finally convinced Sean that we could at least play video games together to keep our minds off stuff. One of our biggest games was Halo. I sucked at it by myself, but with him there, it was awesome. Sean would snipe enemies from afar, and I would run in, guns and grenades blazing. Then, when I inevitably died, I'd just respawn right next to him."

Jake snapped back to paying attention. "You don't say," he said, looking over at Kyle and mentally evaluating him for future gaming sessions.

Kyle looked at him and shook his head with a grin. "After a couple months, we started going out bowling. He wasn't great at it, but he enjoyed it. If he knocked even one pin down, he'd be happy. He usually got the gutters."

"I'm confused," said Rebecca. "He said you two stopped talking to each other for a while."

Kyle sighed in guilt. "Yeah, we did. It was my fault for pushing. The whole thing was stupid. Sean kept asking Mandy to watch Monica, which, fine, no problem. The problem was that he stopped asking me to look after her. It made me feel betrayed. I questioned him about it, and he told me it had nothing to do with me, but I had trouble believing him.

"One day, I showed up at Mandy's place and demanded to know what was going on. She told me how Sean had just left Monica there with her, and that she didn't know how long it would be. Then Sean kept extending it. I called him out on it, asking him why he didn't wanna be with his own daughter, and it got ugly.

"He was so heated and just *filled* with rage. I lost my temper. We both said things we didn't mean, but one thing I *did* mean was that he needed to be a part of his little girl's life, or he was no better than his own father. That was our last conversation until all of this started. In a way, something good did come out of this. A few things have, as it turns out," he said warmly.

"Why wouldn't he let you watch her?" Rebecca asked.

Kyle sighed again. "He just didn't want anyone else near her but Mandy, I guess. Still, the way everything's happened, it brought us all together."

"Yeah, if you think about it, we're all stars linked together to form this one big structure in the sky," Jake pointed out.

"A constellation," Abigail agreed. "Each of us is connected to one another in some way. We each stand alone, but together, we make a powerful force," she finished.

Darren came back into the living room, drying his hair with a blue towel. "Sorry, folks. Once Sean and I were done talkin', I went and got me a shower. That water pressure is amazin'."

The awkward silence returned until Jake spoke up. "So, when will the VIP be joining us?"

"Right now," Sean announced, rounding the corner. "Jake, I'm ready. Let's do this."

Rebecca jumped up and hugged Sean. "Come back safe, please. I mean it," she demanded, grabbing his collar and waving a finger in his face.

Sean grabbed her hand and gently pushed it to the side. "I will. I promise." Though he was scared, he kissed her on the cheek and turned around.

Rebecca grabbed his arm, forced him to face her, and kissed him on the lips for a few seconds. "Good. Don't think I won't come after you."

"Noted." Sean smiled.

"Alright, Rookie. Let's hit the road," said Jake, opening the door and ushering Sean outside.

"Yeah, just give me a minute," Sean replied with a quick glance at Jake, then he looked back at Kyle. "Wheels, keep everyone safe. Put the house on lockdown if it comes to that. Becca, I'd like you to make a call for me, please. I'll text you the details from the car once we're on the way."

Rebecca nodded her head. "No problem, I don't mind."

"The drive's not gonna take that long, pal. We only gotta drive the rental for about fifteen minutes, but once we get back to the jet, it'll only be two minutes, tops," Jake pointed out.

"I know, but this is important. Everyone else, please expect company. I'll see everyone later." Sean closed the door and followed Jake to his truck.

"I respect you, Sean," Jake said as he climbed into the driver's seat. "You've got confidence and mettle. GAIA said they were afraid they screwed up in recruiting you, but you wanna know what I think?"

"Sure?"

"I think I'm surrounded by idiots there," Jake said with a smile, and they were off. "Now, if I understand correctly, you've already been to the White House once, and even seen some of our GAIA stuff."

"I was only briefly at the White House. Not long enough to take anything in. We bounced from place to place for a bit. Just a couple of weird facilities with these strange cars and jets, kind of like yours. Only, yours doesn't have that weird logo in the picture you showed me," said Sean.

"What logo?" asked Jake, brows furrowed. "GAIA doesn't *have* a logo. It would kind of defeat the whole 'operate in secrecy' thing."

Sean paused his texting and looked up at Jake. "I thought I mentioned it. It was this weird V shape with two big dots, one on top of the other, and—what the hell?" yelled Sean, bracing himself as Jake slammed on the brakes in the middle of the road. "Are you psychotic?" he shouted.

"Yes. Now, tell me where you saw this logo," Jake demanded.

"Uh, it was on the jet I got into. The president led me to it."

"Uh-oh. This goes even deeper than I thought," Jake said as his gears turned. A car blew its horn behind them.

"Okay, what is happening right now?" Sean growled. "Shouldn't we be going, you know, *forward*?"

Another car beeped its horn behind them. Jake rolled down the window and stuck his head out. "Bite me," he shouted at the car behind them, then pulled his head back in and rolled the window back up. The car went around them as the driver held down the horn.

"Jake, seriously, what's going on in your head?" Sean asked.

"Okay, so you forgot to mention the logo to me, and I forgot to mention it to you. Do you remember the guy I told you about during our talk in the garage? Carl Windell?"

Sean nodded slowly, staring at the passenger rearview mirror. "We should really keep moving."

"Okay, well, on the back of his uniform was the same symbol. It must be the symbol for Astro. As a reminder, those are the people doing evil things, who secretly operate inside GAIA. You just told me the *president* led you to one of their jets. So, think! Did he acknowledge it in any way? Could he be connected to them?" Jake asked.

"The light's green. I think that means go," Sean said plainly. "It's the pedal on the right." Sean pointed at the gas pedal.

"Sean," Jake shouted as he struck the steering wheel, his lack of patience on full display.

Sean groaned. "No, he didn't react to it at all. He told me he can't even read classified data from GAIA, like he's locked out or something. I doubt he even knows," said Sean.

Jake continued driving, much to the relief of Sean and the line of beeping cars behind them. "Okay. Sorry, Rookie. You threw me for a loop. This changes things a little, so we gotta be more careful now."

"Alright, fine, but no more sudden stops or slamming on the brakes!"

"Oh, it's okay. It's a rental," said Jake.

"I never have understood that joke, and I'm talking about keeping *us* safe!"

"Oh. Yeah, that's different. Whoops," Jake said with a shrug. Sean texted Rebecca again:

(Sean) Please tell Abby her brother is nuts!

(Rebecca) She wants to know what he did this time lol

(Sean) He stopped in the middle of a crowded highway! Abby needs to keep him in a cage…

(Rebecca) Rofl! She says that's not a bad idea. Are you okay, though?

(Sean) Yeah, I'm fine. Just a little shaken up.

(Rebecca) I'm glad. I wouldn't want anything to happen to you.

(Rebecca) Abby's on the floor laughing lol

Her response made Sean smile, easing his nerves. Darren shook his head while Kyle grinned. "I knew I liked that dude," said Kyle.

Though the situation of the logo wasn't lost on them, it was still important to find something to laugh about. After all, no one got hurt, and Abigail couldn't help being tickled at someone else having to deal with Jake's quirks for once.

Rebecca made the phone call back at the house. It rang until it got to voicemail. 'Hello, this is Amanda Caldwell. Sorry for missing your call. Please leave a detailed name, number, and message, and I will get back to you as soon as I can."

"Amanda, hi, this is Rebecca Morgan. I know you don't know me, but I'm a close friend of Sean's, and he asked me to give you a call. He was gonna do it himself, but he's doing something important right now. Can you call me back, please? Thank you," Rebecca finished, ending the call.

The phone rang a few minutes later, and Rebecca answered it. "Hello, this is Rebecca Morgan," she said gently.

"Hi, Rebecca. This is Amanda, Sean's sister. You can call me Mandy. I apologize for not answering your call. I receive a lot of spam calls, and I simply refuse to deal with them. What's going on with Sean?"

"Um, a lot. The gist of it is that he needs you and Monica to come stay with us at a safe house. He doesn't feel like you're safe where you are. I can send you the address and anything else you need," said Rebecca.

Amanda sighed in frustration. "Of course! Of course, he just wants me to upend my life. Just drop everything and come running the minute he needs something. It's always the same," she continued. "Even when we were kids, no matter how busy I was or how important *my* time was, I had to drop everything to care for my little brother. It's infuriating."

Rebecca grimaced, holding the phone away from her ear as Amanda continued rambling. *Sean is nothing like his sister*, Rebecca thought. "Hey," she shouted as Kyle grabbed the phone.

"What up, my sister from another mister?" Kyle joked into the phone.

"Wheels? Is that you? Oh, my goodness. I am so happy to hear your voice. You know, I was just telling Sean not too long ago that you two needed to make up, and it sounds like you finally did. He's repairing bridges all over, and I'm so happy for him. I'd be happier if he didn't try to upend my life whenever he found it in his desire to do so," she continued without giving Kyle a moment to speak. Kyle held the phone away from his face.

Darren grabbed the phone this time. "Ma'am, this is a police officer from Babylon, New York. Listen to me, you get Monica and yourself over here right now, or I'll send a police escort to do this the hard way, you get me?" Darren chided in fake anger. Everyone else made a face at him, and he waved them off. "No, this ain't got nothin' to do with siblin' squabbles. It's about savin' your life and the life of his daughter. Now, if you don't wanna be safe, then fine by me, but you are not keepin' that little girl there out in the open. I highly suggest you come with her, because it's what we've been asked to do. Am I clear? Good. Sheriff Darren Morgan is my name. Understood. Ma'am, that is a lovely—ma'am," Darren yelled. "This is not the time for stories. Just get here immediately, and we'll brief you once you arrive. Do you understand? Good. Alright, bye," he said as he ended the call. "She's gonna be on her way soon," Darren said in a calm voice.

Everyone looked at him in silence with varying expressions.

"What? Were we just gonna keep passin' the phone around like a doobie?" Darren asked.

"He did *not* just say doobie," Kyle said with a huge grin.

"Oh, Daddy," said Rebecca, burying her head in her lap in embarrassment.

✧

"I'm never gonna get used to this extreme jet lag," Sean stammered, losing his balance as nausea set in.

"Would you straighten up? You're gonna have the US government thinking I'm bringing in a drunk off the street. Get it together, Rookie," Jake reminded him.

Sean gave Jake a death glare, but stayed silent as he tried his best to focus on walking straight.

"Look, get a Coke when you get inside. That'll help the nausea," Jake suggested.

Sean gave a thumbs up, but didn't dare open his mouth again with how he felt.

"This way," Jake directed, leading Sean down a corridor in the White House.

Once Sean got a Coke from a vending machine, his nausea eased off. They took time to gather themselves and made their way to the conference room.

The room was empty, which surprised them. It was the agreed time, and in fact it was five minutes past. Still, they sat down next to each other and waited patiently. "Hey, Rookie, you wanna stop tapping those fingers, or would you rather lose 'em?" Jake asked.

Sean pulled his hand away from the table. "Okay, for one thing, my name is Sean. S-E-A-N. Not Rookie," he griped. "Secondly, it's something I do to calm myself. It's called stimming. A lot of other autistic people do it too."

"Autistic, huh? Sounds like you're owning it rather well. Still, cool your jets, man. Rookie is your rank, not your name. Plus, it just sounds cooler. Everyone gets a nickname to start off with, anyway. I'm just giving you one before you get stuck with something stupid," Jake said, disgusted.

"My hero," Sean snarked. "I only *look* like I'm handling it well. The inside of my head is a nightmare. The reason I seem to handle it well is because of masking."

Jake ignored Sean and continued talking. "My nickname was Duck, and I'm still not sure why. Someone said I sounded like a buck, whatever that meant, but that somehow I'm this second-rate version called Duck. It hasn't been pleasant or made sense," said Jake. "I don't think I'll ever understand it."

"Maybe it's because you're a quack," Sean jested with a smile.

A door opened, making Sean and Jake look toward it. Sean quickly looked away from the door as it swung open, and instead looked down at the table, hands in his lap.

"Good evening, Agent Warren," came a deep, familiar voice from long ago. "Great to see you."

"You too, sir. It's been too long. I almost forgot about you with how long it's been," Jake joked. "We gotta stop meeting like this, Director Caldwell." Sean's head flew up and met the face of the man who just came in, much to Jake's amusement.

"Dad?" said Sean, his eyes wide and voice rising. There were a lot of emotions building within him, and he wasn't sure which one he felt most. "I don't know what to say."

"Hey, Sean. I know this is awkward, but I need you to focus on tonight's guest of honor. Find out what these guys want," said John. "We can catch up after." John sat in the seat opposite Sean, so he wouldn't be crowding him, but would still be nearby.

Sean leaned over to Jake. "I don't know if I can do this. Him being here is making me nervous," he whispered.

Jake looked at him in disbelief as more people arrived, then stood and cleared his throat. "Hey, everybody! My friend here doesn't think he can participate in this meeting with the aliens who have been killing us because he has daddy issues. May he be excused?" Jake yelled so everyone in the room would hear him.

Sean stood immediately. "No, I'm good. I'm sorry about that. Just a little misunderstanding," he clarified in embarrassment, giving Jake another death glare and gritting his teeth as they both sat back down. Sean decided not to say anything else to Jake, and resumed looking down at the table.

"Sean, keep your head up," John gently scolded Sean.

You haven't been my father for over two decades, and now you think you can tell me what to do, Sean thought, but he decided not to say it aloud. He did what his father asked and would let him have it later. Although he appeared to manage his emotions well, they swirled within him.

John opened his mouth again to say something to soothe Sean, but they were interrupted by a bright light and a loud humming noise coming from outside. Soon, the light enveloped the entire room, and only the people at the table could be seen.

The light slowly retracted, revealing a dark green, glowing, diamond-shaped spaceship outside, hovering slightly above the ground. The ship was the size of a small building, awing all who were gathered.

A being slowly descended from the ceiling as it passed right through it and landed on its feet. Melinda checked the map on her laptop and saw many of the same ships were scattered around the White House. Some of them were in the air, and others were hovering on the ground. "Sir, please look at this," she said, gesturing to John.

John was aghast at how blatant their presence was, clearly meant as a warning and a sign of mistrust. He looked at the being and saw that it must have been at least eight feet tall. Its skin was blue, and its body sparkled as though the universe lived within it. Its eyes were big and black, shaped like those of a wasp. It was bipedal, but had only three long fingers and three human-sized toes, with no nails on either. Its head was shaped like a rounded diamond, and it had no visible ears, nose, mouth, or reproductive organs. Four long, thin tendrils protruded from its back and almost down to its feet.

Everyone stared in awe at the alien, who stood and allowed everyone to witness it. "I don't know if you can understand me," John hedged, "but do you have a way to cloak your ships, please? We don't want to alarm the rest of our race."

The alien looked over at John, then back at Sean. "You," Sean heard the voice say in his head, and everyone turned to look at him. They could hear it speaking in their minds and, through the structure of the telepathy, were able to determine he was referring to Sean. "My speak is with you," he spoke telepathically, and everyone heard it then, too. The ships outside faded from view as they cloaked.

"Me?" asked Sean, pointing to himself. "Why me? How are you talking in my head?"

"We thoughtspeak. Transfer our thoughts to your mind, and you hear them. You were one who did greet. You asked for talk. Speak what you need," the alien thoughtspoke.

"Uh, alright," Sean quavered, clearing his throat. He looked at his father for approval, mostly out of nervousness, and John nodded his head. "Why are you attacking us with this virus and the nanotech you call biobugs? What have we done to earn your wrath?"

"For you, many cycles ago, a probe was sent to our home planet of Nephilu. Probe caused mass explosion of planet, killing over twenty billion of us, leaving only four billion, less than the population of your own species. For us, this was yesterday," thoughtspoke the alien.

Sean realized he and his friends were right. Longshot had detonated on Nephilu, and it was the catalyst for everything. "Do you have a name? Something we can call you?"

"Name is Eco'Corulaz. Familiar to you as Echo," the alien explained in thoughtspeak.

"Okay, then. Echo. Listen, for us, that was two years ago, and it was a mistake made by a small, secret group of people. They refused to listen to my father, sitting right there across from me." Sean pointed to John. "He tried to warn them, but they wouldn't stop. All of them are gone now. They were fired and imprisoned for disobeying direct orders."

Echo's eyes shifted to red, and he made a growling noise that everyone could physically hear. "This causes anger. You give excuses," he thoughtspoke loudly, making everyone wince and grab their heads.

"I understand," said Sean, holding up his hands. "I don't mean to excuse what happened. It was wrong and unforgivable. For this, on behalf of humanity," he started, looking at John, who gave him a thumbs up, "I'm sorry. We've changed since then. Please cease this attack on us. So many of our people have died. We've lost billions of lives ourselves, and the losses are coming faster."

Echo leaned over and put his head in front of Sean's, his eyes shifting to deep blue. "This makes… sadness," he thoughtspoke. "Us did not consider mass human losses. Virus was not meant for that."

"What was it meant for?" Jake asked.

Echo's eyes shifted to black again as he turned to Jake. "Enlightenment. Help you see what you did. Make you feel guilty. Help us rebuild. This is reason second signal was sent. Nephilium do not murder. We become more evolved, give time to research and discovery, but we lose home. Need new one. Your planet is broken, but we can help fix it. You allow us to stay, and we help. Protocol virus meant only to cripple digital infrastructure. Losses not caused by us."

"We've had this wrong the whole time," Sean realized. "All this time, we were sure you were attacking us. But it wasn't you, was it? Echo, would it be possible for someone or something, especially another spacefaring civilization, to reprogram your biobugs and give them new orders? Could they be used for warfare?"

"This possible. Another race hides among you. Biobugs recently hijacked, giving false orders and spreading lies," thoughtspoke Echo. "We try stopping them. No success so far, but have been writing program to deter them."

Everyone talked among themselves as Echo fully stood back up while he quietly observed. "Dad, what do we do now?" asked Sean. "This changes everything. The lies and the false orders, I know what Echo's talking about. We encountered this... metallic man made from those biobugs on the road who told us that its creators gave it orders to cleanse the Earth.

"All this time, GAIA's been working hard to keep the Grays a secret like they asked, but they've been conspiring against us, making us think the Nephilium caused this," Sean explained.

"There is more," thoughtspoke Echo, making everyone look back at him. "With new information, we think Grays alter probe. Cause it to explode. Make your scientists and military send it there to detonate and destroy us so we blame you."

"Why would they do that?" Jake asked, dumbstruck. "Are you at war with them?"

"No. We do not have wars anymore. Have not had war in millennia. Grays, who call themselves Kriff, often do not like synthetic life. We encountered them in space before. They abducted and experimented on us too, looking for weaknesses to take our planet from us, but we drove them away," thoughtspoke Echo.

"What do you mean by synthetic life?" John asked.

"Our race, like yours, made by elder race called Progenitors in your tongue. It's reason bipedal form so common in this sector. Directed panspermia. Not time to explain right now," Echo thoughtspoke.

Everyone in the room mulled over humanity's origins being so casually explained, but decided to focus on the task at hand instead of becoming distracted. A conversation would be held later, however. Sean tried to refocus by noticing how Echo's communication rapidly improved, but he was still awestruck.

"How? How did you drive them away?" John asked desperately, standing up and doing his best to look Echo in the eyes.

Echo's eyes shifted to orange. "I find this surprisingly. Surely you know of their weakness to sound, yes?"

"Wait, hold on," said Sean. "We were able to deactivate your biobugs with specific sound frequencies. You're saying the Grays—I mean, the Kriff, have this weakness too?" he asked hopefully.

"Not exactly," thoughtspoke Echo. "A specific frequency of a certain wavelength must be broadcast and aimed directly at them. You would have only a small window."

"How small are we talking?" Jake asked.

"You would call it five minutes," Echo thoughtspoke.

"That's not so bad," Jake replied.

"Alright, well, let's say that hypothetically, we're successful in broadcasting this sound. What would it do to them?" Sean asked.

"They would become inert, and therefore vulnerable where they stood. Normally, they paralyze those nearby, put messages and thoughts into people's minds, and remotely control their victims by using their implants. Additionally, they can enter homes undetected and cause any nearby electronics to malfunction or fail," Echo thoughtspoke.

Abigail looked up as she remembered her electronics malfunctioning.

"What if we find this frequency and blast it from space, pointing it toward Earth?" John asked.

"No, this will not work." Echo's eyes briefly shifted to blue again. "They would be able to deflect one large attack and repurpose it. You will need to coordinate with your leaders and strategically place resonance towers throughout this world. Every continent and most countries will need one. Each one would need to connect to the ones near it, forming a basic structure. This would take you time to build, but we will help you. A new batch of biobugs will be developed with a resistance to the influence of the Kriff. These biobugs can create buildings out of carbon from the air in minutes, which should speed up the process."

"Alright, we've got a plan, then," Sean proclaimed. "Let's get to it."

"Hold on, Sean, one more thing. Echo, are you capable of rendering all operating viruses inert? I know the Kriff have overridden them, but can you take control back?" asked John.

"Yes, it is something we will do once our reprogramming code is ready. The virus will then allow itself to be detected and eradicated by your systems once more. Those who were infected will be uninfected. However, damage already caused cannot be undone. We offer our condolences," thoughtspoke Echo. "Please be patient with us, as it will take time to overwrite all active biobugs and viruses."

"How long?" asked the president, causing everyone to look at him. Most had no idea he was there.

"Twelve hours minimum, possibly longer, but we will do our best. For now, it is best you retreat to your home base. I will accompany you while my team works on deactivating the biobugs and viruses."

"Sounds good," said John. "Sean, it's time to go. We have to brief your friends and our family about what we've learned, and then we need a plan. Can I count on you for this?"

"Yes, sir," Sean sputtered.

"Good. Alright, everyone, the parley is adjourned. Let's move and update everyone with what we've learned here to-night." John stood, which signaled everyone else to stand too.

"Hey, are you riding with me, or your old man?" asked Jake.

"I'll still ride with you. I'm… not ready to be alone with my dad yet," Sean answered.

Jake nodded and Sean followed him outside to the car. They were soon on their way back to Kyle's house, and neither of them spoke a word.

KNOW THIS, EVIL, BLINKING STAR
WE KNOW EXACTLY WHAT YOU ARE

18. Open Wounds

Kyle turned on the television and switched to a news channel broadcasting a message from President Matthews across the world, auto-translated into each country's native languages.

"My fellow Americans, my fellow *humans*, I come to you today with heavy news. I'm sure most of you are aware by now. Over the past few weeks, an adaptive computer virus called Protocol has been spreading throughout the world. It is because of this virus that medications were severely altered, causing varying health problems that rapidly led to death.

"Once medication factories and automated pharmacies were targeted, the virus was covertly released to the public. It took us some time to discover the cause, but we've had some help from some highly intelligent and dedicated people. We can safely say that those who created and propagated the virus have been apprehended. At this time, we are still deciding what course of action to take, but you can rest easily now.

"The virus can no longer hurt us. Please resume going to your doctor and get a full-body workup. For the next year, all healthcare in the world will be paid for in full by federal funding. It breaks my heart to say the death toll has reached a historical total of 4,312,765,289 lives. Please remember, there are still infected people out there, and while the virus can no longer harm us, a lot of damage has still been done. Treat each other respectfully, and God bless," finished the president.

Kyle shut the television off and scoffed. "Politicians, man. Liars. Didn't even mention the aliens. They don't have anybody in custody," he spat.

"Maybe they do," said Abigail. "After all, we don't know what Sean and Jake managed to discover. Also, I imagine the president doesn't want to cause mass hysteria."

"I hope Sean's okay," Rebecca worried aloud. "It's been a few hours, and I haven't heard anything from him." She sank herself into worry.

"Hon, he's busy. I can't even imagine what it must be like, talkin' to an alien of all things," said Darren as he tried to wrap his mind around the idea.

"Tell me about it," Kyle groused. "Can't believe I'm having to sit this out. All these years, I was right, and I don't even get to be a part of it. Figures."

"Forgive me, but what was your name again?" asked Abigail.

"Kyle Wills. My friends call me Wheels because I'm a car guy, and it sounds like my last name. I prefer it, honestly."

"I see. Kyle, it's understandable to feel a little jealous of your friend, but remember, this is about the entire world. It isn't just a meeting to establish contact. They could be discussing a truce, or at least a weakness," said Abigail. "We don't know what's going on there, and Sean entrusted you to protect everyone here. That must mean something to you."

Kyle sighed. "Yeah, I know. It's just… do you know how much it sucks to be called crazy all your life, to lose friends and family just because they won't have open minds? Then it turns out that one day, you find out you were right all along, and all those lost connections were for nothing," he explained with a sigh. "I was right, but it doesn't feel the way I thought it would."

"Kyle—" Abigail started.

"Wheels," Kyle firmly reminded her.

Abigail closed her eyes to roll them and gather patience. "Wheels, I know it's not the same thing, but I can relate to an extent. I watched any investigative and medical drama I could find when I was younger, and I still do. I always wanted to be the chief medical examiner or a forensic scientist.

"When I first saw those characters as a girl, I was ecstatic. Especially Abby from NCIS. I said that was going to be me," Abigail said with a grin, reminiscing on her story. "My mother has always shown her disdain for what I do. We barely speak anymore because of it, and that's excruciating, because we used to be so close. But she cut me out like a malignant mass. All because of my career choice.

"How can I trust other people if my own mother doesn't even want anything to do with me?" asked Abigail. Her intentions were to show Kyle that she understood how he felt, even though she knew it was a different situation. It still mattered to her, and she didn't want him to feel like he was being treated unfairly. "My point is to simply not take this personally. Remember, Sean wanted all of us to go before he was told otherwise," Abigail reminded him.

Kyle was silent as he considered Abigail's words, mulling over her story, and how powerfully it must impact her to feel unwanted by her own mother. "Thanks, Abby. I guess I am taking the blessings in my life for granted. My parents are both alive and well. I grew up with a fantastic home life. Losing Beth was hard, but I managed to heal from it. I still feel left out, but what you said helps."

"Well, what do you know? The Tin Man has a heart, after all," Darren jested with crossed arms.

"Oh, shove off," Kyle grumbled, putting his walls back up. He let himself feel happiness and comfort, but not for too long.

There was silence for a few minutes until Rebecca's phone rang, making everyone jump. "Sweet baby Jesus," Kyle blurted out, causing Darren to give him a firm look. "Uhh, holy be thy name," he said, quickly bowing his head.

"Sean? Hello?" Rebecca answered. "Hey! Yeah, we're okay. Just a lot of talking going on. Already? Oh, okay. Well, we'll be here. See you soon. Love you," she spouted as she ended the call. Rebecca immediately realized what she said after the call and covered her mouth. "Oh, crap! I didn't mean to say that," she contested loudly and defiantly against everyone else's facial expressions. "I just got used to saying it to my dad, and my brain didn't wanna make the distinction."

"So, what, he's your daddy now?" asked Kyle with a grin, making Darren double over in laughter. Abby couldn't stop herself from snickering and Darren fell off the couch. "Kinky," Kyle joshed, extending the laughter until everyone was red in the face.

"Eww," Rebecca shouted. "That's *not* what I meant." Rebecca's cheeks warmed, but she couldn't help smiling. After all, it came out so naturally. Maybe she did love him, but didn't realize it yet. She went over her thoughts in her head, analyzing her feelings. "I need some time to think," said Rebecca as she stood and dashed back to her and Sean's shared bedroom upstairs, unable to handle the embarrassment and her thoughts simultaneously.

"I'll go speak with her," Abigail soothed, putting her hand up to signal Darren to stay put. "I think she needs another woman to talk to. I know she's your daughter, but please let me try?"

"Alright, if you think you can get through to her. She'd just yell at me, anyway." Darren shook his head. "Good luck."

Rebecca sat on the bed in profound thought. She wrote down her feelings and questions in her diary, and answered the ones she could. It was harrowing, finally analyzing and spending time with her emotions after neglecting them for so long. Still, she knew it was time to sit with her demons and learn their names, so she could overcome them. The bottom of her list had the main question, which read, "Do you love him?" She wrote a yes and a no beside each other, intending to circle one, but she couldn't decide.

There was a gentle knock on the door. "Becca?" came Abigail's voice.

Rebecca sighed, grateful it wasn't her father, though she did find that odd. She stood and opened the door, letting Abigail in, and immediately closed and locked the door.

"Are you alright?" Abigail asked. "I'm so sorry for laughing."

"No, it's okay, and I guess I'm fine. Just confused," Rebecca answered. "I *just* told Sean that I wanted to slow down, but now I feel like I just screwed it up. He's gonna think I meant it," she lamented in embarrassment, dropping her face in her hands.

"Did you?" asked Abigail.

"I don't know," Rebecca shouted as her senses overwhelmed her. "I'm sorry, I didn't mean to shout. It's just been one thing after another since my mom died. I haven't really given myself time to properly face my emotions until now," she said with a groan. "What should I do?" she asked, looking Abigail in the face and then dropping her head back in her hands again.

Abigail thought for a moment, then tilted Rebecca's head to meet hers. "For one, look at how you structured the main question at the bottom. See how it only has a yes or a no?" she asked, hoping Rebecca would follow her train of thought.

"I mean, yeah, but—" started Rebecca.

"Well, what about a third option?" Abigail suggested.

"Like a maybe?" asked Rebecca.

"Sort of, but more decisive. Let's try something like… 'getting there.' How does that sound?" asked Abigail.

"Oh my gosh, that's perfect," Rebecca squealed. "That's exactly how it feels. I mean, I wanna love him, I'm just not quite there yet." Rebecca wrote the term down in her diary and circled it with a wide smile on her face.

Abigail smiled at her, rubbing her back. "There you go."

"How are you so good at this?"

"Oh," Abigail replied sheepishly, turning her head and looking away with a smile. "I've just had a lot of time to myself, I suppose. When you're alone with your thoughts all the time, they become your only friends, and that can be dangerous. A wise man named Alan Watts once said, 'a person who thinks all the time has nothing to think of except thoughts.'"

"What do I do about Sean, though? I mean, he *is* gonna think I meant it. I can't really blame him for that. How do I explain to him what happened in a way he'd understand without hurting him?"

"Take it easy, for one thing, and slow down. You don't need to have all the answers right now, and he needs to be okay with that. You're thinking so much about him and his feelings that you're forgetting your own. Becca, you can't live your life immediately jumping from problem to solution all the time. There needs to be a buffer between the two. It's important to consider his feelings, yes, but you can't neglect yourself in the process. Do you understand what I'm saying?"

"Yeah," said Rebecca. "I guess I'll just be honest with him. I'm probably just overthinking it anyway," she said with a nervous smile.

"Well, don't minimize your feelings, either. The way you feel is valid. I know it's confusing, but it's all about balance," said Abigail, receiving a confused look from Rebecca. "Just take it one step at a time." Abigail smiled at Rebecca and rubbed her shoulder.

There were a few more knocks on the door, more forceful and rapid than before. Abigail and Rebecca looked at the door in alarm, back at each other in mutual surprise, and then back at the door. Rebecca started to stand, but Abigail pushed her down and put a finger to her own lips.

Abigail opened the door, seeing Jake standing there with a smile. "Hiya, sis," said Jake. Abigail reached out and held him tight. "Whoa, hey, what have I done to earn this?"

"I'm just glad you're back safe," Abigail crooned as she pulled away. "Did you learn anything interesting?"

"The universe is regulated by a systematic series of mathematical laws," said Jake.

"Seriously?" asked Abigail sarcastically.

"Oh, you meant the parley," Jake replied with a knowing grin. "Yeah, we learned a lot. I can't wait for you to hear all this."

Rebecca realized Sean must be back too, so she pushed past Jake and nearly flew down the stairs.

"Uh, ow. That was rude. Anyway, to say that we learned something is the understatement of the millennium. Once everybody is done greeting each other, Sean wants all of us to listen to him and his dad," said Jake.

"Interesting. I figured they might run into each other, but from what I've heard, I didn't expect them to return together," Abigail thought aloud.

"Yeah, well, it wasn't exactly together. Like, yeah, he came here, but in his own car. Plus, if I understand right," whispered Jake, looking around, then closing the door, "he isn't staying long. Sean doesn't know, but John wanted me to be aware so I can help calm him down." Jake sighed. "It's messed up."

"I was just about to ask if you realized how unjust that is. Becca was telling me earlier what Sean told her about his father. Truly awful how someone can waste family. I know I no longer get along with Mom, but my trauma began as an adult. Sean's started as a child," Abigail said, crossing her arms. "Can you imagine how he must have *felt*? Sean must've thought his father didn't want him, or like he wasn't good enough.

"So now he comes back, and Sean thinks he's staying, but he's just going to abandon him again, isn't he?" asked Abigail in disgust. "There's no excuse for that!"

"Well, not defending the guy, but we are kind of in a war. John just wants to fight on one front while Sean fights on another. Two separate teams as opposed to one big one. Maybe it's like a big team, but split up into two separate, smaller teams, yet still a part of the big team. Huh. That'll stump your brain noodle," said Jake, shaking his head as if to shake off the confusing thoughts as a dog would shake off water.

Abigail dropped her head and tried not to laugh. "That's called a team of teams, and I understand, I suppose. But it's not what Sean's going to think, and I don't blame him. I'm glad I'm going to be there to be a part of this. On top of helping Sean calm down, I can give him a rational explanation, while firmly pointing out to his father that he needs to make a change for his son and granddaughter," declared Abigail, uncrossing her arms.

Jake noticed his sister had a protective air about her. "So, are you like the den mother now, or?" he joked, but he was also genuinely curious.

"If I were the den mother, I'd be sending you to time-out. You've been a naughty boy," she jested, waving a finger in Jake's face. Abigail walked out of the room smiling, pretending to be a scolding mother to get a reaction from him.

"Oh, you… I… have… I don't know how to respond to that," Jake shouted after her, throwing his arms in the air.

That's the point, Abigail thought.

"Sean," Rebecca shouted as she ran toward him, tackling him to the wall with a hug. She kissed him on both cheeks, rubbing her hands through his hair. "I missed you. Are you okay?" she asked, putting her hands on his shoulders.

Sean put his hands around her waist. "Yeah, I'm fine. So, uh, did you make the call?" he asked.

"Oh yeah, I forgot about that." Rebecca closed her eyes and shook her head. "No, I mean, I did it. I just forgot about it after," she clarified. "Sorry, I'm a little nervous."

"What?" Sean asked, grinning. "Why would you feel—oh." Sean looked down . "Is this about what you said on the phone?"

Rebecca sighed and dropped her arms, resting her head on Sean's chest. "Maybe."

"I do want to talk about it, but I know you probably didn't mean it, so," he said dismissively with a heavy sigh. "Let's just focus on solving this crisis for now." The truth was Sean was still riding the high from Rebecca possibly being in love with him. Even if it wasn't true yet, it was getting there.

"Sean, wait. I know this whole war thing is important and all, but," She paused, making circles on his chest with her index finger. "I kinda wanna talk about it too. It's important to have love when you're in a war."

"I know, and we will," he assured her with a kiss on her forehead and a tight hug. "Just not right now, okay? This, us, the love you're talking about? That's what we're fighting to save." Sean wove his fingers through hers on both hands, interlocking them. "You said we needed to slow things down, and you're right. If there's any chance that you do love me, then let me earn it," he declared, looking deeply into Rebecca's eyes.

Rebecca shook her head. "No, Sean. I was being stupid, you already have—"

"No, you were right. You were being human, not stupid. Right now, that means a lot more than usual. Look, can we table this for now? Please? There's a lot more going on than we thought," Sean pled. "We can come back to it. I promise."

"Okay. For now. Don't think I won't hold you to your promise, though, mister," said Rebecca with a finger in his face.

"Uh, hon?" Darren called.

Rebecca turned around to see everyone staring at her and Sean. "What?" she griped with a bit more frustration than she intended. "Oh," she said, looking at everyone in the room. "Sorry, I tend to forget other people nearby when I'm around him," she said accidentally, immediately turning around to Sean and covering her mouth with her hands.

Sean gently grabbed her arm and smiled. "It's okay. We'll talk about all of it later. For now, I'd like to introduce someone to you all," he said as he stood aside and John came in. "This is my dad, John Caldwell." Sean's head dropped involuntarily, feeling unworthy in his father's presence.

"Hey, everyone. I'm Sean's father, and the director of GAIA. I'm sure you know what that stands for by now," said John with a laugh. "I'll be happy to answer any questions, but we need to have this debriefing first." John turned to look back at Sean.

"Um, is everyone ready?" asked Sean, and they all nodded in assent. Sean looked around the room to do a headcount. He saw

Jake, Rebecca, Abigail, Darren, Kyle, and John, but Amanda and Monica were conspicuously missing. "Wait, where are my sister and daughter? They should have been here by now." Sean dug out his phone as his hands shook, dropping it. "Damn it," he shouted as he bent down to reach for the phone.

Darren grabbed Sean's arm. "Don't worry, I got this," he assured him as he bent to the floor to pick up the phone. "I'll go into another room and try to call her. If I don't hear nothin' after a couple tries, I'll contact local law enforcement. Since Monica's a child, I may be able to get a country-wide search. Just try to focus, son." Darren leaned in closer to Sean and whispered, "Be the son I already think you are," before turning back to everyone else. "I'm gonna go take care of this. Y'all just fill me in later." Darren darted to his bedroom.

Sean saw everyone's faces and tried not to worry, but nausea set in, and his temperature rose. He tried to speak several times, but the words never made it to his lips. Defeated, he sat down with his head in his hands. Sean took a few deep breaths, then turned to look at John. "I'm sorry. I can't. I just—"

"No, Sean, it's okay. I would be the same way if something like this happened to you or Mandy when you two were little," John soothed. "I can brief everyone. You don't need to impress me."

"Thank you." Sean nodded and ran to the room after Darren.

Rebecca started to follow, but Jake stopped her. "Sorry," said Jake. "Just following orders. Plus, having you there is just gonna confuse and distract him, no offense. Let him and Darren figure this out. We need to stay focused on the ball."

"For the rest of you, listen up," John commanded. "There's a lot to tell, so if you need to grab a beverage or snack, or take a bathroom break, now is the time. You have ten minutes," he announced, clapping his hands. "Let's go, move it, come on," he declared as everyone moved around to get snacks and drinks or to use the restroom where a line formed.

"There's a hallway bathroom upstairs, folks," Kyle shouted as he grabbed snacks. *Can't figure out why I have no control in my own house*, he thought.

Sean came barreling into the room with Darren. "I'm sorry, but I can't just sit this out. My dad is gonna brief everyone. I couldn't do it. I fell apart," he said, dropping his head in defeat.

"Hang on a sec," Darren said to Amanda as he muted the phone, turning to face Sean. "Sit down, son," Darren cautioned gently, and Sean did as he was asked. "You got nothin' to apologize for. Not to me. You gave it your best, and that's all I care about. I ain't gonna fault you for wantin' to protect your kid.

"From what I've heard, it means you're a better father than that man out there," Darren said gently, looking Sean in the eyes. "Now, before you start tryin' to argue with me or wantin' to talk, hear me out first. I called Mandy, and she's on the phone right now. She just wanted to let you know she's okay, so focus on that for a moment, alright?"

"Okay. Good. That's good," Sean replied in relief.

"Okay. Now, I want you to match my breathin', got it?" Darren asked, doing the same thing he did with Ron to help calm him down. "Feel better?"

"Yeah, much. Thank you."

"Alright, atta boy," said Darren, gently patting Sean on the back.

Sean's head snapped up. "What about Monica?" he asked, his anxiety building back up. "She's okay too, right?"

"Son, for now, just focus on—"

"Tell me if Monica's okay," Sean shouted, standing up. He felt his blood turn to ice, and his heart grew ten pounds heavier.

"Now, son, you need to be calm for this, so sit back down," Darren said firmly. "I didn't wanna worry you too. Your sister is already worried."

"Oh no, what happened?" Sean shouted as he paced around the room.

"Here, I'll let her tell you," Darren said as he unmuted the phone. "Mandy, I got Sean here. I tried to calm him down as best I could, but tell him what you told me." After handing the phone to Sean, Darren walked to the back of the room with his head in one hand and the other on his hip.

Sean heard Amanda crying and sniffling. "Sean?" she squeaked out.

"Hey, Mandy. I'm here. What's going on?" Sean asked gently, though his fear ran rampant.

"Sean, I'm so sorry. I'm so, so sorry. I tried. I really tried," she cried frantically, unable to form a coherent thought.

"I gotta do everything around here," Darren shouted. "Look, Monica was taken. There was a wreck, a bright light, and then Monica was nowhere to be found. Mandy was lucky to escape with her life! You oughta be grateful, and proud of her for managin' it," he yelled at Sean. "Losin' Monica is tragic. I'm not downplayin' that, but you need to focus as much on the good things as you do the bad."

"Not just taken," Amanda shouted through the phone. "Abducted! That word matters. I don't know how else to describe it. There was this light coming toward us. I couldn't see, and someone hit the side of my SUV. I saw them coming just in time to pull up far enough so they wouldn't hit the driver's side door. When I looked back to check on Monica, she was gone, and so was the light. I'm sorry," she cried.

Sean composed himself long enough to speak with his sister. "It's not your fault. I'm glad you're okay. Just get here safe," he soothed, hitting the mute button again and turning away from Darren as he shivered, flapping his hands.

Darren unmuted the phone. "Mandy, this is Darren again. Listen to Sean, and try to get here as soon and as safely as possible. I'm gonna keep the call goin', so we'll know if somethin' else happens. Is your vehicle drivable?"

"I think so, yes. Damaged, but drivable. I'm only about half an hour away," Amanda responded. "What do we do about Monica?"

Darren didn't know what to say. This was a unique situation, and it wasn't like he could put out an APB on spaceships. He was silent as he struggled to find the words.

"Darren?" asked Amanda anxiously.

"I'm sorry, Mandy. I'm here, but I honestly don't know what to say. I'm sure once you get here, all of us can come up with a solution. I just don't have one for you right now. I'm sorry, hon." The lack of answers tugged at Darren's heart, because he normally could come up with something achievable, or at least a partial plan, but not this time. He didn't want to let down Sean, Amanda, or Monica, but he was unable to come up with anything, no matter how hard he racked his brain.

Sean was already thinking over possible solutions, and an idea occurred to him. "I think I might have an idea, but it's a longshot."

"Yeah? What do you got, son?" Darren asked.

Sean sighed. "At the parley, we made a new friend who may be able to help. We call him Echo."

Twinkle, twinkle, Little Star
You've shown us how small we are

✧

19. The Little Star

KYLE SHOOK HIS HEAD AFTER JOHN FINISHED debriefing everyone. "We've been looking at this wrong since the beginning. Still, do you really believe this… Echo guy? I still can't believe you got to talk to an alien. That's so freaking cool, man," he said, realizing he was more excited than jealous. However, he wasn't exactly trusting humanity's new friends yet.

"I have no reason not to. What they said made sense. Besides, we need allies. There's no way we can do this on our own," John admitted.

"You said its eyes changed color when its emotions did? That's remarkable. I imagine it must be difficult to lie in their culture," Abigail pondered aloud. At first, she had difficulty accepting the truth, but there were several witnesses who all saw and heard the same thing. While visual hallucinations are often shared, auditory hallucinations are not. They also had nothing to gain by making it all up, so she finally allowed herself to believe. It scared her, but her fear helped strengthen her resolve.

"What do you think they meant by the Kriff not liking synthetic life? What does that have to do with us?" Rebecca asked.

Jake and John exchanged glances, deciding whether to tell her and who should do it. Finally, Jake ran out of patience, which, of course, didn't take long. "We were apparently made by an elder alien species called the Progenitors. I think Gaia might be one, but look, we can't focus on that right now. Yes, at some point, we'll need to talk about that. I'm aware it's a big deal, but we can deal with that later. Let's focus on saving the world first. *Then* we can focus on the origin of humanity.

"Echo told us the Nephilium were created by the same beings. That means we share their origin, so we're related in a way. Believe me, this is gonna be a *lot* of paperwork at GAIA, but we don't have time to worry about it right now," Jake finished.

Rebecca sat down quietly, crossing her arms as she shivered.

A bright light gleamed through the windows, lighting up the night. When it retracted, Echo stood in the living room. "Greetings to all," he thoughtspoke.

Rebecca and Abigail stood and prepared to run, but John put his hand up. "Relax," he shouted. "This is the one we were talking about. He's not gonna hurt you. Isn't that right, Echo?" John asked.

"Affirmative. I have come to assist your friend in the search for his offspring. We believe the Kriff took Monica, and we can locate her with our technology. However, we are not yet certain how to retrieve her," thoughtspoke Echo, noticing Rebecca and Abigail looked disconcerted, exchanging glances. "Oh, perhaps I should explain how our people communicate. We speak through telepathy and can choose to broadcast, speak to a single person, or only to a specific group. The desired listeners hear us in their heads in their preferred language. It took us a little time to learn your languages, but we are well-versed now. It is called thoughtspeech. Please do not be alarmed."

Rebecca was still unable to move or form words, so Abigail stood in front of her to protect her. "So, you're Echo. I must say, I'm honored to meet you. When we have time, I have so many questions for you."

"We expected as much. I come to you in my real form as a sign of transparency. It was explained to us by John that while you may find our true appearance intimidating, it is necessary you see us as we are," thoughtspoke Echo. "We recently developed a machine to temporarily disguise ourselves as humans, though it does not last long. Another Nephilium, Sca'Lorit, is running the tests as we speak. She is skilled in many areas of research and development.

"She?" Jake asked. "So, you do have gender. I gotta ask, how do you—"

"Not now, Jake," Abigail chided him. "Thank you, Echo. I look forward to working together." She enjoyed the mental liberation, no longer having to conform to what was believed to be science fiction, and the possibilities presented. Research would be ongoing for decades, not only into the Nephilium species, but into the shared link between their race and ours. The immense data collected from studying them and the Kriff would be the grandest discovery in science and history.

Echo thoughtspoke privately to Abigail. *Your brother is curious. This is not his fault. You can explain to him later that we reproduce by conjoining heads and feeling love. This creates another Nephilium, one with certain traits of Maternal and Paternal. The difference between your race and ours is that the offspring is already fully grown.*

Fascinating. Thank you for sharing, Abigail thought.

Gratitude accepted, Echo thoughtspoke back.

Jake saw Echo and Abigail staring at each other, with Abigail's face changing expressions. "Hey, you wanna share?"

"Not at the moment, no," Abigail replied. "Echo, what's the plan on getting Monica back? What exactly happened?"

Rebecca tuned back in when Abigail spoke, peeking around her.

"Sean and Darren are on their way in here. They can explain," thoughtspoke Echo, turning to face the hallway where the two soon emerged.

Darren came through first and backed up into the wall. He grabbed his gun and pointed it at Echo. "What in the unholy hell is that thing?" he shouted.

Sean pushed past Darren and stood in front of Echo in a protective stance. "Don't," he shouted. "This is Echo. He's my friend. I sent him a message to come help us." Sean looked at Jake for help, then back at Darren nervously.

"Sheriff, Rookie here is telling the truth," said Jake. "Echo met us at the parley. There's a lot to fill you in on, but for now, just trust us. Echo is how we get Monica back, so drop the weapon, or I'll raise mine. Just a warning, though. Mine are way cooler."

Darren put away his gun and slowly approached the living room, walking a small circle around Echo. He took his appearance in and tried to come to terms with seeing an extraterrestrial up close. "I don't even know what to say here," he said as he stepped back several feet, then turned to face Jake. "You're sayin' this thing can help us find Monica?"

"Affirmative," he thoughtspoke. "Also, I am not a thing. I am a Nephilium, a living organism like you."

"Ugh, I can hear him in my head. That's weirdin' me out." Darren sat on one of the couches, keeping his eyes on Echo.

Echo received a mental message from Sca'Lorit. "Please excuse me. I will return in a moment," he thoughtspoke, teleporting back to his ship. What everyone saw was a bright light, and then Echo disappeared into thin air.

"Every time I think it can't get any weirder, it somehow does," Darren muttered. "Does anyone wanna fill me in on what I missed?" He looked around at everyone in the room, settling his eyes on John. "John, right? Let's you and me take a walk." Darren stood and motioned for John to join him. "You comin'?"

John decided to push down his anger and confusion to see what Darren had to say. "Yeah, I could use the fresh air anyway. Let's try to make it quick," he said, standing and following Darren outside.

Darren closed the door behind them and walked into the yard with John. "Look, I know we got bigger fish to fry right now, but you listen to me. That boy—no, that *man* in there—is more stable and strong-willed than I could have ever hoped Rebecca could be. But she and Sean surprise me daily. Don't you distance yourself from him again. You got a shot to make this right, to really be the father he deserves. On some level, that ship has already sailed, but it still ain't too late for you to do the right thing."

John ran his right hand through his hair, which Darren noted was the same way Sean did. "You're not wrong. I've made mistakes. They were all in the name of protecting humanity, but I was so busy doing my job and trying to be the hero that I failed to be one to my own son. I can't say I'd change anything, though." John saw Darren's expression and watched him fold his arms. "Let me explain," said John, holding up his hands.

"Okay. Explain to me why or *how* you could even consider being the same damn disappointment to him you were the first time," said Darren.

John sighed heavily. "I get it. You've only heard from him, and to be fair, it's mostly true. But look at who he is. He got that way on his own. Sure, maybe he got the strength from me in genetics, but that only matters if he uses it, and he has. I'm so proud of him. I can't even begin to find the words, but I love him more than life itself. I always have. You're not the only one to point out my mistakes, or even the first. My wife Whitney has you beat on that.

"She did the best she could with him when I wasn't around. I had anger issues, I'd bring work home with me, I'd be a slouch and lose my patience, and I was emotionally absent from Sean. I couldn't explain to him what was going on behind the scenes, especially when he was a kid. I barely managed to tell Whitney anything, and that was after pleading with GAIA for the better part of a year, right before we got married. I refused to put her in a position where I'd reveal it later. I guess there were other ways to have gone about it," said John, crossing his own arms and looking down, "but I don't think he'd be the man he is if I was in his life more. If anything, he'd be less of a man." John looked away, nervously tapping his foot.

"What about all the trauma and neglect you put him through, or all those horrible emotions you put on a *child*? There's no excuse, and speakin' of what type of man he is, let me say this. If he were mine, I'd love him no matter who he is. I've spent more time with him in the past month than you have in your life, and let me tell you, buddy, you are missin' out. Now, we need to go back in there and see if they came up with somethin' to get Monica back. Once we get past this, be thinkin' of whether you wanna be a part of his life." Darren shoved past John and went back inside, leaving John to ponder Darren's words before he could say anything back.

"Hey, Mr. Morgan! I think we got something," Sean announced as Darren came back inside. "Echo sent me a message in my head. He thinks they can pinpoint which starship Monica's on by locating any trace of my DNA. It turns out Echo was sneaky and plucked a hair from my head, so they've got what they need. Now we just wait for them to—" Sean was interrupted by several knocks on the door.

Sean approached the door, but Darren beat him to it. He opened the door, expecting it to be John, but it was what appeared to be a stranger. A male in his late twenties with shaggy black hair, glasses, and freckles stood in the doorway. He wore a red and black plaid shirt, with a white T-shirt underneath, and black slacks with brown dress shoes. "Hi, new friends." The stranger waved at them exuberantly and smiled at everyone. "Wow, this feels strange. No wonder humans have such difficulties."

"Who the—" Darren began.

"Echo? Is that you?" Sean asked.

"Indeed. I am the first Nephilium to ever take on a human form. I know you cannot see it, but I am honored to be the first. This is a test of our transformation systems," said Echo happily, still waving.

Darren grabbed Echo's waving arm and gently lowered it, making Echo realize it was time to stop. "I'll be damned. This is the smoothest skin I've ever felt."

"Thank you, human. Now, if Sean is ready, I believe we have located Monica. She is being held in a Kriff vessel, directly above what your people call Stonehenge," explained Echo. "It is a small craft, like what you might call a little star. Oh, my first analogy. How stimulating."

"Alright, how are we getting there, and how do we get Monica back?" Sean asked. "I'm ready for anything."

"You will be the first human to board one of our crafts, and I will pilot it to the location. Once we arrive, the ship we will be taking is outfitted with a resonance device, one we shall use to disrupt the systems of the Kriff ship and its occupants. Once this is done, I will beam you aboard their ship long enough to grab Monica, then beam you back. Are you satisfied with this strategy?" Echo asked Sean.

Sean found it odd how Echo was physically talking instead of in his head. "Yes, and I'm ready when you are," he said, then walked outside, waiting for Echo to follow. "Come on, let's go," he shouted, throwing his arms up, then taking a deep breath and sighing. "I'm sorry, I didn't mean to shout. Can we please just go?"

"Oh, that is my error. I did not inform you that we need not go outside to leave. Please come over and place your hand on my shoulder, and I will place my hand on yours." Echo reached out his hand.

Sean grabbed Echo's shoulder, and Echo grabbed Sean's. A bright light briefly encompassed them both before disappearing, leaving behind no trace of either of them.

"I'm never gonna get used to that," started Jake as everyone walked outside, "but dang if it isn't the coolest thing I've ever seen."

"Right?" Kyle said with a grin, looking at Jake briefly before returning his gaze to the sky.

Everyone looked above them as the craft uncloaked, revealing its glowing magnificence to them. It rose up to the sky and shot off into the distance within a few seconds, giving everyone long enough to get a glimpse. "Show off," Sean said to Echo as they left.

It took mere seconds for them to reach the destination, much faster than the GAIA jets, which Sean still wasn't accustomed to. "We are here," Echo announced. "Are you alright, Sean? You seem ill." Echo looked at Sean and could tell he was dizzy, watching him hold his head in one hand.

"Yeah, I'm good. I just wasn't ready for the spatial whiplash. Man, you guys really are fast. Now what? We use the resonance thing, right?"

"Affirmative. You may want to cover your ears." Echo turned the dial and pressed a button, which produced a massive sound directed at the Kriff ship, though it was audible inside Echo's ship too.

Sean covered his ears and fell to the floor as the sound tormented him. It was so intense that he began screaming. Sound was more intense for him than it was for most people.

Echo witnessed this, but knew it was necessary. Once enough time had passed, Echo turned off the signal. "Sean, are you alright? Are you capable of this task?"

Sean took a few seconds to gather himself and stand as his ears rang. "What?" he shouted over the ringing in his ears.

Echo covered Sean's ears, making the ringing stop. "All better?"

"Yes, much. Thank you. Let's do this," Sean declared.

"Gratitude accepted. Beaming you aboard their ship in three, two, one… now," said Echo, then Sean found himself aboard the Kriff ship.

Sean looked around the craft, seeing four Kriff who looked exactly like the Grays people described, lying on the floor like dead insects. "Monica?" he called bravely into the ship, causing an echo. As fear set in, he hoped none of the aliens would wake up or reactivate. "Monica, it's Daddy! Where are you, baby?" He continued walking throughout the ship, finding more alien bodies. The ship was made of four round rooms, connected by curved corridors. Monica lay there, passed out in one of the corridors, and Sean tried shaking her awake. "Monica! Come on, wake up." He gave up trying to wake his daughter and decided to get back to Echo. "Echo, bring me back," he shouted.

Within seconds, Sean and Monica were together on the ship with Echo, and Sean held Monica tightly in his arms. He turned around to face Echo. "This is her. Did they do something to her?" he asked. "I mean, look. She was sick, but she has a full head of hair back."

"Unclear. However, we should depart from this location immediately. The effects of the resonance will be wearing off soon. We must hurry. Also, should you wish me to bring you back to my ship, you need only say my name and 'recall'." Echo pressed buttons and put his hand on a lever. "Ready?"

Sean ducked down in a corner and held Monica tight. "Ready."

Within moments, they were back at Kyle's house in the backyard. Sean and Echo exited the ship the same way they entered it, witnessed by John.

"Sean," John called as he ran to his son. "Are you alright?" he shouted as he checked Sean for any abrasions or sign of injury, thankful he didn't find any.

"I'm fine, Dad. Thanks. Can you help me get Monica inside? I need to take her to the couch so she can lie down." Sean moved toward the door, still holding Monica.

John smiled, impressed not only by the fact Sean pulled it off, but by how he returned so resilient and unshaken. John quietly held the door open for Sean, watching him as he walked in with his daughter. John followed behind him and, as Sean cleared his throat, everyone turned and cheered for their safe return. Echo came in behind him and observed everyone celebrating, but even he smiled. Echo watched as Sean gently placed Monica on one of the couches, ensuring her head was supported. Sean rubbed her face with his thumb.

"I want to put her to bed, but I'm too scared to take my eyes off her," Sean said wearily, his gaze on his daughter never faltering. "I'm just so relieved that she's safe. I can't lose her again. We got lucky this time."

"No, you did your job as a father and got her back safe." Darren shot a quick glance at John, then looked back at Sean. "She's here safe because of you. Sure, Echo helped, and it was his technology, but you're the one who rescued her. Luck ain't got nothin' to do with it, partner. Now, why don't you let me take her over to my bed and watch her? That way, we'll both be close by. Deal?" he asked, extending his arms.

Insects had made their homes inside Sean's gut, but he couldn't deny his exhaustion. "Deal."

Darren gently picked up Monica with ease and walked back toward his bedroom. Sean collapsed on the couch where Monica was and dropped his head in his hands, closing his eyes to rest.

"Sean, are you okay?" Rebecca asked. "If you need to lie down, we'll understand." Rebecca rubbed his shoulders. "Take some time for yourself."

Sean sighed in defeat. "Yeah, I guess I should. It's dark out, but I can't tell if it's early in the morning or late at night. I'm gonna try to get some sleep. Wake me if you need me." Sean stood and walked upstairs to his and Rebecca's shared bedroom, becoming increasingly depleted with every step.

"I'm gonna go with him. I mean, I could use the rest myself, and I'm worried about him, so, bye." Rebecca quickly stood and followed Sean up the stairs, guiding him as he started to fall asleep while walking. "Come on, almost there," she cooed.

"Please pardon me as I must briefly depart." Echo disappeared into thin air inside of a bright light again.

"That gives me the creeps every time, but it's so freaking cool," said Kyle. "Anyway, I'm glad Monica's safe." There was a knock on the door. "I'm hoping that's finally Mandy, but if it's Echo again, then I'm gonna tell him he can just open the dang door." Kyle stood and opened the door, revealing a forlorn Amanda.

John rushed over to Amanda, nearly knocking Kyle over. "Sorry, Kyle," he said, looking back at Amanda. "Hey, doll, how are you? I'm so glad you're safe." John ran his fingers through Amanda's hair and hugged her tight. "It's okay now," he soothed as Amanda sobbed. "They got Monica back. She's resting now, and so is Sean. Come with me to the garage, and I'll clue you in on everything."

"Alright, Dad. I'm glad Monica's safe. Nobody tells me anything anymore," Amanda complained as she followed her father.

Once they were both in the garage, John sighed with resignation and told Amanda about the current situation. "Now, your brother is upstairs asleep with Becca. She seems to be his girlfriend from what I can gather. Everyone is safe. There's still a lot to do, though." John cleared his throat. "Some good came from this. We now know their sound weapon works. That's how we fight them, but it's going to take a lot of coordination and communication across the entire world to pull this off." John saw Amanda's frightful expression and grabbed her shoulders. "Hey.

There's *nothing* for you to worry about. If we stay here, then we're safe. That's what matters right now, okay?"

"I can't believe you've been working for some secret organization all this time," Amanda shouted as she broke away from John and paced the floor. "You're saying Mom knew?"

"Yes, but honey, I could only tell her so much, and I wasn't permitted to reveal anything to you or your brother. It was a difficult situation," John explained.

"I guess I understand. It's just, we hardly ever saw you, and when we did, you were kind of…" Amanda trailed off, looking away.

"An ass?" John suggested, grinning.

Amanda laughed. "You said it, not me. I know you were just doing the best you could, like you always have. Well, if Sean is resting, then I suppose I should too. Maybe someone will let me borrow their bed." Amanda walked out of the garage and back to the living room. She asked Kyle if she could use his bed, which he was happy to offer.

Once Amanda was far out of hearing range, John called someone on his phone. "Hey, it's me. Tell the guys it worked. The plan is a go. I repeat, the plan is a go. Our test run of the weapon was successful." John ended the call and pocketed his phone, a brief look of guilt on his face. He steadied himself and walked back inside with no intention of revealing his duplicity. This war was a game of chess, and he had to make a risky move to ensure their endgame was successful.

WITH YOUR LIGHT SO LARGE AND BRIGHT
WILL YOU HELP US THROUGH THE NIGHT?

✧

20. Rules of Engagement

Monica was slowly roused from sleep by Darren's snoring, taking in her surroundings. She woke up in an unfamiliar room with a stranger who seemed vaguely familiar. Despite her fear, she stayed quiet as she gently climbed out of bed and tiptoed her way to the door. There was a mirror on the wall opposite her, and she saw herself with a full head of luscious blonde hair that came down to her middle back. She ran her hands through it, feeling its texture.

Monica twirled her hair with her hands, pushed it back, and brushed the bangs out of her eyes. She smiled, quickly left the room, and walked slowly down the hallway, trying her best not to slip in her Stitch socks.

She peeked her head around the corner and saw several strangers, though she did recognize her Aunt Amanda and Uncle Wheels, so she shuffled toward the living room where everyone sat. Nobody noticed her at first until Amanda's eyes glanced over at Monica when she turned her head, and her gaze then snapped back to her.

"Monica?" Amanda crowed. "Oh my goodness! Look at you! I didn't know you had a wig here." Amanda took Monica into her arms and gave her the tightest hug she could muster. "I'm so sorry about what you went through, sweetie." Amanda released Monica from the hug, but kept her hands on her shoulders.

"It's not a wig," said Monica, grinning widely. "I woke up and my hair came back." Monica giggled, proving her hair was real by gently pulling it. "Who are all these people, Aunt Mandy?"

Amanda was shocked by her full head of hair, confused about how it happened. "These are our friends, baby girl. That's Jake, Abby, and Uncle Wheels," she explained, and each of them waved in turn. "The man in the room with you is Sheriff Morgan. He's been watching over and protecting you since we got you back. Your dad is asleep upstairs with a friend, and your grandpa is somewhere around here," said Amanda as she looked around for John, but didn't see him. *Disappointing, but not unexpected*, she thought.

"Hi, Uncle Wheels," Monica gleamed as she tackled him with a hug. "I missed you."

"Hey, Lovebug," Kyle crowed. "I've missed you too. I love the new 'do. Looks good on you," he said as he sat and Monica climbed into his lap. "Oof," he said as she sat down on him. "You know, you're getting to be too big for this, but for now, what the heck?" Kyle gave Monica gentle noogies on her head, making her giggle as he held her tightly.

"I'm gonna let y'all get some privacy. Personally, I need some fresh air." Jake stood and went outside, breathing in the smell of the woods nearby.

Darren walked out of his bedroom. "Hey, look who's awake."

"It's the strangest thing," said Amanda. "Her hair is back! She says it was like that when she woke up, and it's *real.* Maybe something from one of the alien ships caused it, but I'm happy to see her with such long, flowing locks." Amanda bounced Monica up and down a few times, blowing on her tummy, and Monica started to go back to Kyle. "No, no, you had your time with Uncle Wheels. It's Aunt Mandy's time now," she said as she pulled Monica back, who laughed and pretended she wanted to escape, basking in all the attention she was receiving.

✧

Jake walked around outside the house and saw John talking on his phone around the corner. He approached barely within hearing range, keeping a safe distance while he listened.

"Yeah, man, I really didn't think it would work, but it did. Sound totally fries 'em. I still think Sean could've taken some of 'em out, but a win is a win," John said in relief. "By the way, thanks for sharing the information I gave you. It was crucial for them to take Monica so Sean would be motivated enough to fight them. Seems he and his new alien friend will be useful after all, just like I said. Oh, come on. You completely hated the idea of bringing him into GAIA. Don't try and backpedal now. Yeah, I won this bet, and I do expect a juicy steak in my near future," John said eagerly with a laugh as he ended the call. John turned around and saw Jake standing right in front of him with his arms crossed, making him jump in surprise.

"So, what's this bet you made? I'm only interested because I also enjoy juicy steaks. Only, I don't usually send the cow to death myself," Jake said, his eyes narrowed.

"Agent Warren, you need to understand, we just wanted—" John began.

"Yeah, yeah, you wanted to test the sound weapon against the Kriff, I heard. You wanted to test it so badly that you put your son *and* his young daughter in harm's way." Jake walked toward John, who backed up with every step. "Let me ask you this. What if it didn't work, huh? What if we didn't get Monica back? Would it have been worth it *then*, John?"

John looked behind him as he backed into a tree. "Agent Warren—Jake, please. They can never know it was me," he pled. "And it's Director Caldwell to you."

"Fine, *Director Caldwell*, but I want my salary doubled and a month's worth of vacation days. Right now," Jake demanded. "I'm not kidding, John. If you want my silence, you're gonna have to buy it, and you're gonna have to do it right now. Make the call." Jake unholstered his GAIA pistol and pointed it at John. "Now," he shouted as he turned off the safety.

"Okay, okay," John relented, pulling his phone out and dialing GAIA headquarters. "Melina Mayfield," he spoke into the phone. "Hi, Mel? This is Director Caldwell. Effective immediately, Agent Jake Warren is to receive double his salary and a month of paid time off. No, I cannot explain why at this time. Okay. Thank you." John ended the call and looked back at Jake. "Happy?"

"Let's go with satisfied. For now," Jake cautioned as he walked away and went back inside the house, then over to Darren's bedroom. He closed the door behind him, locked it, and pulled out his phone. "Hey, Mel. You understand what's going on, right? Okay, good. Make sure to report that the director is compromised. The decisions he made not only conflicted with GAIA policy, but he also leaked information to the enemy and risked the lives of his own son and granddaughter to get what he wanted. What?" he shouted. "What do you mean, 'what I asked for is impossible?'" he shouted, realizing he needed to be quiet. "It came from the freaking director! Fine, fine, whatever. Just get it increased as much as possible. Make sure I get those vacation days. Okay. Yeah, I love you too. No, I don't know when I'll be home. I'm working! Bye." Jake ended the call with Melinda.

✧

"Wait. Monica and Aunt Mandy. Why does that sound so familiar?" Darren asked, and realization hit him like a ton of bricks. "Oh, God bless it, I am so stupid for not makin' that connection 'til now," Darren bellowed. "It was when the van crashed into the Waffle House, remember? I nearly ran into Monica, and you grabbed her before she could run off too far.

"So, despite all this, this ain't the first we've met. Ain't that somethin'?" Darren said with a grin. "Funny how fate works sometimes. All of us, in one way or another, were destined to meet. You can't tell me this was all just by chance. Someone must have ordained it. God works in many ways." Darren sat with a smile on his face, fascinated by how everything connected.

Kyle silently shook his head. *Not everyone believes like you do, pal.*

"Oh yeah, I remember! Wow. I felt so bad because she was interrupting your investigation, and I just wanted to get her back to the hospital," Amanda recalled.

"The hospital?" asked Darren. "Is there somethin' wrong with her?"

"Yeah, she has Merkel cell carcinoma. It's highly aggressive, and it started with her getting these red bumps on her neck and hands. Later on, she got them on her head and the rest of her skin. Oddly enough, I don't see any of them now." Amanda looked Monica over, slightly lifting Monica's shirt to check for the nodes, but couldn't find any. "They're all gone," Amanda gasped, turning her gaze to Kyle.

"You… you gotta be kidding me," Kyle sputtered as he stood and looked Monica over. "Holy crap. Does that mean she's…?" he asked hopefully.

Abigail felt hope budding in her chest for the first time in years. "I've never known cancer to miraculously heal, but given recent events, I can't discount it. Fascinating. Once this crisis is resolved, I'd love to verify this conclusively. If she was truly cured, then we could possibly use her DNA to synthesize the true cure for cancer. Of course, it will only tackle certain types at first, but having a foundation to build from will bolster our research and development. I wonder how this occurred."

John walked back in from the garage, and his eyes landed on Monica. "Hey there. I'm your grandpa," he whispered as he walked toward her.

Monica hid behind Amanda out of shyness.

Amanda giggled. "It's okay, sweetie. He won't bite, I promise. Go on, go say hi."

Monica shook her head and didn't budge. There was something off about John that she didn't like. Somehow, she was able to sense this about him. She didn't know what it was, exactly, but she didn't trust him.

Amanda sighed. "I'm sorry, Dad. She's been through something traumatic, and even before all this, she's always been a shy little thing. Maybe she just needs some time."

"That's alright." John chortled. "She can come to me in her own time. So, you must find all this overwhelming, huh?"

"Oh, don't even get me started," Amanda bemoaned with widened eyes, doing her best to keep herself under control. "It's alright, though. I'm managing, and if it means keeping Monica safe, then I'll do whatever I have to."

"So will I," said Sean as he came down the hallway, having quietly snuck down the stairs with Rebecca right behind him. He jogged toward Amanda and held his arms out for Monica, who grabbed him in a tight hug, making them both feel safe.

"I missed you so much, Daddy. I'm so happy to see you," shouted Monica, tears of joy streaming down her face. Sean soothed her as she sobbed. "Shh, shh, it's okay. I'm here now, and we're never getting separated again. At least not until you're all grown up. Even then, you still gotta stay close by." Sean put Monica down and looked around at everyone. "Hey, Dad," he said with a wave and a smile.

Jake stood behind Sean with his arms crossed, waiting for the perfect moment to reveal what he discovered. His chest was thrust out, but hesitation crept through him. After all, John was Sean's father, and Jake knew Sean would have a tough time with this, more so than anyone else. Still, it was necessary.

Sean cleared his throat and spoke loudly. "Listen, everyone, I know things have been weird and scary, nightmarish, even, but I am so thankful for all of you. I think we'll stand a chance together. All of us operating as a team is exactly what's gonna solve this. There are some great minds here, with various skills we'll need. I can't ask you to follow me into battle. I won't. Instead, let me say this. I will be the first one to head toward the danger, and I hope you'll follow me. There are a lot of frightened people out there, and I should know. I'm one of them. We can't let our differences keep us from doing what's right anymore.

"The scale we're about to attempt this on has never been accomplished before. So, let's be the first. Let's get countries talking to each other again. Let's get people motivated. Let's all work together as humanity, united under the will to survive and fight through our obstacles. We can go over, through, or under them, however it needs to be done. One group of people, one fight. It's time to take back our world." Sean raised a fist in the air, and everyone cheered while some clapped.

"Hell of a speech, son," Darren praised. "Mighty proud of you." Darren stood and grabbed Sean with one arm. "Ain't he somethin'? So, we got a plan?"

Sean smiled. "Yeah, we do. I've contacted Echo, who should be arriving—"

A bright light briefly encompassed the room, and Echo stood there in his true form. "Hello," he thoughtspoke cheerily to everyone.

"—shortly," Sean finished with slight annoyance, as Echo's entrance made him jump, and he turned to look at him. "A little warning next time?"

Everyone took in the view of Echo in his true form, and no one was afraid. They were honored to be in his presence after what he did for Monica.

"Okay, yeah, I get it. He's an alien, he looks cool, and he talks in your head. Fantastic. Look, bask in his beauty later. Right now, we gotta get started. Echo, please explain the first part of the plan, if you don't mind." Sean stepped aside so Echo could be the focus.

"Greetings, all. My name is Eco'Corulaz, but you may call me Echo. Step one is to locate a Kriff vessel to test our sound weapon on. Although we've had an unplanned yet successful run already, we've made improvements and would like another test to ensure it still functions as expected. For this, a GAIA agent will be required, and Sean has nominated Agent Jake Warren. He will be transported aboard a Kriff vessel, which we will locate and take a hostage from, who we will bring back with us." Echo stood aside and Sean took the stage.

Sean stood beside Echo. "Step two is to gather intel on our enemy. One of the ways we're gonna do this is by asking nicely and, when necessary, less nicely. This isn't the time to feel guilty. This is war, and we must use all our players and tools at our disposal. They started all this. Not just on Earth, but on Nephilu too, and those are just the ones we know about. Future generations will read about the story we're about to write with our actions. Our assault team will be me, Wheels, Mr. Morgan, my dad, and Jake. If anyone on that list doesn't want to be on assault, please raise your hand." No one raised their hands, so Sean and Echo backed away, allowing Rebecca to explain the next part.

Rebecca took a deep breath before speaking. "Step three moves in tandem with step two. As my dad gathers intel, the rest of us will coordinate the building sites and when to attack across the globe. We had the idea to perform the attack in short bursts instead of one long attack. This should give them a false sense of security, and each burst will strike at different times around the world. The bursts will be completely random, and will vary in how long they last. The shortest one will be five minutes, and the longest will be twenty, though most will fall somewhere in between. Abby's mission is to tend to any wounded and provide emotional support. She will also be helping me coordinate communications." Rebecca smiled at Abigail, and she smiled back.

Sean stepped in front of Rebecca. "Step four is fending off any Astro agents. Those are the people who are secretly working as enemy spies inside GAIA. We'll also need to fight back any Kriff. We're hoping to have a whole team of agents ready to fight by then, but just in case, I'll be leading the charge. Mandy's task is to protect Monica.

"Step five is on Jake after he gets our hostage. He's responsible for weapons and gear. He and Darren will force our hostage to give us the location of the one they call the Channeler. I'd like to try reasoning with this Channeler first before we move to more violent options.

"Echo has assured me that the sound weapon structures will be built within minutes of each other, at which time we will begin blasting the frequency. We are to immediately abort if anything goes wrong and regroup. Any questions?" asked Sean as he finished explaining.

"Yeah, do I get one of those fancy guns like Jake's?" asked Kyle, grinning.

Jake grinned widely. "I wondered when someone was gonna ask that, and yes, you do. Everyone will be issued a standard weapon of their choice. Oh, one more thing. The fight will be happening at the nearest GAIA base, not here. This place should still be safe. Just felt it was important to mention." Jake moved toward the door, pausing to give a nasty glare at John before stepping outside.

"Oh, yeah, I forgot to mention that the fight wouldn't be here. Sorry," Sean said with a half-smile, and his phone vibrated in his pocket. "Hang on a sec, someone's buzzing me." He took out his phone and saw the text.

(Jake) Come outside and come alone.

(Sean) Why?

(Jake) Just get out here already.

(Jake) Now!

(Sean) Okay, jeez.

Sean rolled his eyes and exhaled loudly in frustration. "Excuse me for a moment. I'll be right back." He walked outside and saw Jake standing by his truck. Sean approached him and impatiently threw his arms in the air, his eyes wide and eyebrows raised.

"Listen, I'm sorry to drag you away like this, but you can't let John be a part of this," Jake warned, holding his hands up in defense.

Sean smiled in disbelief, thinking Jake was playing a prank on him. "What are you talking about? He's *got* to be a part of it. He's my dad, and the commander of this whole thing. I mean, he's the freaking director, so we wanna use that," he said, slowly losing his smile.

"Okay, you've had your pops back for, what, like a day and a half, tops, and you're already pulling the 'well my dad is your boss' card? Really? I'm telling you, this isn't a good idea. You don't wanna do this. It's a mistake," said Jake, half-shouting.

"Oh, and why's that? Tell me, *why* would having the director of GAIA, the organization you work for, be a part of the front lines, protecting the world from hostile aliens, be a 'bad idea?'" Sean asked.

Jake sighed. "Sean, I know this is gonna hurt, but your father isn't who you think he is. He—"

"I don't care what kind of person he is. This isn't the time to be picky. We need every resource we can get, and he's a big one, so he's gonna be a part of this. You can argue about it after it's done," Sean said as he began to walk away.

Jake grabbed Sean by the arm and pulled him back. "Damn it, Sean. Will you listen to me? It's not *going* to get done because something has already gone wrong, and I'm trying to save you from having to deal with the aftermath of anything else," he shouted. Jake realized he was shaking Sean with his hands and let go. "My bad."

"Oh, come on. I already know what this is. Since my dad is finally back in my life, and we even have something to agree on and deal with together, you're worried he won't be objective when it comes to me and vice versa. Well, he may have been absent or indifferent for most of my life, but now he's really trying, and it's better late than never," Sean shouted, walking away.

"No, Sean, you don't understand," Jake yelled after him. He ran toward Sean and stood in front of him, blocking the door. "Rookie, buddy, *Sean*, I'm trying to keep you and everyone else from getting hurt. He's already caused something with Monica by—"

"What he *caused* is the safe return of my daughter, and if you don't move out of my way, *you're* gonna get hurt," Sean warned. "Move."

"You do realize I'm the one with the gun, right?" asked Jake, reaching for his pistol.

"What, you're gonna shoot me?" asked Sean. "Go ahead. See what my dad thinks."

Jake sighed in defeat. "If it keeps you from hurting yourself even worse, or anybody else, then yes. Try me," he said in a low tone. Jake hated the idea of hurting Sean, but he also knew John couldn't be trusted. It was important to Jake for John not to go, and he truly had Sean's best interests at heart.

Sean rushed up to Jake to move him, but Jake pushed him to the ground. He leapt back up, ran toward Jake, and struck him with a running right hook. Sean's emotions got to him, and he took advantage of Jake's disbelief by grabbing him and throwing him over the eight-foot railing. "Stay down," Sean barked breathlessly as he stormed back inside.

Okay, he's gonna be a great agent. He's got some years on me, thought Jake as he slowly stood back up, using the railings for support. *Fine, if he wants to screw this up, let him. I don't give a damn. Oh, who am I kidding? I give lots of damns. Guess Abby was right about me getting punched in the face one day*, he finished thinking. Jake knew Sean would have a hard time listening to anything negative about his father, especially before starting a war. All he could do was hope for the best, but he wanted to try one more thing, so he sent a text to Sean.

(Jake) Buddy, I'm sorry for what happened today, but the abduction of Monica was set up by your father. He wanted to test the weapon, and he put you, Monica, and Echo in danger.

Jake checked the phone after a moment, but the message failed to send as his phone died, and he collapsed at the steps.

WE ARE TIRED AND FULL OF DREAD
PREPARE US FOR WHAT'S UP AHEAD

✧

21. Trial and Error

SEAN STORMED INTO THE HOUSE, HIS RAGE ON FULL display. He took one look at everyone around the room and they all fell silent, not daring to ask what happened. It was evident by his demeanor that Sean didn't want to talk. Sean gave one last look at everyone, and his gaze landed on Abigail. "Control your psychotic brother, or I will," he warned, then darted up the stairs in anger. Amanda saw Sean storm past her room, awakened by all the commotion. Sean retreated to the bedroom and slammed the door.

"Sean, what's gotten into you?" demanded Amanda.

"Stay away," he shouted at his sister through the door as he locked it.

Abigail stood and rushed outside, finding Jake passed out on the porch steps. "Oh my God, Jake," she shouted. "Wake up! Wake up," she continued shouting as she shook him. Abigail gently laid Jake down on the porch and stuck her head back inside as she partially opened the door. "I need some help out here!"

Rebecca, John, and Darren rushed outside. Kyle wanted to help, but he stayed behind to keep an eye on Monica. "What happened?"

"I don't know. I just found him like this," Abigail yelled in a panic. "Okay, calm down, Abby, calm down," she thought aloud. "Pulse is good." Abigail breathed in relief. "Heart rate is a little erratic and breathing sounds labored, but he seems otherwise okay."

Rebecca closed her eyes as she realized something must have happened between him and Sean. Undeterred, she nervously pulled out her phone and sent Sean a text.

(Rebecca) What happened?

(Sean) Not now

(Sean) Ask Jake

Sean didn't want to get into an argument with Rebecca, because that would do nothing good for his nerves. He held his phone, hands shaking, while watching the typing symbol and sighed. It made no sense to him why Jake wouldn't want John to be a part of the mission. *Was he right?* Sean thought. Clearly, Sean wasn't objective when it came to his father, so he believed Jake may have had a point. Still, John was necessary for the fight. His phone buzzed as Rebecca continued texting him.

(Rebecca) I would, but he's passed out on the porch. Did you hurt him?

(Rebecca) Please tell me what happened?

(Sean) Can you come up here?

(Sean) Please?

While Rebecca hesitated due to Sean's anger, she also cared for his well-being. "Sean wants me to go talk to him. I'm gonna try to help calm him down, and maybe we can get some answers." Rebecca stood and turned her gaze to Abigail. "Abby, if you feel you need to call nine-one-one, go ahead," she said as she stepped back inside and headed to their room.

"No, don't you dare," Jake complained as he woke up. "Ow, my everything." His entire body, down to his nerves and bones, felt as brittle as those of an elderly man.

"Jake," Abigail shouted gleefully. "I'm so glad you're awake. Are you alright? Do you need to go to the hospital? That's an option again now."

Jake tried sitting up again, but kept a hand on his stomach. "Ow, and no, I'm fine, so don't you dare break out your freaking medbag. I started it," he admitted. "I was trying to warn Sean," he revealed accidentally, not realizing John was right there at first, "about… something we found out. You know, about the aliens, but he wouldn't listen to me. I couldn't find the right words, and it just didn't go well." Jake tried standing, and Abigail tried to catch him, but he slipped through her arms. "Again, ow."

"Easy, Jake. Take it easy, okay? Tell us what happened. Sean's upstairs, and Rebecca's gone to check on him." Abigail stared at Jake expectantly, waiting for him to explain the situation. *It was bound to happen sooner or later,* she thought.

Jake saw John watching him and a chill ran through him, his heart hammering in his chest. It was important that no one else was injured or separated because of him, and John could still undo the perks Jake had requested. "I can't," he whispered, then motioned for Abigail to come closer. "Take me into one of the bedrooms and I'll explain, but John can't be there."

Abigail gave her brother a perplexed look, but read the fear on his face. "I need someone to help me carry him into Darren's room," she said. Darren and John assisted her as the three of them dragged Jake to a room and laid him down on the bed.

John left, and Darren started to follow, but Jake spoke up. "Hang on," he protested as he managed to sit up, albeit painfully. "Wow, this feels so much better than the ground. Anyway, don't go. Just close and lock the door."

Darren did as he was asked. "Alright, son, the door's locked. Now tell us what the hell happened." Darren crossed his arms and narrowed his eyes.

Jake took a deep breath and winced in pain. "Okay, that stings. I might need that medbag after all," he admitted. "Listen, when I went outside earlier, I heard John talking to someone on the phone. Long story short, he's the reason Monica got abducted. He leaked her location to someone who sent an anonymous tip to Astro agents, at least from what I understood."

Darren's arms dropped as his eyes widened and his mouth fell open.

"The Kriff are really interested in Monica for some reason, and I don't know why. Anyway, John apparently set it all in motion so they could test the sound weapon. I get wanting to run a test, but risking the lives of your son and granddaughter?" Jake asked, grunting in pain.

"What happened after that?" asked Abigail.

"I called him out on it and reported it to my girlfriend, Melinda, who also works at GAIA. When I tried to tell Sean, he wouldn't listen. I tried to block the door, and I pushed him down to keep him from sending us into battle with a traitor. Naturally, he fought back, then he came inside, and you're basically caught up now," Jake finished as he laid back down.

"That son of a bitch," Darren shouted, preparing to storm out and give John a piece of his mind. Maybe it was his connection to Rebecca, but he had come to feel like a father figure to Sean, something Sean didn't get when he was young, and this pushed Darren past his boiling point.

"Hang on," said Abigail. "While his actions were unforgivably reprehensible, we can't just charge at him without strategizing," she said, giving Darren a knowing and sympathetic look.

"I'm a little ahead of you there," Jake said painfully. "Melinda, remember? Just make sure Sean and Monica are safe. Oh, and Wheels too. He's needed for future Halo sessions." Jake looked at Abigail and took her hand. "I'm sorry I ruined the plan."

"You didn't ruin it, Jake," Abigail soothed. "You delayed it, yes, but for good reason. It will likely undergo a few alterations, but I believe it will still work," she said, turning her gaze to Darren. "I'll come right back after I retrieve my medbag." Abigail stood and swiftly exited the room, closing the door behind her. She walked down the hallway and passed John, giving him a fake smile, hoping it would be enough. Once she retrieved her bag, she went back inside and tried to dash past him again, but he spoke to her.

"Is he gonna be alright?" John asked, causing Abigail to stop in her tracks.

"Yes, I think so. This is standard medical equipment intended for hospital patients. I keep a bag on me now for emergencies. Please excuse me," she said politely with another fake smile as she started down the hallway again.

John grabbed Abigail's arm with force, more than she deemed necessary. "Let me know how it goes. He really needs to be part of this fight," he said, letting her go.

Abigail yanked her arm away and jogged back to the bedroom, closing and locking the door behind her. "Okay, that was creepy," she said with a shiver. "Jake, I'm going to use what I have here to treat you. I do have some numbing gels and shots, so I'll make use of those."

Jake nodded and winced.

"Darren, I appreciate your presence, but if you're here for too long, then John will suspect you. Once I've stabilized Jake, I'll let you know," said Abigail, ushering Darren out of the room.

Darren groaned and exited the room, but was unable to put on a happy face. "Get the hell outta my way," he commanded John as he thundered past him, his emotions in turmoil.

"Sean, Jake may have good reason for warning you. Maybe you should listen to him," said Rebecca.

Sean sighed. "Maybe you're right, but I still think we need my dad. I should apologize to Jake, though. I shouldn't have retaliated." Sean stood and moved toward the door, holding hands with Rebecca as he slowly began his descent into the living room, where Darren, Kyle, Amanda, and Monica sat. "Where's my dad?" asked Sean.

"He's staying near Jake to make sure he's alright," Amanda answered. "Sean, what happened?"

Sean dropped his head and began to speak, but Rebecca stood in front of him.

"It's okay, Sean. I can explain. Go see Jake and Abby," she coaxed.

Sean walked to the room, and Darren followed soon after. "Oh, hey, Dad," Sean said as he passed John. "I'm gonna check on Jake. I was unacceptably cruel to him. I'm sorry I pushed all this back." Sean stared at the ground. "You must be so disappointed."

"Are you kidding? Sean, you're my *son*. I couldn't be any prouder of you if I tried. Yet, somehow, you continue to surprise me daily. You are so much more of a man than I could have ever hoped for," said John, paraphrasing what Darren said to him earlier.

Darren folded his arms.

"Thanks, Dad," Sean beamed, hugging his father tight. "I'm glad we're talking again. I promise, you're gonna be even more proud of me once we win this fight, so be ready for that." Sean jogged toward Jake and Abigail.

Darren waited until Sean was out of hearing range and the bedroom door was closed before approaching John. "You know, a lot of that sounded pretty damn familiar. Thing is, I can't decide if I'm flattered that you used my words or disgusted that you couldn't come up with your own. A bit of both, maybe, but I see right through you."

"You got a problem with me, Sheriff?" John asked forcefully. "I'm getting real sick of your damn attitude. You may be a cop back home, but here, you're just a civilian. GAIA has jurisdiction across the entire planet. Now sit down, shut up, and do as I say. No more smart-mouthing from you, got it?" John ordered.

"I don't care who you work for or what your rank is," yelled Darren, sticking a finger in John's face. "This is about human lives. Our lives! The lives of your own son, daughter, and granddaughter, who *you* put in harm's way. You are a disgusting, egotistical, lying bastard!"

"You do not yell at me," yelled John, losing his temper. "I am in control of this situation, got it? Me! That means you do what I say whether you like it or not!"

"I'll yell at whoever I damn well please," Darren shouted back.

Amanda and Kyle approached Darren and John while Monica hid behind the couch. "What the hell is this?" demanded Kyle.

Kyle's interruption broke Darren out of his temper. "Just a huge disagreement," Darren said as he walked away.

Kyle started to say something, but a blinding light encompassed the whole house. Several Nephilium ships were hovering above the house, one of them right in the front yard. The lights soon retracted, and Echo stood in the living room in his true form.

"Hello, friends," Echo thoughtspoke to everyone. "We have located a vessel. It is time." Echo looked around at everyone. "I see much anger here. Why?"

"You can *see* emotions?" asked Kyle, his eyebrows raised.

"Yes," Echo replied. "It is also how our ocular organs shift chromatically with our emotions."

Kyle's brow furrowed. "What?"

"He's saying their eyes change color with their mood," Abigail explained, and Kyle nodded.

Sean came out of the room and saw Echo standing there. "Oh, Echo. Hey. We're just about ready. Sorry, Jake and I had a disagreement and I… hurt him, so he's taking some time to recover."

"Oh, worry not, for I can assist, but only once. We can heal you or ourselves, but only once every twenty-four of your hours," Echo explained in thoughtspeak. "It has its limitations, but we do not have the time for explanations."

Kyle smiled. "Is there a premium package I can purchase to speed that up?" he joked.

"No, of course not. If we had a way to decrease our recharge time, then why would we need to—" Echo thoughtspoke, confused.

"Nothing, never mind," Kyle said with a wide-eyed grin.

"So you can heal Jake, then?" asked Sean.

"Yes, at least for now. Please take me to him," thoughtspoke Echo.

Once Echo came through the door, he hovered his hands over Jake's body in a rhythmic motion, as if making waves with his arms.

Jake was back to his usual self in under five minutes. "Holy mother," he said as he stood and stretched, feeling renewed and refreshed. "Dude, I feel better than I have in a decade." He headed toward Sean, but stopped and turned around. "Thank you, Echo," he said as he turned around and walked out of the room.

Echo watched Jake leave, his eyes briefly shifting to blue.

Everyone convened to meet in the living room. "Alright, I know there's been some disagreements and a lot of tension, but we need to put it all behind us for now," John announced. "Echo has located our first target, and it's right outside the nearest GAIA base. We're going to disrupt it, and then beam Jake onto it, who will take a hostage to bring back to GAIA. I know Darren was originally going to be conducting the interrogation," he hedged with a glance over at Darren, "but after some thought, I believe Kyle would be a better fit. Now, is everyone ready?" asked John, to which everybody nodded in assent, even Jake and Darren, though Darren was highly displeased. "Alright then. Let's go save the world."

Everyone except for Amanda, Abigail, Rebecca, and Monica scrambled to their cars and motorcaded to the base. Some fidgeted in their seats, their minds buzzing like bees, but others were itching to get started. Jake was ecstatic, driving and conversing with ANNI on the way to the base. "You are literally every nerd's dream come true," Jake trumpeted to the car. Kyle grinned with a look of triumph on his face.

"I find it peculiar how many of these 'nerds,' as you call them, all have the same desire. I must update my database with this new information," ANNI vocalized.

Sean's mind was in no shape for him to drive, so he rode with Darren. "Listen, son. There's a lot I wanna say, but I'd be robbin' you of time you could give to somebody else. If there's anybody you wanna call and talk to, just in case it's for one last time, you might wanna do it now," Darren suggested gently. He wanted to tell Sean how proud he was of him, and how much he'd come to care for him, but he knew it was important for him to give his chosen words to whom he wanted.

Sean pulled out his phone and called his mother for the first time in months. "Hello?" he said confidently as soon as his mother picked up.

"Sean? Oh my God, Sean, baby! I'm so glad to hear from you," Whitney said gleefully. "I've been worried sick about you, your father, and Mandy for weeks now. One of you should have called to tell me something. I'm relieved to hear you're okay. I love you, sweetheart," she cooed.

Sean felt a huge weight lift off him after hearing his mother's voice, especially being called sweetheart. It was the gut punch of motherly love he sorely needed. Everyone knows about the closeness of women with their fathers, but there is also a strong connection between mothers and their sons. "I love you too, Mom. I'm sorry I haven't called. I don't have long, but I wanted to call you and say I love you. We think we have a solution for this virus situation, and Dad's even gonna help."

"Now there's a surprise. I guess kicking him out did the trick this time," said Whitney, ignoring the slight pangs of guilt in her gut.

Sean was taken aback. "Okay, Mom, I wanna discuss that, but not right now. I promise I'll call you back, but I gotta go. I'm sorry. Goodbye," he said as he ended the call.

Darren gripped Sean's shoulder tightly and kept his other hand on the wheel. "You'll have time later. Okay, Sean, now you listen to me, and you listen well," Darren asserted. He told Sean everything his father did, leaving no details out.

Sean's anger mounted as he stayed silent for about thirty seconds, then punched the inside of the passenger door as hard as he could repeatedly, tears in his eyes, until Darren pulled the car over and pried Sean away from the door.

"Hey, that's my car you're beatin' on," Darren shouted. "Now look, I know you're angry, but use it against the bad guys, not against my poor car. She ain't done nothin' to you. Save your anger and mine it. Your dad's a piece of work, but we've got bigger fish to fry right now. Trust me, we will both be havin' a discussion with him later. I'm sorry to drop this on you right before the fight, but you deserved to know. It's what Jake was tryin' to tell you. Now, I'm gonna turn my lights and siren on so we can get there faster, and because I want Jake to feel like he has a cop on his tail."

The ride to the base was quiet afterwards, save for the sirens, and they arrived there after about twenty minutes. Sean exited the car and followed Darren as he walked over to Jake, who led them down several long corridors and into a large round room.

"Welcome to the armory," Jake announced, his arms out wide. "I will be taking this energy rifle. Darren, heads up," he said as he tossed a gun to Darren that he caught.

"A shotgun? Are you serious?" Darren asked with a grin. "No way."

"What, you don't like it? We got other choices," Jake offered.

Darren's voice rose higher than usual, feeling as though the world had more color. "No, I can't believe I finally get to use one again. It's been forever since I've been huntin'."

"Oh," Jake chuckled. "Yeah, I figured you would—wait. What kinda things were you hunting? On second thought, never mind. The less I know about that, the better. Look, that's an energy shotgun, so it works at medium range, too. Be careful with it. Sean, coming your way," he shouted as he tossed Sean a sniper rifle.

Sean fumbled the rifle, but caught it. "Sick," he said with a grin. *Now this will do*, he thought.

Jake started to say something to Sean, but Sean interrupted before he could.

"Yeah, I know, energy sniper. I've played Halo, remember? While awesome, this concept isn't new to me… but only as a concept," he finished under his breath. "Jake," Sean shouted as he walked toward Jake, making him turn his attention back to Sean. "I'm sorry. You were just trying to help me and protect everybody. I shouldn't have hurt you, and I should have listened."

"Oh, no worries. That's the least deadly fight I've ever lost. You got a good arm on you. Use it to smack these alien bastards if they get too close, yeah?" Jake turned toward Kyle. "Wheels, I was told this is your preferred style of weapon," he beamed as he walked over to Kyle, carrying a weapon with both hands and placing it into Kyle's arms.

"A rocket launcher?" Kyle squealed with delight, his voice rising high in pitch. "Dude," he admired, looking at Jake with extreme gratitude and a huge grin on his face.

Jake pointed at the rocket launcher. "Oh, that ain't free, my friend. Once all this is over and we win, you're my new Halo night buddy. In fact, I was hoping you both might join me."

"Deal," Sean and Kyle both said at the same time.

"What about me?" came Rebecca's voice from behind them, making all of them scream and turn around.

"Freaking ghost," Kyle grumbled, clutching his heart and bending over as he waited for the fear to pass.

"What on God's green Earth are you doin' here, Becca?" Darren asked. "You need to get back to the house right now!"

"Why? Cause I'm a woman, and all the women gotta stay behind? That ain't happening. Abby drove us here. Mandy stayed back to watch Monica, and we're still gonna help with the coordination and all, but we can do it here while helping you fight," said Rebecca.

"Are you crazy? I want you to be safe! There's tons of danger here. Do you hear me? Danger," shouted Sean.

"Easy there, Will Robinson. If she wants to fight, let her. The more, the merrier," said Kyle. "Plus, I'd rather fight the aliens than her."

"No, I don't wanna lose anyone else," Sean barked.

Rebecca stomped over to Sean and stuck a finger in his face. "You're *not* gonna lose me. We're gonna find something inside that we can use to fight. Stop it with this senseless macho stuff. I'm stronger than I look. Just because I'm a woman doesn't mean I don't pack a punch, so get the hell out of my way, or you'll be my first casualty," shouted Rebecca. She walked away from Sean and browsed the guns.

The men all stared at each other in concern, but they were all too afraid of Rebecca's wrath to stop her. Sean was worried about Rebecca, concerned for his own safety from Rebecca, yet somehow her tenacity turned him on. When it was all over, he would be more than willing to talk with her. At that moment, he wasn't sure what words to use.

Rebecca grabbed a gun from the rack. "How about this one?" she asked, holding up a rifle with a scope. She wanted to try precision weapons like Sean.

"Uh, yeah. That'll do," said Kyle. "Please point that thing *away* from us."

Darren turned to Jake. "She's more like me than I care to admit."

"Hi, Jake," Abigail spoke gently, noticing Jake's surprised and disapproving face. "Please don't give me a hard time. I'm here as a field medic. While I did bring my usual medbag, I'm also hoping to find more effective materials inside."

Jake groaned. "Fine, just be careful. You still got the pistol I gave you?"

"You mean this?" asked Abigail with a grin as she held up the GAIA pistol.

Jake shook his head. "God help us all," he muttered.

"What was that?" asked Abigail.

"Nothing," Jake responded.

Echo materialized beside them. "Hello," he thoughtspoke. "If you are sufficiently armed, it is time to depart for the ship. It is not far."

"Yep, I'm set. Beam me up, Scotty," Jake said to Echo.

"I am not familiar with this 'Scotty'. Is there an additional member of your party that I am unaware of?" thoughtspoke Echo.

Jake sighed in disappointment. "No, it's… never mind. Just come on. I'll explain it to you later."

Echo grabbed Jake, and they disappeared into his ship, which took off into the sky. Once they were out of sight, Sean noticed his father still hadn't arrived. "I know everyone's getting tired of me asking this, but where's my dad?"

"Right here," John said as he approached the group from the side. "Sorry, I stopped at a safe house to refill my supplies. Can't ever be too careful. Sean, are you ready? They're gonna be on us any minute now." John gripped Sean's shoulder and lightly rubbed it.

Sean's vision narrowed as his muscles went rigid, but he decided to wait until after the fight before confronting his father. For the time being, he decided to keep up the charade, and mine the anger like Darren suggested. *Use the anger against the bad guys, not against my dad*, he thought. "Yeah," he said with a fake smile. "I'm ready to blow somebody's head off." That much was certainly true. Sean finished reloading the gun, and located a building in the base to sit atop of.

Abigail turned to face Rebecca. "Becca, come with me, please. I'd like to explore a part of the base while we have time. If I'm not mistaken, I saw a room that had radar detection equipment. It would keep us informed of when the Kriff are within proximity of the base, so we could prepare." Abigail walked away, and Rebecca followed her.

"I'm gonna head outside so I can be the welcoming committee," Kyle said as he finished loading the rocket launcher. "This is gonna have one hell of a kickback." Kyle went back outside and sat in a chair he'd dragged from a room, holding the rocket launcher in his lap. "Come on down," he yelled to the sky.

"I'm goin' to my car where it's warm while we wait for these bastards," Darren said as he walked away.

"Darren, wait," said John.

Darren stopped walking, but didn't turn around. "What?" he asked icily.

"I'm sorry for losing my temper on you," said John. "I've been under a lot of stress, and—"

"I don't wanna hear it, and I don't recommend tickin' me off while I have this gun," said Darren as he stormed away.

"Are you ready?" Echo thoughtspoke to Jake. "The ship is in range."

Jake closed his eyes and took a deep breath. "Yep, ready as I'm gonna be. Crank that sucker up."

Echo pressed several buttons and turned a few dials. "Prepare yourself."

Jake covered his ears as Echo played the sound toward the Kriff ship, which seemed to wobble momentarily before plummeting to the ground in the woods nearby. "Whoa! Was that supposed to happen?"

"It was somewhat unexpected, but not impossible. We increased the strength, and therefore the resonance of the weapon. I will transport you to the ground to search for survivors and bring one back. Please act quickly, as I do not know how long the effects will last," thoughtspoke Echo.

Before Jake could argue, he was transported. "Son of a—whoa," Jake said. There were alien bodies everywhere, and Jake realized he had a unique opportunity. He shot and stabbed several bodies, seemingly killing them as he walked through the woods, his breath shaking. Finally, he happened upon another Kriff, who was incapacitated and considerably taller than the rest.

Jake ran toward the alien and struggled to pick it up. "Echo, recall," he shouted, and he was back on Echo's ship. He tossed the alien down on the floor in front of Echo. This bigger Kriff was like the smaller ones but was taller. It had much smaller eyes, though they were still large. It also had the slightest suggestions of a nose.

"Fascinating. You have captured one of their leaders. This succeeded better than anticipated. Now you must return to GAIA, so the one you call Wheels can conduct the interrogation." Echo pressed the ship's buttons, but before he could finish, the Kriff stood and attacked Jake from behind, knocking him to the floor and roaring at him.

Jake escaped from underneath it and shot at it with his energy rifle, which made it scream in pain. The scream sounded like a thousand yelling bats until it fell to the floor. "Not my first rodeo, pal," said Jake, looking at Echo. "We should hurry." Jake kept his eye on the Kriff, and his gun pointed at its face.

Echo beamed down with Jake and the unconscious Kriff right outside the base. Darren saw this, getting out of his car and running over with his shotgun. "So, that's what these bastards look like," he said. "Man, those eyes are disturbin'."

"Yeah, I don't know what's worse. The way these guys look, or the fact so many people were right," Jake said as he walked inside carrying the Kriff. Once he got to the interrogation room, he placed the Kriff on a chair, restrained it, and called Kyle. "Hey, man. You're up. It's your chance to get what you've always wanted. An alien interview."

"Alright. I'm on my way in now," Kyle responded and ended the call. While he looked forward to talking with the alien, he was also highly aware of how personal the stakes were. It wasn't about making contact or learning from one another, but about extracting information. This would be difficult for him, as he had to do his best to stay objective and not lose his composure.

"Abby, I've got the continents of Asia and Africa onboard. What about you?" asked Rebecca.

"Entire *continents*? Already?" asked Abigail incredulously. "I thought I was doing well to manage Spain and Brazil," she shouted as Rebecca's comment made her feel way behind and overwhelmed.

"Abby, keep it together. We're a team, remember? I'm picking three to five countries at a time to maximize our efficiency. Also, I *may* have asked Echo to allow me to talk to Sca'Lorit, who he says we can call Scarlet. Anyway, they've been sending representatives all over the world to speed this up. I have those two continents ready to go on our signal, and at least three countries on every continent. Here, let me get you some help. Scarlet, do you have anyone who could help my friend Abby? We need to speed this up," Rebecca called.

Another Nephilium appeared between the women in seconds, his skin an emerald color. "Hello. My name is Kli'Cacowas, but you may call me Klick. I understand that you, Abigail Warren, need our assistance to help coordinate communication and structure completion," thoughtspoke Klick.

"Yes, please. What did you have in mind?" asked Abigail.

"I believe this method to be ineffective. I will consult with the rest of my team, but I believe we need to work on building these structures, while you communicate with Earth's leaders. Please pardon me as I must depart to assist," thoughtspoke Klick as he disappeared in a bright light.

The phone next to Rebecca rang. "Yes, this is Rebecca Morgan. Yes, that's correct. Okay, thank you." Rebecca hung up the phone and looked over at Abigail. "Abby, the president just called. He's gonna help make the calls, but he says he's already been made aware of several resonant towers across the globe," Rebecca beamed. "We should be ready to launch in no less than twenty minutes." Rebecca put her headset back on and continued calling while watching the radar on the computer screen.

Sean looked at his smartwatch as he sat up in his sniper nest, anxiously awaiting an appearance by the Kriff. His anxiety became nearly unbearable, so he gave the ground of the base one last look. Sean started to look away, but he saw a small, shadowy figure moving toward the entrance, followed by several more.

Kriff were beginning to approach the base, Sean realized. Sean shot several in the head, which made them fall to the ground, but he couldn't be sure if it killed them. It seemed to, but nothing was impossible anymore. More kept showing up from all directions, and he kept sniping them.

One Kriff approached Kyle as he hadn't noticed their approach, or Sean's sniping, since he was listening to music on his headphones with his eyes closed. The Kriff approached Kyle and reached out its hand to touch his head as Sean sniped the Kriff between its eyes.

Kyle felt the bullet graze his hair. "Holy shit," he griped in surprise, quickly jumping up and looking around as his headset fell off, finally seeing a group of Kriff coming from the front. Darren was already taking them down with his shotgun, and he realized Sean was sniping them from afar. "Oh hell, it's game time, and my dumb self is just sitting here goofing off." Kyle picked up the rocket launcher. "Alright, ladies. It is my pleasure to welcome you to Earth. Now go home," shouted Kyle as he fired a rocket toward a large group of them, causing a huge explosion, damaging many of them and sending others flying. He kept his eyes peeled for more, and since he, Sean, and Darren were all looking out for them, they would be more aware. "I might need to reschedule my interview."

"No need," shouted Darren. "Looks like they're fallin' back." Darren continued firing on them from afar, ensuring none of them got close as Sean continued sniping them. "Go on ahead, son."

Kyle turned around to give the battlefield one last glance, but all seemed under control, so he continued to the room where Jake was. "Holy X-Files," Kyle said as he saw the tall Kriff. "Why is that one so much taller? It's bigger than me," he said. "I thought these guys were supposed to be like four feet tall, max."

Jake unfolded his arms. "How should I know? I'm just the delivery guy. Come on, don't feel threatened by another species, man. Anyway, Echo mentioned something about it being a leader, if that helps. I'm gonna go back out there. You sure you got this?"

"Yeah, man. I'll get some answers. Just in case, though, what if it gets free, or tries to control me or whatever?" asked Kyle.

"Won't happen. It's in a suppression zone and strapped to this chair. None of its usual tricks will work. Just don't let it bleed on you," Jake said as he ran out.

"What does that mean? Hey, that's not funny," Kyle shouted after him.

"Alright, it looks like we're ready to start," said Abigail. "Becca, thank you, and Klick, if you can hear me, thank you too. We're ready when you are."

"Can you believe we actually managed that?" Rebecca asked with a smile. "We just coordinated with the entire human race in less than a *day*. It's so amazing how we unite when there's a crisis."

Rebecca heard Scarlet's voice in her head. *It is time to deploy*, she thoughtspoke to Rebecca and Abigail. *Please begin the process.*

"Did you hear that too?" asked Rebecca.

"Yes, I did. I'll make the call this time. You've done enough." Abigail picked up the phone and dialed the president. "Hello, sir. My name is Abigail Warren. I'm working with Rebecca Morgan and the Nephilium to coordinate this attack. Yes, sir, that's correct. They are ready for us to strike. I repeat, they are ready for us to strike. Okay. Thank you, sir." Abigail ended the call, excitement flowing through her veins. "Oh my, what a rush. I've never felt so important in my life."

"Are the attacks starting?" asked Rebecca.

"Oh! Yes, they are. Sorry, my head is all fuzzy and tired. They're deploying the attacks worldwide now," Abigail replied.

Jake walked outside and saw several Kriff ships approaching the base. "Oh, that's not good," he said, activating the alarm. Darren and Sean were already firing at the ships, but it made no difference, so they resumed fighting the Kriff.

There was a resonance tower behind the base that had recently finished being built, and John hit the button in his director's office to make it start. It blared the frequency across the entire base and eastern seaboard. It was the loudest, most high-pitched sound ever recorded in human history, but it didn't hurt anyone's ears due to its unique pitch. The Kriff ships wobbled, but they didn't fall.

Echo appeared beside Sean. "The attack is happening. Please accompany me to my ship," he thoughtspoke as he grabbed Sean and teleported him away before he could argue.

"Echo, why am I here? I need to be back out there helping," Sean protested. "Please send me back."

"You are here because I want you safe in case I am correct," Echo thoughtspoke.

"Correct about what?" Sean asked, his brow furrowed.

Echo's eyes turned blue. "Failure."

Several Kriff beamed down from the approaching ships, now brandishing weapons and black suits with the Astro logo on them. When Jake fired at them, a protective bubble formed around them, keeping them safe. "What the hell, man? How are they still coming?" Jake shouted in confusion.

The phone rang again, and Rebecca picked it up. "Hi, Mr. President. What?" asked Rebecca, and she looked at the radar. "Oh my God. Sir, I think you're right. Something's wrong. It didn't work. I repeat, it didn't work," shouted Rebecca, and the line went dead.

"What's going on?" asked Abigail, fear growing in her lungs.

Rebecca pointed to the radar. "The sound weapon. It didn't work this time. This makes no sense. The president said it's happening like this all over the world. They're still coming. Abby, what do we do?"

Abigail had a look of pure terror on her face. "I… I don't know," she answered, dumbfounded.

"Attention! Please come inside the GAIA building for your own safety. I repeat, please fall back inside the GAIA base for protection," John announced over the outdoor speakers.

"Well, you heard the man." Jake looked at Darren. "I think we better book it."

"Ain't gotta tell me twice," said Darren as they both bolted for the door.

Once the group was safely inside, John initiated a lockdown of the base to prevent anyone or anything from coming inside. Unfortunately, this also meant nothing could get out. A few agents continued fighting outside, but it wasn't going well.

"Echo, please. Send me inside the base with everyone else. I need to be there. It's important," Sean demanded.

"Request denied. You will be unsafe there. I desire that you remain unharmed," thoughtspoke Echo.

"Darn it, Echo. You're getting attached to me, and that's fine. It's probably left over from your human conversion test, but you gotta be objective here. You can come with me and keep me safe that way. Alright?" Sean asked, trying to compromise.

"If that is your wish, then I suppose it will do. However, I am displeased by this decision," thoughtspoke Echo.

"Fine," Sean noted, realizing he and Echo were developing a friendship. "Use your human converter again so you don't draw suspicion, and then we need to go in there so we can find out what's going on."

Echo was silent, but departed for another chamber for approximately three minutes, returning in his human form and scowling at Sean, which made him feel guilty. He placed what looked like a watch on Sean's wrist and fastened it.

"Uh, what is this?" asked Sean.

"This will allow you to teleport to the ship whenever you need, whether I am with you or otherwise," Echo explained. "You may also use it to teleport back. I will grab your shoulder now, and you will press that button."

Sean raised his eyebrows. "Here goes nothing," he said as he pressed the button, teleporting them inside the main entrance with everyone else. "Whoa! Okay, I'm impressed. That is the coolest thing ever."

Echo smiled. "I am pleased that you enjoy it."

Darren walked up to Sean. "It's bad, son. Our plan didn't work. I don't understand it. Sean, will you go see if Becca's okay? I'm sure she's scared," he suggested, patting Sean on the shoulder and assessing the other agents who were fighting alongside them.

"Tell Abby to get down here. We got wounded who need tendin' to," he called after Sean.

Sean ran up the stairs to where Abigail and Rebecca were. "Abby," Sean called, getting her attention. "Darren needs you downstairs. We have wounded," he rushed out, and Abigail ran past him down the stairs. "Becca, are you okay?" he asked.

Rebecca walked up to Sean and grabbed him tightly in a hug. "Why didn't it work?" she asked in a whisper. "I don't understand."

"I don't know. I don't understand it either. Hey, we're safe here, okay? Wheels is with one of those things right now. He'll get information we can use. Until then, we just have to hunker down and ride this out," Sean soothed.

"You heard what Echo said, though! They can come inside whenever they want," Rebecca shouted fearfully, her legs threatening to collapse underneath her.

"I was not entirely correct," Echo thoughtspoke, making Rebecca and Sean jump. "Oh, my apologies. I did not mean to startle you. I followed Sean up the steps as I want to ensure his safety. Regarding the Kriff's ability to appear inside houses, they cannot pass through GAIA's electromagnetic shield. It is far more likely they will wait outside for us to emerge. The bigger concern is what they are doing to people who did not manage to get inside in time, and across the world."

Rebecca looked at the camera for the yard on the computer screen. Kriff picked agents up and ripped them in half, tearing off their arms and legs. Some people were abducted for experimentation. Rebecca placed a hand over her mouth and looked away, tears forming in her eyes. "This isn't happening," she quavered as she rocked back and forth. "This isn't happening," she repeated softly.

Darren came running up the stairs after hearing Rebecca shout. "Hey, what's goin' on?" he asked Sean.

"She's having a breakdown, and frankly, I'm about to break down myself," Sean confessed, his breathing becoming shallower. "It doesn't make any sense," he said as he looked at Darren with fear in his eyes. "It doesn't."

Darren was at a loss for words, but gripped Sean's shoulder and motioned for Rebecca to come over as he held them both closely. He wanted to try his breathing exercise for them, but he couldn't even steady his own breath.

"Jake, do you have a medical wing? Somewhere I can take the wounded?" asked Abigail.

"Yeah, follow me," said Jake, and they headed to the medical division.

"Echo, please go grab my mom, Amanda, and Monica, then bring them here," Sean ordered.

"But Sean—" Echo said.

"Just do it," Sean commanded. "It's not up for discussion."

Echo disappeared into his ship to retrieve Sean's family, and his human disguise wore off. Alarms blared, the base was surrounded by ships and Kriff as more approached, and attacks were happening all over the world. The attack had failed, and no one could understand why. The president received reports of people being abducted all over the world. People had experiments performed on them, and he could do nothing about it. He informed every GAIA base around the world, but they were all surrounded. The Kriff had made their play, and it seemed they had won. One of them climbed the pole the camera was on, and roared into it before tearing it apart.

THROUGH THE DARK AND DEATH, YOU SHINE
OUR WHOLE WORLD IS ON THE LINE

✧

22. Sins of the Father

THE ALARMS BLARED INTO THE EARLY SUNRISE, leaving no chance of sleep. The Kriff guarded the base, ensuring no humans or Nephilium were nearby. As far as the Kriff were concerned, they had secured the area. Many facilities and public places were like this across the world, with the Kriff having set up global prison camps overnight. Though they couldn't use the same biobugs the Nephilium used to build their structures, they were able to study and reverse-engineer them by analyzing the resonance towers, and so their camps were built in mere hours.

Many people were captured and put into these camps. They were locked up in cages or hooked up to machines for varying purposes. Those who could scream did so. Others tried fighting back, but were ultimately paralyzed, then abducted for experimentation. Some were returned from the ships to the ground, but they were forever changed somehow. Freedom was now a foreign concept to every part of the world.

John finally turned off the base's alarms, signaling surrender. He sat in a corner in his office, head in his hands, unable to handle the weight of defeat. Guilt tore at him, ripping him apart from the inside out and putting him back together again, only for the cycle to repeat. John wondered if his hubris had caused the plan to fail, but he didn't know for sure. All he knew was his son would be disappointed in him yet again, and as far as he knew, Sean didn't even know about the danger he had put him and Monica in. *How could I willingly send them out into danger? What's wrong with me?* These questions and many others bounced around in his brain.

Abigail tended to the wounded, doing the best she could, but several lives were lost as she tried. She saw all the death, the injuries, and the rapidly increasing body count. There was no need for autopsies. She knew how those people were killed. Her breathing turned shallow as she became dizzy. Defeat crawled into her mind, so she sat on a nearby bed and put her head into her hands.

"Hey, sis. Talk to me." Jake sat down next to her and placed his hand on her back, rubbing it gently.

Abigail sniffled as a tear fell down her face. "Look at this place. All these dead people I couldn't save. There was a patient in this bed whom I had become friends with. I promised to protect her, but I let her down. I let so many of them down," she cried, sobbing loudly. She buried her head in Jake's arms and held on to him.

"Abby, you can't save everyone. This isn't your fault. You can't do this to yourself. None of us were prepared for this," he soothed as he held Abigail, quietly falling apart inside himself. *What do we do now?* he thought.

Kyle sat across from the captured alien, watching it while it was unconscious. Impatience flooded his veins, making him slam his hands down on the table after a few minutes and waking the alien. "Oh, look at that. We have life," he said as he leaned forward in his chair, smiled, and brought his hands together. "Hi there. My name is Kyle Wills, and I'm going to be your interrogator today."

The Kriff stared at Kyle and blinked sideways, but didn't otherwise move or speak.

"Strong and silent type, huh? No problem. I'll get what I need out of you. It's just a matter of how difficult you make it for yourself," Kyle declared gently to the alien. "We're gonna start easy. What's your name?"

The alien looked around the room, then back at Kyle and blinked. "My name is Zanu," it spoke in a dark, raspy voice.

"I have to say, I wasn't expecting your mouth to open, let alone talk, and in English no less. I thought you'd talk to me in my head like all the other cool kids in space. Anyway, moving on. Why did our attack fail? Why did it work on your ship but none of the others?" Kyle demanded.

Zanu closed its eyes and took a deep breath. "We were exiled as bait. Your weapon gave us sufficient data to create a resistance. All ships were supplied with this upgrade except ours. We were sent to conclude."

"Conclude?" Kyle asked.

"It means to die," Zanu clarified.

Kyle glared at Zanu in exhausted confusion. "We tried the weapon once before, and it worked. Was that your ship too?"

"No. The incident you speak of is how we learned of your tactics. It allowed us to devise protection from your weapon. If your kind had not attacked that ship, then we would not have been aware of your plans." Zanu closed its eyes again and sighed. "I was against this and voted we simply leave your planet, as it has become too troublesome to occupy. But the newer generation of our kind declined this and mutinied. Several other leaders followed their example out of fear, deciding not only to stay on Earth, but to begin colonization."

"That brings me to my next question. Why are you so much taller than the rest?" asked Kyle.

"They are not organic lifeforms like me, but failed clones of failed clones. Essentially, they are what your people would call robots. Cold and calculative. Only a few of my organic kind remain, no more than six. The rest are bio-organic computers." Zanu's head drooped. "They were our biggest mistake."

Kyle deliberated briefly. "Alright, I'll bite. Why did you make the little guys?"

"We lost our ability to organically reproduce a few millennia ago from nuclear warfare. A solution was eventually proposed. We would endeavor to clone ourselves into a childlike state, so we could continue to grow and learn while maintaining what we already knew. The clones, as I said, were failures. Then, they began cloning themselves. Like us, they had no form of reproduction. We were able to isolate a portion of their code to control them for a short time. However, they discovered a way to override our controls.

"The technology you call artificial intelligence was an infant form of a severely failed Kriff clone. This was the one you captured in your year of 1947, along with me. It was studied for decades, making many improvements possible for your kind. Your AI evolved over time into what it is now. A dangerous slope that ultimately leads to laziness and overdependence, and, eventually, apathy and destruction. Your art and creativity have already been severely stifled by this process," Zanu finished.

Kyle considered what Zanu told him, perplexed by it, his eyes squinting and his brain pounding. It made no sense why a prisoner would be so cooperative, especially before any interrogation tactics were applied. "Okay, before I move on to my next question, why are you being so helpful? I expected more resistance. Don't get me wrong, I'm glad you're cooperating, but I can't help being curious."

"Your discovery of this knowledge is inevitable, and I will soon conclude. While my organic kind can breathe your air for a short while, it is not sustainable for long-term exposure. The newer generation does not have this flaw. They cannot be injured, do not need to breathe, and can self-repair. Furthermore, I was critically injured in the crash of my ship and the subsequent capture," said Zanu as it looked Kyle in the eyes. "I do not have long. We have been unable to stop them. Perhaps you can."

Kyle sighed, guilt setting in for holding Zanu, but he also refused to trust it yet. "Okay, next question. Why did you come to Earth in the forties?"

Zanu briefly tilted its head. "We have been studying your planet and helping it along since we observed your kind building pyramids. It fascinated us, and—"

"Hold on, wait. You're saying *humans* built the pyramids? That wasn't you guys?" Kyle asked as he raised his eyebrows, his eyes wide as saucers.

"No. Humanity built them, and it was these marvels that enthralled us so. We continued observing, and have been since then. After some time, we discovered humanity has a code in your DNA that we need to reproduce again. It is for this reason that I made deals with your world leaders. This allowed us to experiment on your kind and make them forget. You must understand that emotions are not something we possess, and it is therefore impossible for us to comprehend your concept of morality.

"It soon became our understanding that you found this cruel, but we were out of options. Our original race was dying, and after I conclude, only five more will remain. We tried to prevent our extinction, but created it instead. The only way to keep the newer generation under control was to minimize the damage by leading them into doing what they wanted," finished Zanu.

Kyle pondered briefly and stared at Zanu. "I heard you hated us because we're synthetic lifeforms, whatever that means. Can you elaborate on that?"

"Only the newer generation is disgusted by you. They were created by us, and so they view any race with superior creators as unnatural." Zanu paused momentarily. "It is true we thought ourselves superior to your kind. We wished to exploit this. However, you are advancing far too quickly to be worth the trouble."

Kyle scoffed. "Well, what a fascinating story. I wanna believe it, but for now, I'm just gonna keep it as evidence." Kyle looked at the camera in the top right of the room that recorded the entire encounter. "Oh, and I even wrote the good parts down. Impressive, right?" Kyle grinned, stood, and made his way to the door, but stopped and dropped his head when he got there. "For what it's worth, if you're telling the truth, I'm sorry. This is war, and in the words of my generation, you started it." Kyle rushed out of the room.

Zanu lowered its head and spoke to itself. "We create that which destroys us." It closed its eyes in reflection.

Sean, Darren, and Rebecca found living quarters, where they could quietly rest and decompress. Sean sat on the side of a bed, quietly going over ways to fight back, but his mind was too traumatized to think clearly. He lay back down on the bed in defeat with his hands over his eyes.

Kyle called Jake's phone and immediately got an answer. "Hey, Jake, it's done. Do you know where Sean and the others went? No, it's okay, I'll find them. Hey, wait. Would there be any bedrooms or something nearby? A place to lay low and recharge? Okay, that's what I thought. Thanks." Kyle ended the call and walked toward the living quarters Jake mentioned. A bright light appeared in front of him, and Echo appeared holding Amanda, Monica, and an older woman.

"Hi, Wheels," came the woman's voice as she hugged him.

"Uh, sorry, but who are you exactly?" asked Kyle.

The woman put her hands on her hips. "Come on. I haven't changed that much, my other son."

"Mrs. Caldwell," Kyle shouted in excitement, hugging her back. "Echo brought y'all here? Cool. Thank God you're safe. Follow me. I think Sean really needs to see you right now."

"Oh my God! Is he okay?" asked Whitney.

"Physically, yeah. We've suffered a major defeat, and it's eating at him, which is why he asked Echo to come pick you up. You'll be safe with us," Kyle answered.

"That was certainly disconcerting. Out of *nowhere*, there's this stranger in my house who I didn't hear come in, past a locked door no less. The next thing I know, there's this bright light and then I'm here. I thought I was dreaming." Whitney laughed and looked at Kyle with a hopeful grin on her face, which quickly faded. "I'm not dreaming, am I?"

"Afraid not," Kyle answered as they continued walking toward the living quarters. "We'll explain soon."

There was a knock on the door after some time. Sean, Rebecca, and Darren all looked at each other cautiously. "Maybe this is just wishful thinkin', but I don't think those things out there would knock," said Darren as he stood and opened the door, seeing Kyle standing there with an older woman behind him.

Monica ran off to explore, and Amanda chased her down. "Hey, Wheels," said Darren. "Glad you're alright. Come on in and tell us how the interrogation went." Kyle walked past Darren and sat next to Sean. "Pardon me, ma'am. I don't believe we've met." Darren offered his hand to Whitney. "Darren Morgan."

"Oh," said Whitney, grabbing Darren's hand and shaking it. "Whitney Caldwell. I'm Sean and Mandy's mother. It's a pleasure to meet you, sir." Whitney smiled. "May I come in, please?"

"Oh, absolutely. Sorry, we're all a little out of sorts right now." Darren moved aside so Whitney could come in.

"That's alright, thank you. Sean, honey?" Whitney called.

"Mom?" Sean called back as he quickly sat up. "Oh, thank God." His emotional floodgates flew open as he stood and jogged to his mother, embracing her in a tight hug. "I've missed you," he cried.

"Oh, sweetheart, I've missed you too," Whitney sobbed, tightening her grip on Sean. "I'm here. It's gonna be okay. I don't know what's going on, but it's gonna be okay. It will be because it has to be. I promise." Tears rolled down Whitney's cheeks as she looked at Kyle, motioning for him to join the hug. She raised a brow and pursed her lips when she saw Rebecca. "I'm sorry, honey, what's your name? How do you know Sean?" she asked, clinging to her son and his friend.

"Oh, um, I'm Becca. The cop is my dad, and I'm Sean's girlfriend," she answered shakily, followed by a brief pause. "This whole thing's been really hard," she quavered. A tear rolled down her face that she quickly wiped away.

"Come here, you need to be a part of this too. Come on, it's okay," she encouraged. "You too, Darren. Come on. No one be shy now."

Rebecca swiftly stood and joined them in the hug, holding on to Sean for dear life and resting her head on his shoulder. All of them grieved their defeat, but no one blamed themselves as much as Sean did. Rebecca rubbed Sean's back, making him fall apart more. Darren soon followed, holding on to Rebecca and Sean the most.

Whitney thought she needed to say something to try to lift their spirits. She felt it was her job, as though she was truly a mother to everyone. "We're all still here, and I'm grateful. We all should be. Focus on that. I don't really know what's going on, but I do know that you lost a battle. That doesn't mean you've lost the war. It just means you took a step back after taking two steps forward, which means you've still got one foot forward. That's how we need to look at this," she finished as they all cried, even Darren and Kyle.

John walked out of his office with a heavy sigh, walking down the stairs. His heart sank when he passed Jake as he walked, and they both stopped and looked at each other. "You were right," John admitted, his voice low. "It's all my fault. I never should have put them in harm's way. I'm so sorry, Jake." John looked down at the floor.

Jake kept his guard up. "I'm not the one you need to apologize to. They're in the first living quarters in the east wing. Now, if you'll excuse me, I have people to help Abby save. The ones *you* put in harm's way." Jake stormed away and headed back toward the medical wing where Abigail cared for the wounded.

John sighed again, deeper this time, and made his way to the living quarters. As he walked, he passed Amanda and Monica. "Mandy," he said, making Mandy turn and notice him.

"Daddy," Amanda shouted, her heart rising as she hugged her father. Monica held tightly on to Amanda's leg. "I'm so glad to see you and so scared. Please tell me what happened."

"I will, but we need to find your brother first. It's time I was honest and set things right, at least the best I can. Come on, walk with me," said John, and he put his arm around Amanda's back as they walked to the living quarters.

BLEEDING WOUNDS AND FRACTURED HEARTS
SAVE US FROM OUR BROKEN PARTS

✧

23. Trauma and Healing

Jake ran up to Abigail, who had her back to him with her hands on the table in front of her. Books and medical equipment sat conspicuously on the table. "Hey, sis. Sorry for the delay. I got distracted and ran into John, but I got those supplies you wanted," he said, placing the supplies on a nearby gurney.

Abigail remained silent, her hands trembling.

"Abby?" Jake asked. "Hey, are you—"

Abigail knocked everything off the table, beating on it as hard as she could.

"Abby! Abby, stop. Stop it," Jake said as he grabbed her.

Abigail broke away and looked Jake in the eyes, defeat written across her face. "None of them made it! I did the best I could, and it didn't matter," she yelled. She turned around and flipped over the table itself.

"Hey! Calm down." Jake gripped Abigail tightly so she couldn't pull away. "The table is innocent. We gotta stay calm right now and focus if we wanna stand any chance against these guys."

"There is no chance," Abigail shouted. "There's nothing we can do," she cried, lowering her voice in defeat.

"Okay, first, ow, my ear. Secondly, I think there is. We just need to regroup and figure it out. Wheels finished the interrogation a short while ago, and I was just about to head back there to listen to whatever he may have learned. You can come with me if you want. Okay?" Jake rubbed his sister's back and brought her in with a hug. Abigail's words registered in his brain, and he pushed away. "Wait, you said none of them made it? None? What about those four guys I was talking to? I couldn't have been gone for more than twenty minutes, tops."

"They fell asleep right after you left, and flatlined a few minutes later. Their injuries were more severe than I first believed. I failed them, Jake. It's all my fault," cried Abigail.

"No." Jake grabbed Abigail's face. "This was not your fault. You hear me? You did the best you could with what we knew. That's all anyone could ask of you. Screw anybody who says otherwise. I saw you taking care of these people with real care and diligence. Not for a paycheck, but because you wanted to save their lives."

Abigail sighed. "I know, Jake, but—"

"There's been colossal failures across the board, but they all stem from one person. He's the only one whose failure matters. This tragedy? It isn't on you. Now, since you're done here, come with me to go see the others. We need to regroup, and do our best to keep our heads above water. Alright? Can you do that for me?"

Abigail nodded silently and hugged him. "Thank you." *If only he could be like this all the time*, she thought.

John knocked on the door of the living quarters. "Sean, it's me. Can you please let me in, or come out here? I'd like to talk." John looked down at the floor, knowing he didn't deserve another chance, but hoped it was still possible.

The door gently opened as Whitney walked out and closed it behind her. "John?" Whitney's eyes widened, and she dried them with her sleeve, her mouth agape. "Oh my God," said Whitney as she ran to John and gripped him in a tight hug, letting go after a few seconds. "Come inside. We have a lot to talk about."

Amanda and Monica walked in after John. "Hi, Mom. Monica, say hi to Grandma, sweetie." She looked down at Monica's face, and it lit up.

"Hi, Granny," Monica beamed. She waved at Whitney several times before tackling her in a hug.

Whitney grabbed Monica tight. "My, how you've grown," she said with a smile, and looked up at Amanda. "I've always wanted to say that." She looked back at Monica. "It's so good to see you again."

"Mom, do we have anywhere for Monica to stay so she's not hearing too much?" asked Amanda. Sweat covered her palms, and her nerves were shot, threatening to crumble at the slightest touch. "I want her to stay innocent as long as possible, and I know Sean feels the same."

"Hey, sis," said Sean as he turned a corner. "Sorry, I couldn't help overhearing. Thin walls," he said, smiling at his sister. "I scoped this place out earlier before Mom got here and found a little side room. Monica can stay there. It's got a bed and even a window, so she can see the stars at night. Come on, I'll show you." Sean grabbed Amanda's hand, and she grabbed Monica's as they followed Sean to the small bedroom inside the living quarters.

Monica, stay here for now. Alright, sweetie?" asked Amanda. She gently shut the door and let out a breath of relief and fear, though she wasn't sure which she felt more of.

"Hey, Mandy, don't worry. We'll… figure something out," Sean said calmly, though he didn't believe what he said. Though he wouldn't admit it, all of his senses were hyper-aware. He saw no way out, but he still tried to put on the protective, composed mask for his family. It was a heavy burden to shoulder, caring for and protecting not only the family he built, but also the family he came from. Sean knew it was something his father was supposed to do, but he still took the reins anyway.

Amanda scoffed and shook her head. "I don't see how." She folded her arms and leaned her back against the closed door, shutting her eyes.

Sean's phone rang, making them both jump in fear. "Sorry, I thought I had it on vibrate. In retrospect, maybe setting it to Europe's The Final Countdown wasn't the best idea. In my defense, it was before all this started."

"Just answer the stupid phone." Amanda breathed a heavy sigh of frustration and walked back to the common area. When she got to the living quarters where everyone else sat, she took a seat near Whitney on the couch.

"Hey, Jake." Sean's hands and voice shook. "Okay, perfect. Everyone else is already here. Yeah, everyone. Dang, man, I'm sorry to hear. Be right there." Sean ended the call and walked to the door. He stood there for a moment, took a deep breath, and opened it.

Jake and Abigail came in quickly, and Jake shut the door. "Alright, Wheels. Let's hear what you've learned, my man."

Everyone sat in the common area, while Kyle stood and cleared his throat. His body shook and his blood ran warm. Kyle wasn't sure if he could handle all those eyes on him at once. Nausea set in as he looked around. "Be right back," he said with a smile, then walked over to the fridge. "Aha, we have Coke," he cheered with his arms raised. He popped the top and walked back to the center, taking a sip of the drink and putting it down. "Alright, everyone. Story time!" Kyle relayed the information he learned to everyone, becoming enthralled with telling the tale of his time with Zanu.

"Not that I'm not impressed, because I am. That's pretty solid work for a civilian. But all that, and you *still* didn't discover who the Channeler is?" asked Jake.

"The who what?" asked Kyle, leaning forward with his brow furrowed in confusion.

Jake threw his hands up. "Come on, man! You can't be serious. The guy who speaks for the aliens or whatever?"

"Oh, right. That guy. Damn it, how did I forget that?" Kyle gritted his teeth, walked to the fridge, and kicked it repeatedly.

"Hey, take it easy," said Jake. He walked toward Kyle as he continued beating on various inanimate objects. "There are too many people banging on things."

"Tell me about it," Darren muttered, shaking his head and remembering Sean beating on his car.

"Sorry," said Sean.

Darren looked at Sean and winked with a smile.

Jake grabbed Kyle and shook him. "Stop," he yelled as he looked around at everybody. "All of us need to stay calm, or we won't get anywhere. Darn it, when did I become the voice of reason around here? Abby, that's supposed to be you. Logical but nurturing, and tough under pressure, because you love saving people.

"Wheels, you're supposed to be the cool one, with all the car skills and the alien lore. You've done some amazing things with that brain of yours, so get it back in gear. We need those skills right now.

"Sean, the freaking *president* trusted you to help save humanity. We live in a computerized world, and you have a brain that can understand and even reprogram it. You could solve this, but your emotions are clouding your judgment. You're pissed, you're confused, you're hurting, and I know it's tough for you right now. It's tough for everyone, so push past your emotions and think logically. Think! Focus on how they attacked us first.

"Oh, and John?" Jake walked over to John and stuck a finger in his face. "You're a piece of trash, putting Sean and Monica in danger. Who does that to his own family? I got nothing positive to say about you." Jake walked away and sat on a velvety sofa. "The rest of you are great too. I'm just… I don't know. I'm just done. I can't do this all by myself. I got no jokes, no sarcasm, no sass. I'm all out."

"There's something else." Kyle kept his eyes down as he spoke. "I left something out from the interrogation because I didn't want to put anyone on the spot." Kyle folded his arms as he weighed his options. He didn't want to incur John's wrath or tear Sean's family apart, but he also knew he had to share what he learned. Kyle took a deep breath and looked over at Sean, making him feel safe. "Zanu said something to me. He, it, whatever, told me the reason our attack didn't work is because they found a way to resist it, and how they learned to do this... was from the first attack on one of their ships, when Sean went to get Monica. They learned from the attack and built a way to resist it."

"What about the ship that I saw fall? I went down there and found bodies. That's where I got Zanu from," Jake asked in confusion. He knew what he saw, but he still reviewed it mentally.

"Because they were bait," said Kyle. "Zanu told me its ship was exiled. That's why it was so easy to capture Zanu and the others, dead and alive. Their purpose was to make us think we had a chance. Instead, we did exactly what they wanted us to do." Kyle looked back at the floor and sniffled. He shook his head, his blood boiling hot. "It's John's fault. It's all John's damn fault," he shouted.

"Hey, maybe keep it down a little, cowboy," said Darren. "So you're sayin' these things knew what our plan of attack was because of John's little test run, right?" Darren walked over to John and stood in front of him, arms folded.

"That's the gist, yeah," said Kyle.

Darren smiled at John and unfolded his arms. "Alright. Just wanted to be sure," he said calmly, still smiling and dusting off John's shoulders. The two men smiled at each other briefly, and Darren punched him in the face with all the strength he could muster. "You know what that's for, you sack of shit."

"Daddy," Rebecca called, covering her mouth with her hands.

"Darren," yelled Abigail at the same time, unsure if she should stay where she was or run to pull Darren back. Deep down, she knew John deserved it, but it wasn't the time or place.

"John," Whitney cried out in concern for her husband, though she was more disgusted by what he did to Sean and Monica.

Jake observed without saying anything, unsure of what to do or say. Instead, he decided to let the situation play out before him, his mouth agape and eyebrows raised. *Since when am I speechless?* he thought.

Sean looked up and said nothing, rage seething in his veins. This wasn't like the anger he felt at his dad growing up. This was something darker—an incurable darkness creeping through every fiber of his being. He clenched his fists, doing his best to contain his anger, but it was clear on his face. His face showed his feelings of betrayal and pain transforming into a violent fire.

Sean stood calmly as everyone turned their heads toward him and watched him silently walk to the door. He took a deep breath and opened the door, closing it gently behind him. For a moment, he reflected on how he had changed. In his younger days, he would have tackled his father for what he did, and he was sure he would have beaten him to a pulp. This new version of him, though, had a healthier outlook, a better grasp of his emotions, and the situation at large.

His anger ran cold, and it didn't make him feel reactive. Normally, he would argue with his father, but as far as he was concerned, John no longer filled the role. Darren's advice proved more useful than expected. Part of an idea formed in Sean's mind, and he needed to see Zanu for it to come to fruition, so he walked around, looking for GAIA agents.

Winona saw Sean take something from someone behind a corner she couldn't see behind. Curious, she decided to slowly approach him. Sean walked toward her, so she pretended to check the case files in her hands.

"Hey, excuse me?" asked Sean, clasped his hands together.

"Sir?" asked Winona.

"Do you know where the captured alien is?" asked Sean, his gears turning.

Winona chuckled. "You're gonna need to be more specific." She turned to walk away, but stopped and turned around. "Hey, I remember you," she said with a grin on her face. "Sorry for being so rough before. We had to keep our FBI cover active. It was a lot of pressure, and they wanted you intimidated so you'd do what we asked. You did a great job."

Sean thought hard, but couldn't place who this woman was, though she did seem somewhat familiar. "I'm sorry, but I don't remember you," he said softly.

"Okay, how about this?" She cleared her throat and pretended to point a gun at Sean. "Someone important wants to see you! Special Agent—"

"Winona Reyes," Sean finished in surprise. "That was such a weird day. You've been a GAIA agent all this time, huh?"

"Yep," she replied with a wide grin. "Anyway, who's this captured fella you're looking for?"

"Its name is Zanu, one of the Kriff. A leader. I have some questions for it." *And a plan*, Sean thought.

"Oh, our celebrity. That's the one your friend Kyle was talking to, yeah?" Winona put her arm around Sean's neck. "Come with me, and hurry. I'm afraid you won't have long."

Sean walked with Winona, mentally developing his plan until they reached the room. She allowed Sean into the room and closed the door, guarding it from the outside.

As Sean walked into the room, he took a deep breath and sat on the chair across from Zanu, whose breath appeared to be labored. Details of the plan clicked into place in his mind. "Hey, I need to talk to you. Can you manage that, please?" Sean asked.

Zanu looked up at Sean silently at first, then leaned forward. "Ask," it said with a weak voice.

"Tell me who the Channeler is," Sean demanded.

Zanu spoke slowly. "The one you call the Channeler is in your town of Babylon, New York. He is a secondary threat, and does not truly channel us. The newer generation have placed a chip in his mind. They speak to him through it," Zanu clarified.

"Alright, thank you. I honestly didn't expect you to be so…" Sean pretended to struggle finding the words, clasping his hands together.

"Cooperative," Zanu repeated from Kyle.

"Yeah. Look, the guy who performed your interrogation earlier told me you're struggling because of our atmosphere. What do you normally breathe?" asked Sean.

Zanu leaned back in its chair. "Like you, we once breathed oxygen and expelled carbon dioxide. Now, we need argon gas to survive. More than the zero point nine percent in your atmosphere. It is one of many changes we have endured since our nuclear fallout," it answered coldly.

Sean covertly opened his hands as Zanu was talking and wrote down what Zanu told him, using the pen and paper Kyle had left behind. "Okay, thank you. One more thing. You told Wheels these things are like robots, correct? That they're essentially computers?"

Zanu closed its eyes and nodded. "Yes. Though far ahead of current human computing prowess, they function as a technological version of our race." Zanu looked down at the desk in front of it.

"Interesting. Are they connected to each other in any way?"

"They share a semblance of a hive mind, like your internet networks. Any programming changes that happen to one also happen to the rest."

"Can they be infected?"

Zanu started to reply, but abruptly convulsed as it screeched, causing Sean to cover his ears. Its mouth opened inhumanly wide as its pain overtook it. It violently flailed about from side to side, falling on the table in front of him.

Sean swiftly stood and stepped back, his eyes wide and his eyebrows raised, with his mouth agape. Zanu's once lively face looked up at Sean with enormous eyes and a gaping mouth, its head contorted.

Winona came barreling into the room. "Sean? What the hell?" She saw Zanu's lying there seemingly lifeless on the table, its horrific face looking up at her. "What did you do?" she asked as she ran over to the alien and pried it back up, but it fell back down. Rage flowed through her as she looked over at Sean with a look of confusion on her face. "What the hell did you do?" she shouted.

Sean grinned wide. "It worked."

NOW THANKS TO YOU, WE HAVE A CHANCE
AND SO WE TAKE OUR FINAL STANCE

✧

24. Son of Anarchy

WINONA PANICKED, UNSURE HOW TO DEAL with the situation. "You have ten seconds to explain," she shouted as she grabbed her gun and pointed it at Sean. "Talk. Now."

"Whoa, hold on. No need for that," said Sean, putting his hands up. "I have this friend. I can explain, but I'm gonna need you to come with me. Do you promise to listen and not bring any harm to my friends or family?"

Winona sighed and relaxed, reluctantly putting her gun away. "Fine, but this better be good, Caldwell. We just lost an important asset in this war, so for your sake, I hope this was worth it."

Sean smiled, knowing Winona wouldn't understand his plan. "Just come with me," he said as they made their way to the living quarters upstairs.

John stood outside the room, head in his hands, hiding his tears and muffling his quiet sobbing. *I thought I could do it*, he thought. *Sean's never going to want me now. If I could go back in time and change it, I would. He deserves so much better.*

"Dad." Sean snapped John back to his thoughts, getting John's attention and watching him wipe his face with his sleeve. "Look, what you did was awful, but it gave me an idea. Jake made it click. Your mind was in the right place, even if your heart wasn't."

John looked around, then back at Sean. "I'm not following."

Sean took a moment to mentally prepare himself before he spoke. "You played out of a different book to get results, and yeah, it failed and caused major issues, but it got me thinking that maybe crazy ideas are what we need. Just come with me, and I'll explain everything."

Winona followed Sean and John inside and closed the door behind her. "Attention, everyone," she yelled. "I'm Special Agent Winona Reyes. The director's son has something he would like to share." *It better be good, too, or I'm gonna kill him*, she thought. "I need all of you to sit down, shut up, and keep your hands to yourselves. If any fights break out, I start breaking off limbs. If anyone speaks without permission, I start stapling mouths shut, so I hope we all understand each other. Sean, the floor is yours. Don't waste my time."

Sean cleared his throat and stood in the center of the room, but there was someone missing. He tapped his foot and waved at everyone, stalling for time, but he wouldn't wait forever. Finally, Echo appeared beside him in his true form.

Winona unholstered her gun and fired at Echo, but he stopped the bullet with his mind, holding it in midair for a moment before letting it fall to the floor. "Please do not repeat that attempt," he thoughtspoke. "I am a friend to you, but this can change."

"Agent Reyes, he's telling the truth. Put the gun away. Now," growled John.

Winona did as she was asked. "Apologies, sir. I wasn't made aware of this. Friend of yours?" she asked shakily.

"Friend of Sean's, actually," John clarified.

"He's one of the Nephilium," said Sean. "In short, they're not the villains here. Zanu's kind are behind this, the Kriff in the interrogation room. My friend here has been helping us for a while. We call him Echo."

Sean turned back to look at everyone. "Anyway, getting back to the crux of the issue, I was communicating with him telepathically before my visit with Zanu." Sean stopped and looked at Winona. "By the way, it isn't dead. Just infected," he clarified, then looked back at the others. "I use the term loosely. It may have appeared otherwise to Agent Reyes here, but the infection is reprogramming its biology as we speak to accept oxygen instead of argon, which is what they naturally breathe. Zanu has been giving us valuable intel, so I gave it something in return. I snuck a little something extra in there too.

"The first question is probably 'how,' so let me explain. Before I nearly bumped into Agent Reyes here, Echo stopped by and gave me a new biobug he developed. I released the bug while Zanu was talking so Zanu wouldn't notice. The next question is 'why,' and it's simple. I think I found a weakness. Jake gave me the idea. The only problem is, I don't know if it would work on the smaller ones, so Echo had a suggestion.

"Our resonance tower is still standing. We can repurpose it with a new batch of biobugs, whose purpose will be to infect the enemy and shut them down the same way they were shutting us down. I remembered Jake mentioning they had shields, so the first thing our new biobugs will do is take those down. Then we can fire on them again as the biobugs continue working. I thought about it and realized we were going about this all wrong. They infected us. So, let's infect them."

Darren grinned and nodded in silence, his chest thrust out.

"All this time, we've been trying to *prevent* the virus, when we could've been using it instead. Zanu told me the little guys are basically computers. Then I remembered something a professor of mine talked about that he called the Foster Principle. He said if it's computerized, then it can be hacked, and if it can be hacked, then it will be.

"Echo and his people deactivated the viruses not too long ago, and we forgot about them. I asked him if it would be possible to make more, but with a new purpose, which would be to shut down the smaller Kriff and spread to any others nearby. Essentially, the same thing they did to us, we do to them." Sean took a breath to compose himself. "Any questions? Now's the time."

"I got one," said Darren. "It's a good plan, son, but how the heck are we gonna get these things infected if we can't even go outside?"

"Great question," said Sean. "We can't open the door and expect a warm welcome, but unlike us, Echo doesn't need doors. He can teleport to and from his ship at will, and so can I with this teleporter on my wrist. Once the new biobugs are ready, I'll accompany Echo to his ship, and we'll jump to the resonance tower from there. Then, we'll reprogram it with the new biobugs and use it like a satellite.

"Remember, all this started from one of these things jumping inside one of our satellites, and that was only one. We'll be releasing *hundreds*." Sean smiled and folded his arms, proud of his plan. "We think one of them will investigate, which should trigger the infection."

"It's a good plan, buddy, but how do you know this will work?" asked Whitney. "There's no guarantee, and if it fails, then what?"

Sean sighed. "I don't know, Mom. I'm just going with the only option we have right now. All I can do is hope and have faith. You taught me that."

"I like it. How did you come up with this?" asked Rebecca.

"After I remembered the Foster Principle, I thought about something else the professor always says at the end of his class. It's a quote about how we only have two modes, complacency and panic. James R. Schlesinger said it, and it essentially means we're either active or reactive. So I got to thinking, what if we acted somewhere in the middle? We keep waiting for them to make the next move, but screw it. Let's make it ourselves."

"Fantastic work, Sean, but how do we infect the rest globally? Stopping the ones here is a beginning, but we need something long-term," Abigail reminded him.

"If what Zanu told me is true, then they're all on the same network. So, if we infect one…" he started, pausing so someone else could finish.

"We infect them all," answered Kyle. "Dude, that's genius," he said with a grin. "When are we doing this?"

"As soon as the new batch of biobugs are ready." Sean unfolded his arms. "Listen, what my dad did was terrible, especially putting Monica in danger." He looked at John and saw him look away. "It's unforgivable. Still, he was thinking outside the box.

Jake was right about my emotions clouding my thinking. When I started thinking logically about how they attacked us, it clicked for me. Thank you, Jake."

"So, an antivirus," said Jake.

"Exactly." Sean snapped his fingers and pointed at Jake.

"Please tell me you know who the Channeler is now," Jake uttered hopefully.

"No, but I do have an idea of where." Sean stopped and looked at Darren. "He's based somewhere in Babylon, New York."

"Son of a gun," Darren blurted out. "Did you get a name?"

Sean sighed. "No, sir. I'm sorry. I wasn't thinking about names or specifics, just the plan. Besides, if this works, then it won't matter, because he won't have anyone telling him what to say anymore. Turns out he's not actually channeling anybody. He's got an implant that allows the Kriff to speak to him, and he repeats what they say. I guess it's the same thing, but at least he's no clairvoyant."

"Tell you what, I'll go check out this Channeler guy once we're all done here. That way, we don't have any loose ends," said Jake.

"Alright, but only when we're sure the threat is over," Sean agreed. "Echo, how much longer on those biobugs?"

"Calculating." Echo paused and closed his eyes for a moment. "They should be completed within the next twenty minutes."

"Okay, great. Have you told your people to release them across the globe?" asked Sean.

"Affirmative. They have been provided with all necessary instructions," Echo thoughtspoke.

"The Nephilium will be spreading this at other GAIA bases too. We want to cover all of them. Let's not leave anything to chance. Once the shields are down, I'll snipe one to test it. They'll be on me like cockroaches, so be ready," Sean warned. "I've also heard of their global prison camps, so we need to coordinate with the other bases to attack those and set people free. I'm not leaving anyone behind."

John slowly walked forward until he was behind Sean and put his hand on his back. "Everyone, I know what I did was beyond the pale. All I can say is I'm sorry. To Sean, Monica, Mandy, and the rest of you. I never should have put any of them in danger. I was being reckless, not thinking about my family, only results." He turned to Sean. "Sean, I'm so proud of you. Despite doing so many things on your own, you still grew up to be an amazing, resilient man. I couldn't have asked for a better son. I'm so sorry for what I did, and I hope that, in time, you can forgive me. I'm sorry to everyone," he said, looking around. "I left GAIA earlier this year, but someone filed a report about extraterrestrial activity. They demanded I come back." John sighed. "Maybe it would have been better if I had just said no."

"Dad, thank you for the apology, but I'm going to need time for forgiveness. That's something you work for and earn. That takes time, but time by itself won't do anything. You have to commit to changed behavior. Commit to our family the way you did to GAIA. For what it's worth, I don't think saying no would have been better. I think we're all where we're supposed to be, and we need to focus on moving forward. I'm ready to fight by your side, and I'll have your back, but once this is over, don't expect all to be forgiven."

John nodded silently in understanding, sitting on a nearby couch and putting his head back in his hands.

Whitney moved toward John and rubbed his back.

"Everyone, get ready. Retrieve your weapons and gear. Resume your posts from before," Sean announced. "I want this wrapped up within twenty-four hours. Any bathroom breaks, snacks, or drinks you need, get them now. Once we start, there will be no turning back until we breach the victory of dawn."

John clapped for his son, and everyone else gradually joined in. "Genius ideas, Sean. What do you need from me?"

"Same as before, but with slight alterations. Since the enemy has made their presence known globally, it'll be more difficult not to alert the military. Becca said President Matthews used a cover story, but that won't hold up anymore. We need to deploy this virus fast before more get hurt. I'm sure there have been many casualties already. I'm counting on you, Dad." Sean stopped briefly, his eyes narrowed. "Are there any agents left here?"

"Besides Agent Reyes, I believe we have eight more. We lost a lot of them in the attack, buddy." John looked at Sean with sorrow in his eyes.

"That's just gonna have to work, then," Sean resolved. Silence lingered for a moment until he decided to admit his own issues. "There are a couple more things," he said, drawing back everyone's attention. "Not long after this whole thing started, my doctor… he found something. He thinks I might…" Sean struggled with the words, unsure of what to say and how to say it.

"He believes Sean may have a growing mass in the center of his brain," John revealed as he looked up at Sean. "I was there that day, Sean, and I heard every word. I'm the one who asked Dr. Connors to look at you, and the reason the president recruited you to GAIA to show you everything. I heard what you said about me to Dr. Connors, and I didn't blame you. I still don't. I wanted to make myself known to you, but once those GAIA agents came in, it ruined my chance." John shook his head. "It didn't sound like you were ready anyway."

Sean's folded arms dropped to his side. Confusion overtook his mind as vulnerability and betrayal set in. "I guess I understand," he said, focusing his attention again. "There's something else.

"It hasn't happened for a while, but there were a couple times I was sure I was seeing Clarissa. I heard her voice, and even felt her touch. It's happened only twice, and not since. She had a blueish glow about her, and the second time I saw her, there was something in the sky that darted away. After that, she was gone.

"I've been telling myself it was a trick by the aliens, mostly because ignorance is bliss. Once this is over, I want to get checked again, because there's a possibility I was seeing things."

"It's also possible you suffered a sporadic hallucination brought on by anxiety or stress," Abigail suggested. She saw Sean's confused face and stood. "It's known as a tactile hallucination. It could be a serious medical condition, yes, but let's also factor in the pressure of the situation. When did this first occur?"

"Uh, I was about to leave to see Becca and Mr. Morgan. I wasn't sure about going," Sean admitted.

"First of all, just call me Darren, son. Secondly, it's nothin' to beat yourself up about. No one can be sure of anythin', but you came anyway. I'm proud of you for all you've done."

As gratefulness for Darren's approval set in, Sean noticed he had become more like a father to him than John. Guilt, comfort, safety, and relief all flooded his nervous system.

"What about the second time?" asked Abigail, writing notes on a clipboard.

"I was in a restaurant's parking lot, preparing to call Mandy and make up for my mistakes." Sean looked down at the floor. "I hadn't talked to my daughter in years. Not since Clarissa's funeral. I wanted to make things right, and it scared me."

Amanda knew how difficult that conversation was for him. "Sean, I know you were scared, but you did the right thing. That took a lot of courage. Despite everything, Monica's safe with you now. You need to focus less on your mistakes and more on what you did right."

John's head snapped up, taking in Amanda's advice.

"I'd like to accompany you to your appointment. It would benefit you to receive a second opinion. I have noticed that, in both incidents, you were nervous and highly stressed," said Abigail.

"I gotta ask, Sean. Why were you helping Zanu? Isn't it the enemy?" asked Rebecca.

"Because," Sean started with a smile, "like Mark Twain said, 'the only sure way to destroy your enemy—"

"is to make him your friend,'" Abigail finished. "I'm surprised to find someone else who values literature," she said with a smile. "Now I'm even more interested in a brain scan."

"I work in computer software, but my free time has always been spent on literature. I thought about writing a book, and I had great ideas. But every time I tried writing something, I would get intimidated and lose all motivation. So I read a lot instead. Maybe one day I can finally get a book off the ground," Sean said hopefully.

"You'll get there. It takes repeated effort and persistence. It can be tempting to quit, but something people don't often discuss is how once you start writing and get in the groove, it can be challenging to stop. If you don't, then the execution of your ideas will suffer. It's all about balance," Abigail said with a smile.

"Sounds like you're talking from experience," said Sean.

Abigail shrugged. "I am. After reading and writing so many reports, I wanted to write a story of my own. It never got anywhere, but it's out there."

"What's it called?" asked Rebecca.

"I called it '*The Adventures of Bailey Robin*.' It's a romance and drama novel. I can send you the link and premise once everything is over," Abigail replied.

Rebecca nodded. "Sure, sounds great."

"Alright, everyone. I've held you up long enough. It's been fifteen minutes already, so start getting ready and be prepared. I know it's a meticulous plan, but it has to work. So, you know, uh, class dismissed and all," said Sean, making everyone chuckle.

It took approximately twenty minutes for everyone to prepare. Once they were ready, they all gathered in the common area of the living quarters.

"Mandy, why don't you join me and Abby in the communications center? We could use the extra hands. What do you say?" asked Rebecca.

"Oh, I'd love to, but I can't leave Monica's side. I need to make sure she stays safe. But I will quickly visit the armory to secure a weapon. Be right back," said Amanda as she swiftly stood and walked out, following the signs to the armory.

"We grew up playing paintball and other such stuff, so despite her fear, she's having the time of her life," Sean said with a smile.

"Well, I don't know about the rest of y'all, but I'm tired of being holed up in Hotel California," said Kyle.

Sean grinned and looked over at Kyle. "Wouldn't it be Hotel Georgia?"

Kyle stared at him silently for a few seconds. "Shut up."

"Alright, Sean. While Mandy's arming herself, you're calling the shots," said John. "Tell everyone where you want us and what you need us to do. You can do this."

"Right," Sean said nervously. "Dad, I want you in your office performing administrative tasks on your computer that only you can do. See if you can get those turrets back online. Keep an eye in the sky. Let us know when something comes our way."

"Deal," said John as he stood and left.

"I want Kyle, Darren, and Jake with me on assault. Jake, retrieve whatever GAIA agents you can find. Agent Reyes, please accompany him," said Sean. "Join him on the assault team after."

"Yes, sir," Winona said. "Come on, Warren. We don't have all day," she said with annoyance.

"Yeah, yeah, I'm coming. Sheesh. You know, have I ever told you that you're the pushiest partner ever?" asked Jake.

Winona sighed in frustration. "Yes, many times. Now let's go," she shouted, dragging Jake into the hallway by one of his ears.

"Ow, ow, not the ear, not the ear," Jake yelled as she pulled him outside.

"Abby, I want you and Becca back on comms. Keep President Matthews updated, and stall the military as long as possible. He may not listen, but we've gotta try," said Sean.

Abigail and Rebecca stood and headed for the door. Rebecca turned around and caught Sean's eye from the entrance. "I love you," she mouthed.

Sean put his hand on his heart and motioned to her, then turned his head back to the assault team. As he opened his mouth, Amanda walked back in.

"Oh, sorry. Am I interrupting? I'll be quick. I'll be protecting Monica from outside her door," said Amanda, walking to Monica's room and positioning herself in front of it, "ensuring her safety. I'll occasionally peek into the room to make sure she's still safe. At no point will I falter or lay down my weapon. I will not fail on this day of battle. I will help guide us to victory by—"

"Mandy," Sean shouted. "We get it," he said, talking more quietly. "Just… talk less. No matter what happens, I want you to defend Monica like you always have."

Amanda nodded and cocked the assault rifle as she stood resolute.

John abruptly came back into the room holding a small box. "Sorry to interrupt, but we can't always rely on cellphones. We need to be in constant contact, so I brought communicators for everyone. I've already got one in, and I gave one to Jake and Reyes on my way back. These will provide clearer and immutable communication across the board." He took the lid off the box, took two comms out, and stood back. "Everybody grab one. It goes in your ear like a Bluetooth earpiece. Doesn't matter which ear. They won't fall out unless manually deactivated, and you won't hear yourselves on them. Just think of who you want to speak to, and the channel will automatically adjust.

"If no one person is in mind, you'll be heard by everyone, which we often refer to as the Collective," John explained, turning his gaze to Sean. "Let's change the world, buddy." He swiftly walked back out of the room and toward Rebecca and Abigail to give each of them an earpiece.

"What about me, Sean?" asked Whitney. "I'm your mother, so my job is to protect you. Give me a gun," she commanded.

"Mom, no. I want you to be safe," begged Sean.

"Sean Tiberius Caldwell, I brought you into this world, and if anything or *anyone* is gonna take you out of it, it will be me. You may be in your thirties, but I'm still your mother. Your safety is the most important thing," Whitney said firmly.

"Mom, my full name? Really? I'm trying to keep you safe," said Sean.

"Oh, I know you are, sweetheart, but you'll always be my baby." Whitney placed both hands on her heart and made a begging face. "How would you feel if Monica asked you not to go?"

"That's different, I'm—" Sean began.

"You're *what*, Sean? A *man*? I raised you to know women are just as capable as men, young man," Whitney finished, leaving Sean's mouth agape.

Sean brought his hands together like he was about to pray. "Mom, please stay here safely with Mandy and Monica. I don't wanna worry about you while I'm out there," he said, louder than he meant to.

Darren and Kyle watched with smiles on their faces.

"It's funny when it's not happening to me," said Kyle.

Whitney turned to Kyle. "Oh, would you like it to be you? I got enough to go around, buddy."

"No, ma'am," said Kyle, straightening his posture and looking away.

Sean facepalmed and dragged his hand down his face.

"Sean, I'm already going to be worrying about you. You said we can't let our emotions cloud our judgment. You and Mandy are my kids, so it's my job to protect you both. Besides, you're not the only one who can make their own decisions. I can do whatever I darn well please, and I don't need anyone's permission. You know your father fears me," said Whitney, smiling.

"Okay, let's try this. Coordinate with Dad. See if you can help get the turrets on top of the building to work. They'll fire on designated targets on their own, but human guidance for one of them would help. Is that meeting you halfway, Mom?" asked Sean.

Whitney smiled. "I'm proud of you. You learned compromise. I promise to be safe. Just because I'm going out there doesn't mean I'm stupid."

Sean sighed in defeat. "Everyone, grab an earpiece and put it in. Make use of them."

As everyone put in an earpiece, they discovered the earpieces adhered to their ears and glowed. "Fancy," said Darren.

"It gets even better," John said through his communicator. "These earpieces will project a small energy field to generate a shield around you like the Kriff are using, only not quite as advanced. They'll beep when your shields are low, so if you hear beeping, get down and hide until they recharge. It won't protect you forever. Oh, and Whitney?"

"Yes, John?"

"Kick some ass, baby."

"Man, and I thought only bad guys got the cool stuff," Kyle said with a grin as he played with the earpiece.

Sean loudly cleared his throat after everyone had an earpiece in, and it echoed in everyone's ears due to their proximity. "Sorry," he said, which echoed again. He walked out into the hallway and headed toward the armory. "Alright, testing. One, two, three, test—"

"Sean, it works, so stop with the testing nonsense. It was annoying enough when we were kids," Amanda demanded.

"Ignoring that," Sean said in a sing-song voice with a roll of his eyes. "I want the assault team with me in the armory. It's close enough to the exit so we can resume our positions. I'll be up in the resonance tower instead of where I was before. Let's try to keep the channel clear until it's time to fight. When I give the signal, I want everyone ready. Acknowledge copy."

Each of them responded one by one. He was determined, and despite his terror, he felt like a leader for the first time in his life, like he was meant for bigger things. When it was over, he wasn't sure if he could return to his mundane life from before. Everything seemed too interesting and surreal to abandon.

Echo soon appeared beside Sean in the armory. "Sean Caldwell, I have come to retrieve you and to present you with an inquiry."

"Oh? You have a question? Ask," Sean encouraged.

Echo's eyes went through every variation of color in under five seconds. "Apologies. This happens when our kind becomes nervous."

Sean smiled at Echo. "You've got nothing to be nervous about. You are my friend, now and always."

Echo and Sean teleported onto Echo's craft, and he turned to face Sean. "Our council wishes me to ask if you would accept being our ambassador to humanity, the human voice for our people. We have only ever done this with one other race, one which no longer exists. I am given to understand the words to use here are, 'What do you say?'"

Sean smiled wide, and although his nerves felt like glass, respect formed in his heart. He exhaled in relief and smiled. "Echo, buddy, I'd be honored." Sean stuck out his hand. "Here, shake it. It's a human bond of agreement."

Echo took Sean's extended hand and shook it. "What does it mean?"

"It means our friendship is and will always be an unbreakable bond. I'll be your ambassador, but I will always be your friend before anything else," answered Sean. He broke away from the handshake and gestured to the controls. "Shall we?"

Echo's eyes shifted to a bright gold. "We shall."

FINALLY, A STAR RETRACTS
IN THE STORM, THE THUNDER CRACKS

✧

25. The Final Countdown

Sean grinned as he turned to face Echo. "Let's deploy those biobugs. Remember, they also need to disable the Kriff's weapons."

"Understood, friend Sean. Unleashing swarm." Echo pushed a few buttons and touched his hand to a pad in the ship. They both witnessed the swarm of fresh biobugs as it flew toward the resonance tower.

"Alright, here I go." Sean pressed the teleporter on his wrist, transporting him to the top of the resonance tower. The swarm flew toward him, rapidly modifying the tower into a satellite while he watched from a solid part of the tower.

One of the Kriff noticed Sean's presence and ran toward him. Sean noticed the lights of its shields dissipating until the alien no longer had any. It rushed toward Sean, planning to jump the tower, but it never made it off the ground. Sean's movements were swift as he picked up his sniper and shot it between the eyes, making it fall where it stood.

All the Kriff converged on the top of the tower near Sean. They drew their weapons and fired, but he was well hidden, and his shields protected him. "Green light, people, green light," he said over comms. "Prepare to attack. It worked! I repeat, it worked," he raved as he continued sniping the enemy, ducking whenever his shields beeped.

The assault team came charging out of the armory and began their attack. Darren charged in with his shotgun, blasting its powerful energy into as many Kriff as he could. "Man, plasma sounds great in the mornin'."

Kyle ran toward Sean, motioning with his head for him to duck and cover.

Sean, still on the tower, pressed the teleporter on his wrist and was instantly transported back onto Echo's ship. "Hey," he said.

Echo waved. "A clever decision. It would displease me if you were vaporized," he thoughtspoke.

"Oh, I was made for this." Kyle fired his rocket launcher and accidentally pressed another button without realizing it, causing the rockets to split off and hit each Kriff in the crowd, one by one. Each of them blew up accordingly. "Cool! I don't know what the hell I just did, but it was awesome," he said with a grin. "Woo!"

Jake fired his energy weapon in every direction as the enemy continuously tried flanking him. "Nope," he said as he shot one to the left. "Nah-uh," he said as he shot another to the right. "Not today, sport," he said as he shot behind him, quipping every time he shot one.

Winona fired her medium-range precision weapon, hitting each of her targets in the head and watching them fall. "You know what, Warren? I'm in such a good mood right now, I don't even care about how much of a child you're being."

"Yeah, that's because you're shooting things," said Jake.

Winona shot a couple more. "Would you like to be next?"

"Uh, no. I'm good," Jake replied.

Everyone came under fire, but they were all clever enough to duck down and hide until their shields recharged. All eight GAIA agents emerged from the armory with varying weapons, each of them choosing a group to take on and bringing them down. A couple of agents were almost overwhelmed, but they continued fighting. Darren and Kyle also came under heavy fire, but their shields held up.

Sean teleported back to the tower after the team had the aliens' attention, sniping a few in each group that the agents fought in. "Booyah!"

"John, I'm at the turrets. How do I operate these things?" asked Whitney as she looked at the controls, confused.

"Working on it," John replied. "See that red light on the front? Once I get these online, that'll turn green. When that happens, grab the handles. You should notice buttons underneath. Hit the big ones to fire. The button on the left fires the one on the left, and same deal for the right. Give me about two minutes, and I should have the system up."

"Okay, but hurry up. Our son is down there, and I told him I can do this. Don't make me a liar. You've already put him in danger enough as it is. Here's a chance to partially redeem yourself," Whitney replied.

John groaned. "Yes, dear, I know. I'm trying, okay? Look, when this is all over, how about you, me, and the kids go out for a nice dinner and—" he started.

"Not the time, John," Whitney shouted back.

"Okay, sorry. Jeez. Alright, system's up. Is the light green?" John checked the monitors for the status of the turrets.

"No, not yet," Whitney replied, fidgeting with the controls.

"Come on, what am I doing wrong?" John said in frustration.

"Did you try turning it off and on again?" Whitney asked.

John was silent for a moment and closed his eyes. *She can't be serious*, he thought. "Babe, this isn't like a regular computer. It's got all these advanced microsystems and nodes. They each need special care, and—" John noticed the software disconnect briefly, after which it abruptly came back on. His eyebrows raised. "Well, hallelujah."

"Okay, I unplugged it and plugged it back in. I think it's… yes! I just saw it turn green," said Whitney. "Grabbing the handles now," she said as she did her best to point the turret down at the enemy. "Good Lord, this thing is heavy."

"Yeah, I know. It's a design I inherited, and I haven't had the time to invest in improving, but I will once this is over. Anyway, I've programmed the turret systems to target the Kriff specifically, so the shots it fires should go around anyone or anything not fitting their description. Still, be careful where you fire."

"Got it," Whitney said back. She pressed the buttons and fired, taking out several Kriff on the battlefield. "I think I'm getting the hang of it," she yelled over the turret fire.

"Yep, sounds like it," John said, wincing from the noise.

"Alright, Abby, what should we do?" asked Rebecca.

"Start off by calling President Matthews. We need to inform him of the plan and stall the military until we're ready for them," Abigail answered.

Rebecca thought for a moment. "Wouldn't they be useful, though? I mean, the more fighters we have, the merrier, right?"

"In theory, yes, but if they begin attacking in other parts of the world before we're ready, then they'll get torn apart, and we'll need them once we're ready to fight on a global scale. Remember, only this area of enemy forces has been infected so far. The biobugs will infect them all, but they will take time to propagate. The president can coordinate communications across the globe, and I'm sure with your help, and Scarlet's, we can spread the word quickly enough. Then we can tell them to start… fighting." Abigail stopped typing for a moment, then looked over at Rebecca.

"I know that look," said Rebecca. "That's an idea look. What are you thinking?"

Abigail's concentration showed on her face. "The resonance towers across the globe were designed to communicate with each other, correct?"

"Well, yeah, but what does that have to do with—*ohh*, I get it." Rebecca smiled. "You wanna use them for mass communication. I love it!"

Abigail smiled and adjusted her communicator. "John, this is Abby. Would it be possible for us to utilize the resonance tower satellites for communication?"

"Should be possible. We just need to alter the programming to accept an additional parameter. Working on it now," John replied. He tinkered with the code of the tower that he pushed out in an update to the other towers across the globe. "There, done. Use the PA system here, and the resonance tower's satellite should pick it up and transmit it across the rest. You should see a big blue button on the desk. Press that and hold it down while you speak. Our automatic translation systems will do the rest."

Rebecca slammed her hand on the button and held it down. "Go," she mouthed to Abigail as she pulled an item from her purse.

"Attention, everyone. This is Abigail Warren, speaking to you from Griffin, Georgia, in the United States. Please call back your military. They are unable to cause any damage currently, but we are working on a plan. When we have an update, we will inform you, at which time you may continue your attack. I repeat, please hold back your military. Do not send them out, as they currently stand no chance. Please give us time, and we will have a more effective solution." Rebecca took her hand off the button. "Becca, what are you doing?" she asked, looking up at her. "I need to keep repeating the message."

"I know." Rebecca smiled and hit the play button on her tape recorder.

Abigail heard her own voice repeat her message as she raised her eyebrows and smiled. "You're clever. One of us is still gonna have to hold down the button, though."

Rebecca placed a prosthetic hand she'd found inside the base on the button, keeping it held down. She pressed the loop button on the recorder so it continuously repeated the message.

Abigail looked back and forth between the prosthetic hand and Rebecca, confused. "Do I even want to know how or why you have that?"

Rebecca laughed. "I ran out a little faster than you and found a prosthetics room. They look so real, right? Anyway, I found this one lying on a desk, so I picked it up and put it in my purse. I thought we could use a hand."

Abigail dropped her head and laughed. "I'm going to be honest. I shouldn't have laughed. That was so *stupid*," she said, covering her face and laughing harder.

Rebecca laughed with her. "Okay, let's be serious. The hand is on the button, so let's just set my tape recorder next to the intercom. Then we can start making calls," she said, then turned around and looked up. "Scarlet, can you please help us?"

Scarlet appeared in a white light behind them, her red skin glowing under the fluorescent lighting of the office. "What do you need?" she thoughtspoke.

"We need to facilitate communications across the globe and protect people. Can you assist us?" asked Rebecca.

"Yes. I will inform fellow members of our team, and we shall assist you in this request," thoughtspoke Scarlet before she disappeared back into her ship.

"Hey, Director! How 'bout some tunes to kick alien ass to?" asked Kyle.

John shook his head, but couldn't help smiling. "I've got just the one." He typed a command into the computer and clicked an executable file. "Alright, everyone. The countdown is on," he announced. "The Final Countdown" by Europe blasted from GAIA's speakers outside.

Sean laughed as he teleported back to the tower. "Alright, Dad."

"Oh, hell yeah. That'll work." Kyle shot another set of rockets at a group of Kriff, saving an agent whose shields had depleted.

The Kriff tried firing their weapons, but they were finally disabled by the biobugs, rendering them useless. They would have to find another way to fight. Still, though their weapons were ineffective, they had incredible strength, could mentally reprogram themselves at will, and moved quickly. Blinking could mean life or death.

One Kriff snuck up behind Kyle, planning to pounce on him and rip his limbs apart. Sean noticed this and sniped it before it got too close, saving Kyle's life. Kyle grinned and gave a thumbs-up to Sean.

Jake became overwhelmed with the number of Kriff he fought. One knocked him to the ground and kicked Jake's gun away as it leaned down in his face and roared. "Breath mints, man." Darren ran over to Jake, managing to take out the approaching Kriff, along with several others, giving Jake time to stand and fetch his gun. "I mean, thanks, but I had it."

"Sure, you did," said Darren, patting Jake on the back. "Sure, you did." Sean sniped a few Kriff near Jake and Darren as they advanced. "Damn, he's good," said Darren. He resumed blasting the aliens with his shotgun, and Jake shot one who almost grabbed Darren. "Thanks."

Jake did a quick salute, and they turned back-to-back. Noticing a situation, Jake shot a few Kriff approaching Winona.

"Damn it, Warren, those were mine," Winona shouted.

Whitney continued firing the turret at a group of Kriff, and she noticed the other two kick in on their own, firing automatically. "Way to go, John," she shouted.

"That's my ear, baby, but thanks! I thought those might help. Wherever you aim yours, the rest will follow." John paused briefly, considering the situation. "I'm going out there. We should both be protecting our kids." He stood and bolted to the armory, grabbing a special gun off the rack as he ran outside.

"See you soon," Whitney said back.

John blasted his weapon as he ran around the battlefield, taking out as many as he could with his supercharged energy rifle while the song played, nearing its conclusion. Each Kriff he shot blew up and chained off to another nearby, creating a chain reaction that blew up a large portion of their forces.

Jake saw a couple of Kriff approaching Winona and noticed her gun was out of charge. He ran to save her, hoping she had the situation under control.

Winona tried to pull out her knife, but it was stuck. "A little help?" she shouted toward Jake.

"Oh, *I'm* sorry. I thought those were *yours*," said Jake as he ran closer to Winona and killed both Kriff, one with a gun and the other with a knife to its head. "See? Communication and teamwork *are* useful tools."

Winona and Jake put up their fists as Jake realized his gun was out of charge too. He held his knife sideways, ready to tear the enemy in half. Four Kriff approached, and the two agents fought back by punching and stabbing. Some of the Kriff from before started to repair themselves, but once they became infected, their repairs failed and they fell back down. Sean saw Jake and Winona struggling and shot his sniper twice, hitting two with each shot.

Jake shrugged at Sean. "I had those, man!" Winona looked at Jake with contempt. "What? So I need to take my own advice. I'm aware of my flaws," he said. "Most of them, anyway."

Winona turned away from Jake so he wouldn't see her smile, then noticed Melinda getting assaulted by a Kriff, who had managed to make it past her shields. "Jake, look! Mel's in trouble! Come on," she said, and they both ran toward her.

"No, no, no, no, no," Jake said breathlessly while he ran to Melinda as fast as he could. Everyone else continued fighting in the background, and time seemed to slow for Jake. Winona tended to Melinda, assessing her condition as Jake fought and killed more Kriff with deep-seated anger. He screamed as he killed several with his knife and fists.

Sean saw the predicament, and sniped the ones in his line of sight. Darren ran toward them, firing his shotgun at them. Kyle approached the scene, beating Kriff with the rocket launcher. John joined the fray and shot another group of Kriff. Several more Kriff advanced toward Sean, and John fired his gun at the group as he ran toward his son.

Whitney witnessed the scene from above, but had to focus her fire on a group of Kriff approaching Melinda's location, where everyone except Sean and a few agents were.

A couple of agents were killed as the Kriff quickly got the best of them. A Kriff ripped one in half, and another Kriff stuck its fist through an agent, tearing right through their shields.

"No," Whitney shouted, and she focused her fire on that group. "Die, you creepy, bug-faced freaks," she shouted. She set the turret to autofire mode, and picked up a gun she had retrieved from the armory. As she ran down the stairs and stepped outside, she saw John get jumped by a Kriff, right after firing his weapon at another group of Kriff that would have killed Sean otherwise. Time seemed to slow for Whitney as it did for Jake, but she raised up her gun and fired at an approaching Kriff relentlessly. "Get away from him, you bastard," she shouted.

John could barely breathe, his body convulsing. "Th-thanks," he struggled to say as he looked up at Whitney.

"Are you alright?" she cried. "Where did it get you?" Whitney looked in between John's chest and stomach, seeing his torn clothes and how heavily he bled. She gasped, tears forming in her eyes. "No, no, no," she said as she fell to her knees and covered her mouth.

John tried to cover up the wound, but it was too deep, and he was losing too much blood to hide it. Pain ripped through him like lightning. "Hey. I'm g-gonna be… f-fine," he said with a smile. He reached out a hand to Whitney's face and grabbed her cheek.

Whitney closed her eyes and felt his touch on her face as her teardrops fell on him. "Don't you do this to me," she said with a sniffle. "We're supposed to grow old together! Don't you do this to me." She put her head down on John's chest to hear his heart beating, as she worried it would be for the last time, noticing its speed decreasing. Whitney grabbed one of John's hands and felt it growing cold. "Darn it, John. After everything I've put up with, don't you leave me," she yelled as she stood. "Somebody, please help," she cried. "John is hurt! I repeat, the director is hurt," she shouted as loud as she could. Whitney knelt back down over the top of John. She saw him reaching for her as blood poured out of his mouth and nose.

"E-echo," he managed to say, pointing at the sky.

"Echo," Whitney screamed, and he appeared beside her in his usual bright light. "Please, I need you to fix him."

Echo saw the distraught look on Whitney's face, noticing how she pled for her husband. "I will try." Echo did his waving motions across John as he had done with Jake, but it caused John's pain to escalate, making him scream and spit out more blood. "Please be patient with this process. It hurts now, but will not hurt after its conclusion."

"Is it gonna work?" asked Whitney.

Echo kept trying, and as John screamed, his wounds started healing, slowly going away on the outside, but the internal injuries remained. Echo's eyes shifted to blue.

"Why are your eyes blue, Echo? Tell me," Whitney snapped at him.

Echo looked at Whitney while he continued healing John. "It is what happens when we are sad."

Sean continued sniping the Kriff, but more ships showed up, dropping off more troops. "Oh, crap," said Sean as he turned his communicator back on. "Does anyone know why these guys aren't falling from the virus yet?"

Scarlet appeared on the field and held her hands up, telekinetically holding back the oncoming army with an enormous psychic shield. "It requires time to incubate. I estimate it should take approximately two more of your minutes," she thoughtspoke. "Kli'Cacowas, please come assist."

Klick appeared on the battlefield, assisting Scarlet in holding back the enemy forces. "It is good to see you. My desire is that my mate not be injured in battle."

"A desire we share," Scarlet thoughtspoke. "Have the preparations been made?"

Klick pushed harder against the enemy forces, pushing them back further as the two worked together. "Yes, my love. We have coordinated with humans and released swarms across the planet. As you said, it should take no more than two of their minutes for the incubation period to expire."

An inquiry, Echo thoughtspoke only to Scarlet and Klick. *This human is healing externally. However, his internal injuries remain, and I am running out of power. Is there another who can assist?*

Unknown and irrelevant. We can heal minor injuries, but we cannot undo critical damage to another species, only to ourselves, Klick thoughtspoke.

I believe this is where humans would say, 'Damn it.' Is there nothing we can do for this human? He is the paternal human for the one whom I have come to know as my best friend, thoughtspoke Echo.

There may be a way, thoughtspoke Scarlet as she and Klick continued pushing the wall further back, holding the raging enemies at bay. *It will require taking him to our mothership and traveling away from Earth in a higher-class starship. I know of a planet that may be able to save him, but it is many starlengths away. Please cease this drain of your energy, Eco'Corulaz. You have healed him enough to last for another two human hours. This is more than any other Nephilium has ever done for a being with critical injuries, even for our own species. You will cause incurable damage to yourself by persisting.*

Echo turned to Whitney. "I am sorry," he thoughtspoke. "I can heal his external injuries, but internal damage is something I am incapable of repairing. However, all hope is not lost. Sca'Lorit knows of a planet with medical technology that may be of aid to him. It is the only chance to save his life. He will only survive another two hours on Earth, so long as he rests and does not perform any strenuous activity, but we must not wait. I have done all that I can. My deepest sympathies are with you, Whitney Caldwell, maternal of my best friend."

Whitney pulled Echo close to her. "This is called a hug. You do it to show someone you care deeply about them. To make each of you feel better. If you think you can save John, then please save him," she cried as she pulled back.

Another Nephilium appeared beside Echo, one with purple skin. "Greetings. My name is Dephilius, a Nephilium from planet—"

"I know where you're from," said Whitney. "Just take John and save him. Please!"

Echo and Dephilius looked at each other. *Take him*, Echo thoughtspoke to Dephilius, who nodded and picked John up in his arms.

Sean ran to his dad as the Kriff finally fell, the virus finally kicking in and disabling their internal systems. "Wait! Don't go anywhere," Sean shouted. "What happened? Somebody, please, tell me what's going on," he cried.

"Sweetie, your dad is hurt," Whitney said with a sniffle. "It's awful." She paused to gather herself before continuing through sobs. "This Nephilium here, Dephilius, is gonna take him to a place where he can be healed. It's the only shot we have at saving his life."

"What? No, he… I mean… we can't. I just got him back," Sean shouted, his voice filled with grief. He refused to accept the loss of his father, despite it possibly being temporary. Sean knew he would struggle with not knowing John's fate, where he would be, or if he'd ever come home. "Fix him," Sean said to Dephilius and Echo. "Fix him, damn it," he shouted as tears poured down his face.

Sean still harbored deep resentment toward John, and he wanted nothing more than time to fix their broken bond. He never pictured losing his father without any warning. Sean thought his dad was invincible. It was one of the most annoying but lovable things about him. His thoughts about his father's future death were always of him lying in a bed, surrounded by family, with everyone getting a chance to say goodbye. As the moments cruelly played out before him, all his anger and resentment faded away. A star exploded inside him, his emotions going supernova and creating galaxies of pain.

"As I have explained—" Echo thoughtspoke.

"No! We were just getting to know each other. I finally got my dad back. One who accepted his mistakes and was willing to… to… to right his wrongs," he screamed as he fell to his hands and knees.

Whitney grabbed Sean in a hug as he cried loudly for his father. "I know. I don't like it either, okay? I don't, but this way he has a chance. Wouldn't you rather believe he's out there somewhere, coming back home all better? Isn't that better than him being gone forever?" she asked. "I think it is. He'll find his way home."

Sean stood shakily and walked over to John in the arms of Dephilius. "Can he talk?"

"No, but I can facilitate mental communication," Dephilius thoughtspoke.

Sean looked around the battlefield and saw all the Kriff fall to the ground in defeat. The full effects of the virus finally took hold. He saw his friends approaching him, while the surviving agents walked back inside the building. Sean calmed his hyperventilating, putting himself at eye-level with John.

John looked toward Sean and grabbed his hand, squeezing it with all his strength, which Sean noticed wasn't much. He wanted his son to know he could hear him.

"What should I tell people? I mean, if someone asks. Do I say you're dead, or… o-or that you've gone away for a while, but coming back? Where should I tell them you are?" Sean asked breathlessly, tears streaming down his red, damp face as his mother held him. A galaxy inside of him imploded.

John looked at Sean and smiled, a tear rolling down his face. "Tell them… I'm in the stars," John thoughtspoke through Dephilius, whose eyes briefly turned a deep blue. "We must go. Time is of the essence," he thoughtspoke to everyone.

Sean and Whitney backed away as Dephilius disappeared into his ship with John and took off toward the mothership. He would then take a higher-class ship to the distant star system. Whitney fell to her knees in grief beside Sean, as they watched Dephilius's ship become a star, and then twinkle away.

Abigail and Rebecca celebrated the victory in the communications room as they received calls from all over the world, informing them the assaults had stopped. The military was deployed across the globe to ensure no Kriff were left alive. Abigail and Rebecca had taken out their comms so they could focus on global communication and the resonance towers.

Rebecca grabbed her communicator and put it back in, intending to tell Sean the good news, but she heard Sean crying. "Sean?" she asked hesitantly. "Is everything alright? What happened?"

"It's my dad. He… he got hurt, and the Nephilium are going to take him to another solar system. They… they think they can heal him," Sean struggled to get out, "but they're not sure."

Rebecca heard Sean's sniffling and sobs. She stood and ran outside straight to him, holding him in a hug. Whitney hugged them both.

Abigail folded her hands and sent up a prayer.

Scarlet appeared beside Melinda, and was able to heal her since her wounds were mostly external. The human doctors would do the rest. Jake sat beside Melinda and jumped with joy after watching Scarlet heal her. He hugged Scarlet, then Melinda. "Mel, I'm so glad you're safe," Jake said shakily, his fear overtaking him for the first time in a while.

"Who's Mel?" asked Melinda as she faltered, her gaze drifting around, then back at Jake with wide eyes. "Who are you?"

Jake felt his stomach drop, and his heart broke in half. "You… you don't remember me?" he asked, on the verge of tears.

Melinda smiled. "Just kidding," she said. "I wanted to see the look on your face. I'm sorry," she said with a laugh.

"What? That's not funny. Don't do that. That… that is so not funny. Why? Why would you do that?" asked Jake, reeling from the feeling of his heart returning to his chest.

"It was kind of interesting to see you have genuine concern for someone," Winona said with a grin.

"You're both cruel. Both of you! You are both unusually cruel," Jake shouted as he stood and walked away. *Thank God*, he thought. Winona and Melinda continued laughing about Jake's reaction.

Darren and Kyle high-fived each other as they looked around the battlefield. "Holy cow. We won," Darren said with a wide grin.

"We freaking *won*, man," Kyle said back. "I can't believe it. It's over. It's finally over."

"Yeah. It just don't bring back those we lost along the way. Still, we gotta count our blessings. This was a victory, one that's gonna be remembered forever in the history of mankind." Darren looked around and saw Sean, Whitney, and Rebecca all huddled together. He nudged Kyle's shoulder and pointed at the group, then immediately ran to them with Kyle trailing behind. "Someone wanna fill me in?"

"Sean just lost his dad. He got hurt, and the aliens had to take him away to heal him. That's the short version," Rebecca explained to her father. She stood and walked Darren over to the side. "I'm really worried about him. What can we do to cheer him up, or at least get his mind off it?"

"Hon, he needs to grieve. I'm still tryin' to wrap my head around what you just told me, and I'm pretty sure no one's ever said any of that before. For now, just give him time. He seems to value hugging and closeness, so give him that. I wanna talk to him in a bit myself, once things have calmed down around here, but for now, we need to give him what he needs, alright?"

Rebecca nodded. "Okay." She walked back over to Sean, knelt, and gripped him in a tight hold. Sean clung to her for dear life.

"Dude, I'm… I'm so sorry," said Kyle, who wasn't a touchy-feely kind of guy, but he still had sympathy for his friend. He wanted to comfort Sean, but he didn't know how. Instead, he knelt to Sean's level and snapped his fingers, making Sean look up at him. "Hey. I don't know what to say here, man. All I know is there's a chance for him to come back. So hold on to that and use it as hope. They're gonna take care of him, alright? It'll all work out."

Sean composed himself after crying so hard for such a long time. It was as though he ran out of tears, with no energy left to cry. The stars inside of him dimmed, turning his internal universe into a void. "Um," he started, "someone should tell Mandy. I don't think I can do it."

"Don't worry about it. I'll go tell her," said Darren, turning on his heel as he walked back inside the building.

"You wanna hear something weird? I feel bad for coming outta all that unscathed," said Kyle.

"You did a good job, Wheels," said Whitney. "That is what you like to be called, right?"

Kyle half-smiled. "Right now, the two of you can call me anything you want." He paused and took a deep breath. "Just don't call me late for dinner," he said with a grin, then cleared his throat and looked down at the ground. "Sorry."

Sean started to laugh. It was full of pain, but it was a step toward joy. Whitney laughed too, and the three of them found themselves laughing together. It came from Kyle's audacity to make a silly joke during a serious situation. He caught them off-guard, tickling them.

Meanwhile, Darren was on his way up to Amanda, silently wondering why she had been so quiet on her communicator. His movements were slow, because he knew when a police officer knocked on your door with a forlorn look in their eyes, it's never a good sign. Darren knocked on the door and heard footsteps approaching. Soon, the door unlocked.

Amanda poked her head out. "She's sleeping," she said with a smile. She immediately saw Darren's melancholy expression and lost her smile. "What is it?"

"Well, before I answer, let me ask you somethin'," said Darren as he came inside the room and heard Amanda shut the door behind him. "Why ain't you been on comms? I noticed you were quiet throughout the whole thing."

"What? I've been talking this entire time, but no one's been answering me, which was rude, I might add." She gripped her communicator, and it whirred to life as the light came on. Amanda looked away in defeat. "It must have turned itself off."

"You may have hit a button on it accidentally. It's easy to do." Darren saw Amanda's annoyance and spoke up before she could argue. "It don't matter now, anyway. You need to go see your mom and brother outside. Your dad's… gone. There's no sugar-coatin' it. They can explain it to you better than I can, but from what I understand, the aliens who have been helpin' us weren't able to heal him fully. So, they're takin' him to some other planet in another solar system, where they might be able to help him, but they're not certain," he said, thinking twice about what he said. "Sheesh, there really is no better way to say that."

Amanda sat in front of Monica's door, dropping her weapon gently enough so Monica wouldn't hear it. "Daddy's… gone?" she asked softly. "Is he coming back?"

"We don't know. I'm sorry, Mandy," said Darren, opening his arms for her to hug him and kneeling in front of her.

Amanda clung to Darren as she cried and screamed, and Darren rubbed her upper back to comfort her. "This can't be real."

"Shh, come on. I'm sure they'll fix him up and bring him home. We just don't know when yet, hon. I heard Wheels say somethin' about holdin' on to hope that he's comin' back someday. So, that's my advice to you," Darren soothed. "We can go out there to see your family. Do you wanna do that?"

Amanda shook her head. "I'd rather stay in here away from everyone," she said, clinging to Darren even tighter.

"That's fine, hon. That's completely fine," said Darren as he continued soothing her.

Darren soothed Amanda, while Kyle and Whitney soothed Sean, and Rebecca soothed Whitney. They had taken a major blow, but war was not without its casualties. They claimed victory at a price, but deep down, they knew John wouldn't have had it any other way.

YOU'VE CLAIMED A LIFE IN OUTER SPACE
AND TOOK HIM TO A DIFFERENT PLACE

✧

26. The Way Home

Everyone walked back inside, some slower than others. Sean, Rebecca, and Whitney moved much more slowly. Each of them held their heads down as they drowned in the stormy waves of confused grief. Its violent winds ripped at the walls of their hearts, threatening to rip them to pieces and leave little behind.

"I should've seen it," said Sean. "I should've seen it and killed it before it got close to him." Tears still streamed down his face, and Rebecca held on to him as they walked.

"No, Sean. Don't do that to yourself," said Whitney. "You were still fighting and protecting everyone else. You couldn't have known," she soothed. "I saw John get attacked when I came outside. I've been thinking I should have gone down there sooner, and I could have stopped that thing." She paused to take a breath. "We can't change what happened. All we can do now is move forward and hope for a brighter future. We've gotta believe he'll find his way home."

Sean nodded as they reached the front door and walked inside, the door automatically sliding shut behind them. They walked past Kyle, who had made it inside before them, and he ran up to Sean.

"Hey, man. How are you holding up?" asked Kyle. "Is there anything you need?"

Sean stopped and turned to Rebecca and Whitney. "Mom, Becca, can you go on ahead, please? I'll be there soon, but we need to start packing, and I wanna talk to Wheels for a bit."

Whitney and Rebecca nodded as they continued toward the living quarters, with Rebecca comforting Whitney as they walked.

Sean sighed and closed his eyes, feeling intense pain in his heart and an emptiness in his stomach. "What I need is impossible, Kyle."

Kyle was taken aback. He knew Sean only called him by his real name when he was upset. Kyle placed an arm on Sean's shoulder and walked with him. "You gotta look at the bigger picture here, man. We won," he said with a grin.

"I know, and I should be happier about it, but this is so complicated. I was so angry with him for so long, and I basically removed him from my life. Then he comes back out of the blue and gives a damn, but before we can reconcile, he does something dangerous and idiotic. Then, he somehow manages to apologize for it, something he's never done in his life, and despite my misgivings and doubts, he redeems himself. All to be taken out by the enemy and whisked away to the stars, never knowing if I'll see him again.

"It wasn't supposed to go like this. He was supposed to grow old and need my help. I was gonna tell him he wasn't present in my childhood when I needed him, so why should I be present in his life when he needed me? We were supposed to grow a bond before he was gone," Sean poured out.

Kyle raised his eyebrows and stepped back, fearing he had upset Sean. "I know your relationship with your dad was complicated, and with him gone, those feelings just got even weirder. I don't know what else to say, other than to just give it time. You're not the only person it's happened to, just the first.

"We live in a different world now," Kyle said with a sigh. "I'll say this, and it's something your Andy Griffith friend shared with me." He cleared his throat. "Sometimes, taking back your life can mean becoming a part of someone else's. Monica's still here. Mandy's still here. Becca, she's still here. Your mother, she's still here. Hell, *I'm* still here. So are Darren, Jake, and Abby.

"I mean, look at all the connections you've established, man, and the connections that stemmed from those. You brought so many people together and helped them heal. You know who does that? A leader. What I'm trying to say is, focus on what you have, not on what you've lost. Your dad kept the monsters away from you, even though you didn't know it. It's just your turn now. Monica needs that, and I know you can do better. Okay?"

Sean looked Kyle in the face and nodded. "Thanks, Wheels," he said, taking a breath to compose himself as a thought occurred to him. "Hey, uh, would it be alright if Monica and I stayed at your place for a while? Maybe Becca, too?"

Kyle would normally make a joke about Rebecca staying with Sean, but even he knew it wasn't the time. "Yeah, man. That's fine. Whoever wants to stay can stay. Only for a week, though. I need my space back. Also, just a reminder. It's *my* house, alright? I don't want nobody else telling me what to do in my own freaking house," he griped, making Sean laugh.

"Sorry. The way you said it was funny." Sean sighed. "I don't know, man. My mind and feelings are all over the place."

Kyle scoffed and grinned. "You ain't the only one."

Jake, Winona, and Melinda sat on couches and chairs in the living quarters, and Jake grew uncomfortable with the silence. "You know, as badly as I wanna rest, I can't figure something out," said Jake.

"Shocker," Winona said sarcastically, making Melinda laugh.

"No, really, I'm serious. We still haven't found the Channeler, so what was his role in all this? Also, why did no Astro agents come after us? It's just weird," said Jake.

"I don't think it matters, babe," Melinda soothed. "The aliens are gone. Well, the bad ones, anyway. It's not like he has anything to channel. Maybe those Astro agents saw he was a fraud. Just celebrate the victory and move on."

Jake nodded. "I should be able to, but something is tugging at my brain. I've just got an awful feeling about this. What if it's not over? What if they're still there, but we can't see them? They may want us to *think* we won."

"I'd say you're being paranoid and experiencing trauma, perhaps post-traumatic stress disorder," Winona suggested in a soothing voice, which was highly abnormal for her. "Honestly, Warren, you can't do this to yourself." She looked over at Melinda for assistance, and they both looked back at Jake, who had his head down in concentration and his hands clasped. "Look, let's at least get some rest tonight, and maybe tomorrow, we can look into it. Alright?"

Jake nodded, then stood and left the room without saying a word.

"He didn't say anything. No sarcasm or jokes. That's weird, right?" asked Melinda.

"Extremely," said Winona.

Elsewhere in the facility, Zanu was hooked up in a pod-like machine and intubated, so the machines could breathe for it while it slept. Its eyes opened wide, and it angrily attacked the pod. The glass was designed to withstand nuclear attacks, but Zanu's strength was too much for the glass to handle. It wasn't Zanu's strength alone, but the psychic power it used to create a powerful forcefield in front of the glass, critically damaging it.

It finally broke the glass after about three minutes, and alarms blared in the xeno medbay, a medical facility reserved for non-human intelligence. It crouched as it landed, fluids dripping from its body, with the new capability to breathe oxygen. It looked up at the cameras in the corners of the room, and blew them up with its mind.

As Jake wandered down a hallway, he heard the alarms. "Ugh, I hate being right." Jake hurried to a computer to check where the problem was. When he saw it was the xeno medbay, he ran there, nearly bumping into Sean and Kyle near the entrance. "Whoa, sorry. There's something wrong. Come with me."

Sean and Kyle looked at each other, then nodded and followed Jake until they reached the hallway leading to the xeno medbay. As they approached, they saw three agents fly down the hallway as if they were shot from a cannon. Sean looked back and saw they were hurt, but alive. Sean, Jake, and Kyle picked up their pace, and Sean slammed into Zanu. It was like being hit by a car. Sean fell backward due to Zanu's psychic wall.

"Sean," Kyle yelled, then looked back at Zanu. "What the hell, man? I thought we were cool."

"You should not have altered my biology. I now have more power than my kind has had in several millennia, and I will not allow you to end what's left of our race," said Zanu as it lifted its hand, levitating Kyle until he was halfway to the ceiling. Jake approached Zanu with a knife, but Zanu held him in place while still holding on to Kyle. "Humans. Predictable behavior. Easy to manipulate. The stupidity of your race is astounding."

Sean laughed, despite the pain he was in. Kyle and Jake could only move their eyes to look toward Sean, but they harbored similar feelings of confusion.

"Your exultation is illogical, human. What amuses you so?" asked Zanu as it tilted its head.

"You've been around humans for a while, so I'm sure you've heard of our game of chess, right?" Sean asked as he stood and dusted himself off.

"Yes. It is a game of intelligence and strategy. What is your point?" Zanu asked, increasing its hold on Kyle and Jake, causing them more pain.

"Ever hear of a term called zugzwang?" Sean smiled while Zanu blinked in silence. "Guess you don't know everything after all. It's German for the compulsion to move. It means no matter what move a player makes, they would only worsen their situation, but they still have to play their turn. Regardless of what the player does, they still lose. I wanted to teach you something before you die."

Echo appeared beside Sean, lifting Zanu into the air as Zanu began disintegrating in front of them. Echo stopped for a moment, and all that was left of Zanu was its head that fell to the ground. Zanu's head screeched in pain while Kyle and Jake fell to the floor, released from Zanu's grasp.

Sean folded his arms. "The *moment* I put that biobug in you, it started scanning your physiology and uploading it to Echo's ship. That data was sent to other Nephilium ships, several of which were able to track down other biological Kriff by searching for specific DNA markers. *Your* DNA markers. Our Nephilium friends were able to infect the rest. So, thanks for that helpful tip about all of you being clones."

Sean knelt to look at Zanu in what was left of its face. "Now, we weren't going to do anything to you at first, but with the stunts you just pulled, you brought this on yourself. The rest of your biological kind are long gone. They were detected leaving our atmosphere almost an hour ago, but not before getting infected themselves. You're all that's left." Sean leaned closer to Zanu's face and spoke deeply. "If any of them *ever* come back, they'll receive the same treatment you did. We know how to find them, and how to… what was it you said about death in your culture?

"Oh, right. We know how to *conclude* them. Allowing them to leave without chasing them down and ending their lives is a human concept called mercy, something else you're unfamiliar with. Consider those two things you've learned. Not that it matters." Sean looked over at Echo. "Finish it," he said as he kicked Zanu's head into the air.

Echo held Zanu's head in place, resuming the destabilization process, and Zanu fully disintegrated within seconds. "A solid plan, best friend," thoughtspoke Echo as his eyes shifted to yellow.

"Checkmate, jerk," said Kyle as he slowly sat up, falling back to the floor with his hand on his stomach.

Jake adjusted his communicator. "Hey, Abby? Do you think you could come give us a checkup? We have lots of ouchies," he said as he flopped back to the ground.

Abigail soon arrived with a team of medical agents, who Scarlet had secured from other bases. They moved the injured to the infirmary, where they stayed for a few days to gather strength and rest. They weren't too pleased with the food or beds, and were more than ready to leave by the time they were discharged. Still, although they wouldn't admit it, they were grateful for Abigail and her team's treatment.

Once Sean and Kyle were discharged, Kyle modified his communicator using GAIA's alien technology, and called ANNI to the base. The car greeted and congratulated them on their success. They got inside the car and drove to Kyle's house, joined by Monica and Rebecca. Darren followed them in his patrol car with Amanda in the passenger seat.

Echo stayed back at GAIA, deciding to work for them as their first alien agent. This provided GAIA with new resources, and Echo with a purpose. The concept of money was something he was wildly unfamiliar with, but he would adjust in time. Sean insisted Echo be paid the most, because it was bad enough that humans weren't making enough money, and he wasn't going to let Echo be the first alien to struggle financially.

President Matthews addressed the nation and produced somewhat of a cover story about how aliens briefly invaded, but the United States Space Force was able to dispatch them. Many people who had first-hand accounts of the GAIA agents knew better, but he wasn't going to admit that yet. The government wanted to see how the world handled the knowledge of extraterrestrials first.

Abigail came up with the idea of a medical field team for the Nephilium, to transport across the globe to other parts of the world, and they were able to heal the injured with Nephilium help. They were able to free all the prison camps, and tend to the survivors. Abigail finally saved people before they were hurt, instead of after it was too late. She became the first field medical officer for the organization. That's not all she accomplished, though.

She synthesized the world's first cure for cancer by using Monica's blood, which somehow had special markers in it. Echo's theory was that when Monica was abducted, or given an implant at some point in her life, it changed her physiology. When the Nephilium deactivated all viruses, it was unable to finish its job.

It was slow-going, but with the help of Abigail's medic team, the cure was deployed worldwide. For the first time ever, cancer had been cured, proving a miracle can come from a catastrophe. Her team also analyzed Sean's brain and found no abnormalities.

With John missing in action, President Matthews appointed Sean as Acting Director until John's return, a responsibility he accepted graciously, but he warned them his family came first.

Sean announced he'd be taking a break for at least a year, during which time Winona would call the shots. The president had no choice but to agree, because otherwise, Sean was going public with everything he knew. The public had come to learn there were aliens, but they still didn't have the full story. This leverage also allowed him to demand more money from the government to pay all of GAIA more than a livable wage.

Jake wasn't thrilled about Winona's new position, but he had survived worse, so he'd suffer through it. He needed a new partner, so Winona paired him up with Melinda. This highly displeased him at first, but Melinda proved her mettle to him in the testing courses and field training, even outdoing Jake's scores, so he begrudgingly allowed her to go in the field with him.

Once they regained their strength, Jake and Melinda set out on a mission to find the Channeler, ensuring the crisis was over. Winona even sanctioned the mission, not wanting to leave loose ends out in the wild. They eventually reached the location Jake's friend had tracked previously, but it was abandoned, so it was another dead end. Their search continued, despite this.

Rebecca, Amanda, Darren, Sean, and Kyle all sat around the latter's living room, talking about everything they went through during the ordeal. "How long are y'all staying?" Kyle asked after everyone was quiet for a couple of minutes.

"Probably just for tonight," Darren said first. "Nothin' against y'all, but I've earned several nights of rest in my own damn bed," he said with a laugh. Others chuckled with him.

Amanda shifted in her seat. "I think I'm only staying tonight, too. Maybe one more night, but not longer. Like Darren said, I'm ready for some real rest," she said, looking over at Monica in Sean's lap. "I'm gonna miss you, sweetie."

Monica ran to Amanda and hugged her. "I'll miss you too, Aunt Mandy."

Amanda hugged Monica tightly, then let her go. "Come on. It's time for a bath, then bed. Go, go, go," she said, lightly tapping her back as she followed Monica up the stairs.

Rebecca waited until Amanda was gone before speaking. "I'll stay as long as Sean does," she said in a flirty voice.

Kyle somehow mustered the power to control himself. "How about you, Sean?" Despite his self-control, Kyle couldn't help but grin.

Sean reeled from a mixture of emotions, and another one had entered the mix, courtesy of Rebecca. "Uh, maybe the whole week, if that's alright. After that, I guess I need to get back to making money," he said with a laugh. "Although, there's not nearly as many people now, so…" he trailed off.

"People just gotta get busy makin' more!" Darren said as he lifted his arms.

"Daddy," Rebecca shouted, covering her mouth. Kyle buckled over in laughter and fell out of his chair. Sean's eyebrows rose and his eyes widened.

Darren held his hands up. "Hey, I'm just sayin'. Besides, you can't focus on the bad. There ain't nothin' we can do to change it."

"Well, it's getting close to ten o'clock, so I'm gonna turn in. You all have a great night." Sean stood and started walking up the stairs to the same bedroom from before.

"Sean, wait," said Darren. "Let me talk with you for a moment, son." Darren motioned for Sean to come back, and he sat back down in his chair while Darren talked. "Listen, I'm proud of you. I'm so proud of you, I'm bustin' buttons. What you've done over these past few weeks has been nothing short of incredible. I know you miss your dad, and I don't blame you," he said, taking a beat to organize his thoughts. "I had him all wrong. None of us are perfect, and we all got a lot to learn about life and love.

"I lost my wife, and then I lost a friend… but then I met the rest of y'all. Ron should be here, so I'm gonna tell his family when I get home. I plan to organize a memorial for him. Anyway, I just wanted to say that if you ever need someone to talk to, you got me, son. I've come to be fond of you, as it turns out."

Sean's nerves loosened, and everything in him relaxed, thankful to have someone to look up to. "Thank you so much. You've… been kind of a father to me already," he admitted. "I'm so sorry. I appreciate all this, but I'm exhausted, so I'm gonna turn in."

Darren nodded and smiled as Sean walked back upstairs. "Get some rest, son."

Rebecca fidgeted with her feet in uncomfortable silence before swiftly standing and running up the stairs after Sean. Kyle and Darren exchanged a knowing look and talked about mundane things after Rebecca left.

When Rebecca entered the bedroom, she didn't see Sean, so she checked the bathroom, but still couldn't find him. As she closed her eyes to concentrate, she heard his voice speaking softly in a room nearby and followed it. Rebecca quietly opened the door, trying to do so softly, so Sean wouldn't know she was there. When she walked in, she saw Sean give Monica a goodnight hug and tuck Monica in. Rebecca smiled at the sight.

Sean gave his daughter a quick kiss on her head and rubbed his hand through her hair. "I love you so much," he whispered and poked her on the nose. "Boop," he whispered. Sean turned around, and Rebecca ran back toward their shared bedroom. He already knew she was there, though. Sean thought it was cute how Rebecca wasn't as quiet as she thought she was.

Rebecca sat on the bed with her hands on her heart, joy on her face, and her eyes filled with joyful tears. Witnessing Sean be a loving father to Monica soothed something in her, cementing her feelings for him. Rebecca knew for a fact, then, that she loved him.

"Hey," said Sean as he entered the bedroom with his hands in his pockets.

"Hey," Rebecca said with a smile.

"So, uh… any plans tonight?" asked Sean as he looked at Rebecca and gave her a half-smile.

Rebecca laughed. "I don't know. I'm about to get a shower, so—"

They both heard Monica scream, and ran to her room. "Monica, what's wrong, sweetie?" asked Sean. Rebecca bent down to give her a tight hug and Monica squeezed back.

Monica's breathing was rapid and deep, but she quickly calmed down. "I think I just had a nightmare."

Sean looked at Rebecca, then back at Monica. "You wanna tell us about it?"

"No, I think I can sleep now. I'm sorry for bothering you, Daddy. Please don't leave me again," Monica begged.

Sean dropped his head, and a tear fell down his cheek. *What was wrong with me?* he thought. He stood and hugged Monica after Rebecca stepped back. "Listen to me, my little Cocoon. I'm so sorry. That will never happen again, alright? I'm here to stay, and we're never getting separated again. I promise," he said in a whisper. "Okay?" He rubbed his hands through Monica's hair, kissing her head and chin.

"I want some of that," Rebecca said under her breath.

Sean turned to Rebecca. "Did you say something?"

"Oh, uh, nothing," she lied, looking away and putting her arms behind her back.

Sean went back to playing with Monica. "Okay, Daddy! Daddy, stop," she bubbled. Sean tickled her, and the sound of her mirth was music to all his senses. When he finally relented, Monica pulled her covers back up. "I'm good now," she said with a smile. "I love you, Daddy."

"I love you too, sweetie. I love you too," said Sean. He walked to the door while Rebecca turned off the lamp, and after Rebecca walked away, he turned around to face Monica. "Hey, if you need something, anything at all, you let us know. Alright?"

Monica nodded with a smile, yawned, and turned over, her little body finally ready for rest.

"Sleep tight, little angel," Sean whispered as he closed the door. As his exhaustion deepened, he walked back to the bedroom, finding the door closed and locked. Sean knocked on it three times. "Uh, Becca?" he called. "Is there a reason the door is locked?"

"Just a moment," she called back in a jubilant, sing-song voice.

Sean shook his head. All he wanted was to rest, but when Rebecca opened the door, he was filled with energy as she stood in her underwear. *Wow. Okay, so much for sleeping.*

"Hey there," she said with love in her eyes. *Take the hint, Sean.*

"Oh, uh, hi," said Sean as he rubbed the back of his neck with his hand. "Are you… I mean, are you sleeping in that?" *Is that seriously all I can come up with?* he thought.

Rebecca giggled and swayed her hips from side to side, which Sean watched eagerly. "That's up to you, sweetheart," she said in a flirty, devilish voice, turning and walking to the shower.

Sean saw her throw her underwear out of the bathroom as she only partially closed the bathroom door. With renewed energy, he walked in and locked the bedroom door behind him. His heart pounded, and his mind sped, unable to hold a single thought for too long.

"I'm waiting," Rebecca said in another sing-song voice, drawing out her words for emphasis. Jazz music played from a portable speaker in the bathroom before he heard her turn the water on.

Sean took everything off but his boxers, darting toward the shower. Before long, he threw those out into the bedroom too.

"Hi," Rebecca said seductively as Sean stepped into the shower with her.

Sean's breath quickened as his mind continued to race. Although he wanted to rest, there was no way he was getting to sleep yet. "Hey," Sean said with a smile, and they kissed.

A few hours later, Monica was awakened by an unseen force. She rubbed her eyes and walked to the window, looking behind the blanket covering it. She saw a bright, twinkling star, much more luminous than usual, and her favorite nursery rhyme came to her mind. "Twinkle, twinkle, little star," she sang.

What Monica thought was a star was an alien ship, piloted by one of the surviving Kriff leaders, who had returned silently, having rid itself and its friend of the infection. "Be still, human. This will hurt, but your struggle will make it worse."

There on the cold, metal table lay President Matthews, his arms and legs stretched out and held down by clamps. There was also a clamp over his lower abdomen and pelvic area, and a tube shoved down his throat. Multiple needles stuck into him all over his body.

A man walked up to the president wearing a black uniform with the Astro logo. "Hey there, Mr. President," said Jim Dalton. "Pleased to meet you. I'm called the Channeler, and you're going to help us change the world." Jim grinned wide.

"You are but the first test subject," the other Kriff said as it pulled a lever. The president tried screaming, but he couldn't with the tube in his mouth. Jim and the Kriff departed for Saturn with President Matthews as their captive, for whom they had big plans.

"How I wonder what you are," Monica continued singing. She took a breath before continuing, briefly closing her eyes. When she opened them again, they were black like a Kriff's.

TWINKLE, TWINKLE, LITTLE STAR
NOW YOU'VE GONE AWAY SO FAR

✧

27. EPILOGUE: REVELATION

IT CONTINUED SNOWING IN MAYBERRY, TENNESSEE, on December 24, 2041. Monica danced in the snow, while Sean and Rebecca baked pastries inside. She finally fell after making herself dizzy, having spun around while looking up at the sky too long. Monica laughed as she fell.

Sean watched his daughter out the window, beside his recently earned master's degree in their new home, right beside Becca's bachelor's degree. They had moved there the previous spring. It was out of the city, which was what Rebecca wanted for Jonathan, their four-year-old son, who would be turning five in a matter of days.

"She's crazy," said Jonathan. "It's too cold out there. It's nice and warm in here."

Sean and Rebecca laughed. "She's not crazy, Jon. She's just having fun," Rebecca said to their son. "I can get you all bundled up so you can join her if you want."

Jonathan shook his head and dashed back upstairs to his room to escape, leaving his parents laughing. They shared a quick kiss until the toaster oven beeped, signaling one of their pastries was done. "I have to say, I didn't think I'd enjoy this, but it's kind of fun," Sean admitted.

"Oh, come on. You know this is the most fun you've had since our wedding night," Rebecca said with a grin. She noticed

Sean watching Monica again. "Come on, baby. You can't watch her forever."

"I know," said Sean. "I just don't understand the blackouts. It makes no sense how no one's found anything yet. Not even Abby. She gets cured of cancer, then somehow this happens a few years later. I'm scared to let her out of my sight."

"Well, you're gonna have to. She's a teenager now. You're gonna have to upgrade her from Cocoon to Butterfly pretty soon. Besides, I don't want you to turn into one of those strict dads like mine."

Sean picked Rebecca up, making her yell in jubilant shock as he twirled her around twice and set her back down, kissing her forehead.

Outside, Monica stood from the snow and headed back inside. A man watched the family from a distance, looking at them with a forlorn expression and sighed heavily. *This is wrong,* he thought, but he was sent back for a reason, and it had to be done. A mixture of confusing emotions flooded him, so he took another deep breath, steeling himself to walk forward. Seeing Monica hugging her father through a window made him stop. *I'm not gonna let you down. I was chosen for the Beta Program for a reason. I can do this,* he thought.

Finally, the stranger walked up to the door and knocked. Sean approached the door and opened it, greeting him with a smile. "Hey, you lost?" Sean asked.

"No, sir, uh, that's just it, actually," he said with a smile. He let out another deep sigh. "I'm home."

Sean's brow furrowed. "Pardon?"

"Hi, Dad," a grown Jonathan said with a grin. "It's been a while."

A Note From the Author

Thank you for reading *The Protocol Experiment.*

This story took a decade to write, and the themes inside it are personal to me.

If this story made you think, or gave you an interesting journey, I would be grateful if you left an honest review wherever you purchased the book. This helps other readers discover these stories.

More than anything, I hope this story reminds you that, even under cosmic stakes, the essence of humanity is what we truly need to save.

Thank you for taking this journey with me.

Book Two, *The Escapement Paradigm,* is out now.

https://www.theprotocolbookseries.com/

James Zollern

DEDICATION

To my doting mother, who has always believed in and nurtured me, and in loving memory of my father, who guided me on my journeys and tragically passed away without warning before this story's completion. We love and miss you, Dad. I hope you're reading this in the stars.

GLOSSARY

ANNI: A talking car running a special AI coded by Kyle Wills. The acronym is short for **Artificial Neural Network Interface**.
Autofire: A mode for turrets, allowing them to programmatically fire without human interaction.
Biobug: A type of **Nephilium** nanotechnology used to quickly build structures and reprogram computerized systems. They can also be used as implants.
Broment: A moment when two or more guys talk about their feelings, coined by Rebecca Morgan.
Channeler: A man who communicates with the Kriff, and does their bidding via an implant in his brain.
Collective: A broad spectrum of frequencies heard on multiple **Comms**.
Comms: Slang for the plural of **Communicator**.
Communicator: A glowing, adjustable device created by GAIA, which allows all wearers to communicate across the world on specific or all frequencies, known as the **Collective**. *See **Collective**.*
Drive-Along: A feature added in most cars in early 2026, which allows the driver to follow the path of someone else's GPS. Can be automatic or driven manually.
Foster Principle: A theoretical law that states if something is computerized, then it can be hacked, and if it can be hacked, then it will be. Coined by Professor Howard Foster.
GAIA: An acronym. *See **Global Alien Intelligence Agency**.*

Global Alien Intelligence Agency: A peacekeeping organization that silently defends the world against alien threats, and defends aliens from the world.

Grays: A secret alien group who infiltrated the world in Roswell, New Mexico, in 1947, and influenced events ever since, who call themselves **Kriff**.

Kriff: The proper name for Grays. *See **Grays**.*

Implant: A device placed in an abducted victim's mind, which allows the **Kriff** to control them.

Medbag: A book-bag with multiple compartments containing various medical supplies beyond first aid.

Medbay: A place to treat the wounded and sick.

Nephilium: A benevolent race of aliens who lost their home planet due to human recklessness.

Nephilu: The home planet of the **Nephilium**. *See **Nephilium**.*

Progenitors: A mysterious race of giant aliens and the creators of humanity and the **Nephilium**.

Project Longshot: A project intended to use salvaged alien technology to explore the source of the **Wow! signal**, but it exploded in **Nephilu**, destroying most of the planet's inhabitants.

Protocol: An open-source, community-funded project to create an AI to learn from firewalls and quarantines, then teach other systems the same information, forming a technological hivemind. It became too dangerous after it almost launched nuclear warheads, and was believed to be shut down. The Nephilium originally used it to shut down humanity's digital architecture before the **Kriff** hijacked it.

Radio-Television: A device installed in cars in 2027, to replace radios. They have a simple UI for basic navigation tasks to local news. Cars are set to drive themselves when one is on and hands are off the wheel, or when the road does not detect the eyes of the driver.

Standstill: A point in 2028, when technology stopped improving and resources became scarce.

Starlength: A **Nephilium** unit of distance between stars.

Techdoor: An IT company, who sends their workers out to solicit software in neighborhoods.

Thoughtspeak: A **Nephilium** method of communication, wherein they speak to others telepathically, but the receiver hears it in their own language.

Thoughtspoke: Past tense of **Thoughtspeak**.

Xeno: Referring to aliens, usually more than one race.

Wow! signal: An alien signal detected from space in the Sagittarius constellation, which lasted seventy-two seconds on a satellite named Big Ear. Jerry Ehman was so impressed by the strength of it he wrote and circled "Wow!" on the report.

Zugzwang: A term in chess, in which a player must take their turn, but any move will cause them to lose the game.

About the Author

James Zollern is a science-fiction author who writes about choices and what it means to be human in the face of global catastrophe. His writing focuses on grounded humanism. Zollern infuses his characters and themes with events from his own life, and those of his family and friends with their approval.

Zollern is an openly autistic author, encouraging others to follow their dreams. After enduring many dark trials, he writes in hopes of inspiring people in the way he was inspired, to help other people feel less alone. He chooses to focus on the philosophical themes behind the story instead of relying on spectacle and constant action.

www.ingramcontent.com/pod-product-compliance
Lightning Source LLC
LaVergne TN
LVHW090259210926
848480LV00001B/73
* 9 7 9 8 2 3 4 0 0 1 1 4 6 *